A PLUME BOOK

READY, SET, SOLD!

MICHAEL CORBETT is the Real Estate and Lifestyle expert of NBC's number-one news magazine *Extra*. He is also the host and senior supervising producer of *Extra's Mansions & Millionaires*, the hour-long weekend series that gives viewers a sneak peak of the extraordinary mansions, yachts, and hobbies of the rich and famous.

Corbett is a nationally known real estate authority appearing regularly on CNN, ABC, HGTV, and TLC. He lectures at conventions across the country, including the Real Estate & Wealth Expo along with Donald Trump, Suze Orman, and Anthony Robbins.

An accomplished author, Corbett has been sharing his real estate expertise with his first bestselling book, *Find It, Fix It, Flip It!: Make Millions in Real Estate—One House at a Time*. In it he shares his strategies, tips, and never-before-revealed insider techniques that have helped him make a fortune in real estate. Corbett wrote the book for aspiring flippers, first-time home buyers, or any homeowner who wants to create big profits and own their ultimate dream home—mortgage free.

This TV star turned real estate entrepreneur has been buying, renovating, and selling homes for more than twenty years. His company, Highland Properties, which he founded while starring in his first daytime drama *Ryan's Hope*, has bought, restored, and sold dozens of homes and apartment buildings.

While juggling real estate and an acting career, Corbett made his mark in daytime television. He was voted "Daytime's Most Lovable Cad" by *People* magazine, for his red-hot starring roles in three different soap operas. He first starred for three years on *Ryan's Hope* for ABC, next for four years on *Search for Tomorrow* for NBC, and then for eight years he played David Kimball in the CBS number-one daytime ratings grabber in the United States, Canada, and Europe, *The Young and the Restless*.

Visit his Web site at www.MichaelCorbett.com

READY, SET, SOLD!

Make *$10,000 to $100,000* **MORE**

When You Sell Your Home!

Michael Corbett

A PLUME BOOK

PLUME
Published by Penguin Group
Penguin Group (USA) Inc., 375 Hudson Street, New York, New York 10014, U.S.A.
Penguin Group (Canada), 90 Eglinton Avenue East, Suite 700, Toronto, Ontario,
Canada M4P 2Y3 (a division of Pearson Penguin Canada Inc.)
Penguin Books Ltd., 80 Strand, London WC2R 0RL, England
Penguin Ireland, 25 St. Stephen's Green, Dublin 2, Ireland (a division of Penguin Books Ltd.)
Penguin Group (Australia), 250 Camberwell Road, Camberwell, Victoria 3124, Australia
(a division of Pearson Australia Group Pty. Ltd.)
Penguin Books India Pvt. Ltd., 11 Community Centre, Panchsheel Park,
New Delhi – 110 017, India
Penguin Group (NZ), 67 Apollo Drive, Mairangi Bay, Auckland 1311,
New Zealand (a division of Pearson New Zealand Ltd.)
Penguin Books (South Africa) (Pty.) Ltd., 24 Sturdee Avenue, Rosebank,
Johannesburg 2196, South Africa

Penguin Books Ltd., Registered Offices: 80 Strand, London WC2R 0RL, England

First published by Plume, a member of Penguin Group (USA) Inc.

First Printing, March 2007
1   3   5   7   9   10   8   6   4   2

Copyright © Michael Corbett, 2007
All rights reserved

⊕ REGISTERED TRADEMARK—MARCA REGISTRADA

LIBRARY OF CONGRESS CATALOGING-IN-PUBLICATION DATA
Corbett, Michael, 1960–
Ready, set, sold! : make $10,000 to $100,000 more when you sell your
home! / by Michael Corbett.
310 p. cm.
ISBN 978-0-452-28813-3
1. House selling. 2. Dwellings—Remodeling. I. Title.
HD1379.C67   2007
643'.12—dc22
2006036376

Printed in the United States of America
Set in Berkeley Old Style
Designed by Joseph Rutt

ACKNOWLEDGMENTS

When an author writes a book, especially a second book, many people naturally become part of the process. First and foremost, I want to thank my publisher, Trena Keating at Plume, and the entire Plume staff, including Emily Haynes, Marie Coolman, and Mary Pomponio. Plume has been enormously supportive and played a huge role in the success of my first book, *Find It, Fix It, Flip It!*, which made this second work a pleasure to write.

I want to thank my literary agent, Bonnie Solow, who works with so many bestselling authors that I am just grateful to be on her prestigious short list of clients. Bonnie is always available and encouraging.

I am also grateful to be able to work with an extraordinary personal support team. Kristin Loberg, a wonderful writer herself, has been my cheerleader when my deadlines were looming ("hang in there, you are doing great"). Mindi Meader, who is responsible for my Web site, www.MichaelCorbett.com, and all the illustrations in this book, is very talented. Also, I need to thank Scott Khouri, an incredible organizer, and Milt Sutchin, my manager.

Of course I must thank my friends and family: Cheryl, Greg, and my always-supportive mom, Margaret.

CONTENTS

PART II: SET

PART III: SOLD!

INTRODUCTION

Let's get right to it. Why did I write this book? Because I want *you* to make more money when you sell your house. That's right. That's it. That's the reason!

Ever since the successful publication of my first book, *Find It, Fix It, Flip It!: Make Millions in Real Estate—One House at a Time,* I have been lecturing around the country to real estate professionals and investors about how to find, fix, and flip homes; that is, how to buy houses and resell them for top prices. Then it hit me. Why should the real estate pros and investors be the only ones to make top-dollar sales when they sell their houses? Why should they be the only ones to know all the secrets, tips, and techniques that snag the buyers willing to make full-price offers?

I realized that it's the *average home seller* who *really* needs to know how to make the most of the sale of his or her home. It is *you*, the home seller with one house. One house that is your nest egg, your main financial investment. *You* are the one who could truly benefit from knowing how to make $10,000 to $100,000 *more* when you sell that home. For many home sellers, that additional money could be the difference that pays off your credit card bills or even funds your child's college education.

I have seen too many home sellers throw away money and destroy the value of their home simply because they didn't know better. The techniques presented in this book work. And they are making savvy home sellers big money every day. Now it's *your* turn. It's not rocket science. It doesn't take a huge investment of cash. It just takes a methodical approach. *Ready, Set, Sold!* takes you step by step through the process and reveals all the crucial insider secrets, as well as my personal techniques and essential tips that you need to know. Having the ability to share all this information with you, and to help empower your life, is why I have written *Ready, Set, Sold!*

DOES THE THOUGHT OF SELLING YOUR
HOME OVERWHELM YOU?

Does the thought of selling overwhelm you? Are you afraid of the process because you're not sure how it works from start to finish? Do you fear that you'll sell for far less than your house is worth, or be unable to sell at all? Would you like to know how to make more money when you sell? Would you like to learn how to save money where other unknowing homeowners are throwing it away?

Would you like to increase the value of your home by $10,000 in one weekend? Would you like to sell your home for much more than you ever imagined? Do you dream of a big financial gain but worry about not knowing all the secrets to selling successfully—and quickly? Do you want to know how real estate professionals sell their own homes to maximize their cash-out? If you said yes to any of these questions, then you are holding the right book in your hands! *Ready, Set, Sold!* is your solution to gaining the knowledge, expertise, and guidance you need.

HOME SELLERS ARE THROWING AWAY MONEY

As a real estate investor and homeowner myself, I have bought and sold dozens of houses and made handsome profits on each one in every type of market—hot, cold, and lukewarm. I have also walked through hundreds of homes for sale. It frustrates me to watch home sellers make reckless yet fixable mistakes that sabotage the successful and profitable sale of their homes. In any real estate market, especially a soft one, every home seller *must* employ certain techniques and meet certain buyers' expectations to maximize equity, create additional profits, avoid costly oversights, and squeeze more money out of the sale. I call these the *Ready, Set, Sold!* (RSS) techniques. Most home sellers don't realize that they need only spend pennies to make thousands of dollars more when they sell.

• •

Most home sellers don't realize that they need only spend pennies to make thousands of dollars more when they sell.

• •

I WANT TO HELP YOU, JUST AS OTHERS HAVE HELPED ME

Helping others on their road to financial freedom through real estate is deeply satisfying. In fact, the personal satisfaction I felt in helping thousands achieve their real estate dreams with my first book compelled me to continue sharing my message with others who could also benefit. I'm a big believer that one person's success can be inspiration for others. I've been very fortunate to have learned from some of the best professionals, including designers and real estate experts, in the business, and I'm thrilled to be sharing this knowledge with you.

HOW I BECAME AN "EXPERT"

First of all, no one is born an expert in anything. I am the first to admit that. And I am also the first to tell everyone, "If I can do this, *anyone* can do it!" All it takes is a little know-how and a lot of motivation. No kidding: I have lectured to 25,000 people at once, given interviews on CNN, and taught successful home selling on all the major TV networks. And every time I do, I gladly admit that if I can learn how to do it . . . so can you!

I happen to love real estate, architecture, and real estate finance. But my love affair with this field began long before I decided to write books about how to successfully sell homes for more money or how to flip houses and create financial freedom. When I was eight years old, I used to ride my bicycle to the nicer part of town and take photographs of people's houses. My father had bought me some basic photography equipment and I set up a darkroom in a closet in our basement. I made 8" × 10" enlargements and framed them. Armed with my MICHAEL COR-BETT PHOTOGRAPHER business cards, I went back to the homeowners and sold those photos. If they didn't want to buy them, I would say, "I would like to give you this as a gift, and if you would care to make a donation, here is a self-addressed envelope."

Even then, I wanted to show people how great their homes could look. The photos probably weren't all that good, but people wanted to reward my eight-year-old sense of business initiative and optimism.

If you have read my first book, I apologize to you for telling the same personal story here. But if you haven't, then the following is how my career has unfolded thus far.

Fast forward several years. Okay, okay, *many* years. After college at the University of Pennsylvania and Boston University I moved to New York City to become an actor. I was lucky enough to land a Broadway show, and was discovered one night by a casting director who offered me a contract for the ABC soap opera *Ryan's Hope*. That first season, I received my first bonus-overage check for $10,000. I was nineteen years old.

I knew nothing about real estate or renovations. But I always had an interest in architecture and I had heard that real estate was a very good investment. To be perfectly honest, I think I was just trying to impress my dad. I thought if I could buy a house in my hometown, Collingswood, New Jersey, maybe being an actor wouldn't look like such a bad choice after all. So with that first check from *Ryan's Hope* and a big dose of guarded optimism, I bought the house next door to my grandmother's. I fumbled my way through the process and managed to fix it up, applying what would later become my set-to-sell techniques, and put it back on the market. Thanks to good instincts, I actually made a profit.

During my entire fifteen years on daytime television, I continued to buy, fix up, live in, and sell dozens of homes. In the past six years, I've had the great fortune to combine both my career in television and my love of real estate through hosting the number-one-rated nightly news magazine, NBC's *Extra* and *Extra's Mansions & Millionaires*. I make regular appearances as a real estate and home expert on CNN *Nightly News*; HGTV; *Fine Living*; TLC home shows, including *Renovation Generation*; the Discovery Channel; PAX; Fox; and *Good Day Live,* as well as local news and radio programs nationwide.

I've been fortunate enough to share the stage with great speakers such as Donald Trump, Suze Orman, and Anthony Robbins. I've been able to teach and lecture about successful house selling to thousands of people. In fact, one of these lectures, with the Real Estate & Wealth Expo in San Francisco, was attended by 65,000 people.

This is me hosting Extra's Mansions & Millionaires *on location in Monte Carlo during July 2006. I was writing this book in between takes—literally.*

THE *READY, SET, SOLD!*
TECHNIQUES ARE INVALUABLE

The very same techniques that allow the pros to turn undervalued houses into extraordinary homes selling for top dollar are the techniques *every* home seller must use. In addition to mastering the basic principles of the selling process, you're going to learn how to turn your house into a buyer's dream home without spending a fortune or taking months to do it. Yes, there are ways to upgrade your home easily and cheaply. Yes, there are ways to avoid endless negotiations with buyers by focusing on necessary repairs prior to going on the market. And yes, there are ways to turn a low-ball offer into a great offer that ultimately puts the ball in your court. You're going to learn it all—plus more—in the upcoming chapters.

MAKE *MORE* MONEY WHEN YOU SELL

Why lose hard-earned equity and real estate profits by overlooking simple adjustments? As a home seller, you could easily pocket five, ten, twenty, and even a hundred thousand dollars more when you sell your home if you just apply these simple, inexpensive, and often cost-free techniques. Here's a small slice of some of what you're going to accomplish with this book:

- Maximize the value of your home *before* you put it on the market

- Make your house worth $10,000+ more in a weekend

- Repair the essentials quickly, easily, and cheaply

- Create a *lifestyle* and get your house into picture-perfect condition

- Implement emotion-grabbing design secrets that cost nothing, but tug at buyers' hearts

- Dress your home by staging it so that buyers pay more than the asking price

- Decide whether to use a Realtor

- Price the house appropriately

- Spot a winning offer

- Know what to offer a buyer so you get what you really want

- Keep negotiations in your favor

- Navigate the escrow process like an expert

- Eliminate excessive hidden closing fees

- Avoid paying taxes on your profits

KNOWLEDGE IN REAL ESTATE = PROFIT

Just knowing the pitfalls and traps, and avoiding the most common mistakes sellers make—the Ten Sins of Selling—alone will save you thousands and boost your bank account on sale day. Reading this book will give you the knowledge and insider expertise to breeze through what would otherwise be a very complicated process. Selling a home is a huge and complicated financial transaction. Some people do it only once or twice in their lifetimes. The knowledge to do it well should be available and readily accessible to all! And now it is.

READY, SET, SOLD! IS YOUR INSURANCE AGAINST A VOLATILE MARKET

Markets run hot and they run cold, but no matter what the market and economy are doing, one truth always remains constant: No one wants to throw away money. So whatever the market direction, if you don't apply these techniques, you may as well leave that ten, twenty, fifty, or hundred thousand dollars cash in a trunk somewhere in the basement or attic. In a hot market, the techniques outlined in this book allow you to be at the top of the home-selling charts; and in a cooling market the RSS method is a *must* to claim and hold on to every bit of equity you can from the sale of your home.

In a hot market, the techniques outlined in this book allow you to be at the top of the home-selling charts; and in a cooling market the RSS method is a must to claim and hold on to every bit of equity you can from the sale of your home.

FROM MODEST TO MANSION

Don't think your modest abode will benefit from the RSS method? Au contraire! RSS principles apply to every price level of home. The same selling techniques that will enhance a $100,000 sixteen-hundred-square-foot home in Idaho will apply to a $750,000 four-bedroom Tudor in Dallas, and a $3 million mansion in Southern California. In this game, the RSS techniques are applicable to all types of houses and all price ranges. Every home will benefit from the RSS moneymaking tips. And whether you've got a manor or a modest one-bedroom, there's money to be saved at every step of the way.

THREE PARTS TO *READY, SET, SOLD!*

Think your house is ready to sell tomorrow? Do you believe your house is ready to be sold for top dollar? Think again. Your house is NOT ready for a top-dollar sale. I'll show you why your house isn't in tip-top shape in Part One: *Ready,* where I prepare you for your upcoming sales process. Then I'll show you how to get your house in mint condition in Part Two: *Set,* where I will teach you the five set-to-sell techniques that are truly transformational and will stir a feeding frenzy among buyers. And finally, in Part Three: *Sold!,* I'll take you through all the nitty-gritty steps of actually selling your house and saving thousands in the process. So, if you are thinking of selling your house, or are about to put your house on the market, read on. You are about to learn the RSS techniques that will *make you $10,000 to $100,000 more when you sell your house.*

READY, SET, SOLD!

Part One

READY

One

HOW TO MAKE MORE MONEY WHEN YOU SELL

Many home sellers foolishly begin the selling process by blindly jumping in and putting their home up for sale, leaving the outcome to the whims of the Realtors, the market, the buyers, and chance. Well, it's time for you to take charge of selling your home—you need to go from *victim* to *victor*! This book sheds light on the entire process, from how to find the right Realtor to picking up your cash-out check on sale day. You're now going to *take control* of the sale of your house, and *not be controlled* by the sale of your house.

Too many home sellers sit back and simply let a sale happen. I see it all the time. Don't let the sale of your house happen by default. I have a friend who lets his entire life unfold by default, never taking action, just letting things happen. And, not surprisingly, he's never happy with the outcome.

Many people remark, *I don't know anything about this process,* or *I don't have time to do any repairs or work on the house; I just want to sell it and get out!* Well, I say you DO have the time. You HAVE TO have the time. It's not hard and it's not rocket science. It doesn't cost you a lot of money, and ultimately the techniques you'll employ won't take days, weeks, or months to complete. Actually, the *Ready, Set, Sold!* techniques will help every homeowner make their house sale process easier, less stressful, and much more profitable. Even if you apply only one of the hundreds of RSS techniques and tips, you would stand to save or make anywhere from $1,000 to $10,000, or even $100,000 *more*, on the sale of your home!

TAKING THE PANIC OUT OF SELLING YOUR HOUSE

Wow, you have decided to sell your house. Here you go. How are you feeling? Excited? Sounds like a fun and easy process. Yeah, right! If you are anything like the more than 5 million other home sellers each year, then that is certainly *not* what you are feeling. It's more like fear, panic. These are probably the first feelings that overwhelm you when you ponder the idea of selling your home. Will you be able to get the price you want? Will you sell in the time frame you have in mind? Can you really do relatively easy improvements and make a great deal more money?

Time for a Deep Breath

Right from the start I want you to take a deep breath and put a lid on stress. Yes, selling your home is one of the most stressful processes you can endure. It ranks up there with a divorce or family tragedy. It may even be connected to one of those events. If you have lived in your home for more than three, five, or ten years, the mere thought of selling it can be downright paralyzing. Okay, traumatic. Not only are you thinking about how you're going to handle all the paperwork, the Realtors, and the onslaught of buyers lumbering through your home, or worse—no buyers interested enough to lumber—you are also full of anxiety at the thought of packing up all of your belongings, wading through the dust and cobwebs, and getting ready to actually move! Well, your first instincts are right: It *is* a traumatic process!

The Three Fears About Selling Your Home

In 2005, "rogue economist" Steven D. Levitt and *New York Times* writer Stephen J. Dubner came out with their popular book *Freakonomics*, in which they explore "the hidden side of everything." One of the topics they explore is real estate, and what it feels like to be a house seller. As they so eloquently put it, home sellers have three major concerns as they prepare to put their house on the market:

- They are too attached emotionally to their home to sell it.
- The house will sell for less than it is worth.
- The house will not sell at all.

Rest assured, this book addresses these three legitimate worries. You're going to face these concerns head-on and blow them out of the water. You will get past each of these fears . . . and then go several steps further:

- You will not only emotionally detach from your home so you can sell it, but you also *will* be able to easily and seamlessly change how you think about your home and be able to transform it into a product to sell.

- You will not only implement the steps you need to take to sell your home for what it's worth, but you also *will* be able to increase your house's worth by $10,000 to $100,000.

- And not only will you utilize the techniques that will get your house sold, but you also *will* sell it faster.

THREE RSS STRATEGIES TO MAKE MORE MONEY WHEN YOU SELL

1. Get top dollar for your house

2. Save money every step of the process

3. Avoid the ten biggest home-selling mistakes

Luckily, you don't need a fancy degree or innate talent to learn the secrets of selling a home for top dollar. Getting the most money for your house simply requires following a step-by-step process. By arming yourself with the proper knowledge, you'll make more money when you sell by maximizing the value of your home. You are going to use all the set-to-sell techniques that insider real estate professionals employ to generate lofty price tags when they put *their* houses on the market. In addition, I won't let you be among the hundreds of thousands of home sellers who throw away money because they commit one or more of the ten costliest home-selling mistakes. And if you follow my recipe for closing-day success, you'll save thousands of dollars there as well.

So let's get your house Ready, Set, and Sold!

STRATEGY #1: GET TOP DOLLAR

- Maximize the actual value of your home

- Increase your home's emotional appeal and perceived value

- Create a positive experience for your potential buyers

- Don't sell your "house"—sell a *home* and a *lifestyle*

Your own home will be worth more when you discover how to uncover its hidden and otherwise "buried" treasures. And I mean buried! When you strip your house and de-clutter, you will reveal the home that lies beneath all your possessions. Somewhere under there is a house that buyers will pay top dollar for. You will be able to hatch that butterfly from its caterpillar cocoon! Once you learn that you're not going to sell your *house*—you're going to sell a *home* and a *lifestyle*—you'll hold the key that unlocks every buyer's checkbook.

Once you learn that you're not going to sell your house—you're going to sell a home and a lifestyle—you'll hold the key that unlocks every buyer's checkbook.

STRATEGY #2: SAVE MONEY ON EVERY PHASE OF THE SALE PROCESS

- Save on commissions and fees

- Price perfectly

- Negotiate the best deal possible, putting more money into your pocket

- Save money on closing cost and expenses

Every phase of the house-sale process offers dozens of opportunities to save money and uncover hidden savings.

Knowing where you can save on commissions and fees, and where you shouldn't even try, is key. Working hand in hand with your Realtors, lawyers, escrow officers, and title companies is another key to success when selling. You need to be able to optimize their performance and motivate them to work not just *for* you, but *with* you. When they are truly on your team, they will fight for you and your wallet.

Pricing your home perfectly is an art. You need to be educated so that you and your Realtor can put your house on the market at the price that gets you top dollar without overpricing. Perfect pricing is a key to saving you thousands of dollars.

Negotiating is a skill that needs to be learned. But knowing what to ask for and where to give and take is crucial when closing the deal that is a win-win for both you and your buyer.

During the *closing* process you'll want to know how to spot junk fees, garbage fees, or whatever you want to call them. This can save you thousands. Unknowledgeable home sellers pay them every time. You won't have to!

STRATEGY #3: AVOID THE TEN BIGGEST HOME-SELLING MISTAKES

On average, home sellers make up to five of these costly mistakes in every house sale. And each and every one of these mistakes comes with a hefty price tag. Learn to identify and eliminate all of these, and you can save yourself thousands—even tens of thousands—of dollars. They truly are sins, because home sellers are just burning money by committing them. And the most frustrating part is that they are all easy sins to confess and rectify!

Top Ten Sins of Selling

1. **Selling your house "For Sale by Owner."** Trying to sell your home by yourself is sheer madness. You need the expertise of a professional. Home sellers who do it themselves often end up selling for far less. Chapter 4 will explain why.

2. **Neglecting necessary repairs prior to sale.** You will lose money if you don't take care of repairs *before* the house goes on the market. I'll review the ones you'll need to make in the "Repair to Sell" section in Chapter 7.

3. **Refusing to remove your clutter and junk prior to the sale.** Clutter eats equity and kills deals. Learn how to de-clutter in the "Save It, Store It, Sell It, Chuck It" section in Chapter 6.

4. **Selling your house empty.** Selling an empty house makes buyers feel the same way—empty. I will show you how to dress your house for sale in Chapters 11 and 12.

5. **Mispricing your home.** Overpricing or underpricing your house is a huge money-losing mistake. Chapter 13 teaches you how to know the competition and set the right price.

6. **Not setting the stage for sale day.** You must create a showplace for your buyers on sale day. Buyers purchase with their hearts

and not their heads. You'll set the stage for an emotional experience by using Chapters 11 and 12.

7. **Letting your ego get in the way when negotiating.** Too many sellers take negotiations personally and lose out on creating a win-win deal. Chapter 16 explains how to take your ego out of the equation and put your head back into it.

8. **Neglecting to complete a full set of disclosures prior to closing.** I've watched too many home sellers pay out big bucks because they didn't "reveal it all." Chapter 15 will tell you everything you'll need to tell.

9. **Mistiming the sale and losing out on maximum tax benefits.** Even one day mistimed can cost you tens of thousands in extra taxes. Don't be left a day late and many dollars short. Learn your taxes and timing issues as I explain them in Chapter 3.

10. **Overlooking junk fees and extra expenses at closing.** Home sellers throw thousands away by not requesting and confirming a list of fees and expenses long before closing day. Chapter 17 on the escrow process tells you the fees to pay and the ones to refute.

Face it, you can't afford to lose money either through neglect, indifference, or ignorance of the selling process. Read on, and you'll learn how to be sin-free every step of the way.

THE EIGHT *READY, SET, SOLD!* STEPS TO SELLING

Following the steps to *Ready, Set, Sold!* success is very easy. Don't get overwhelmed here. Most of the steps are in a linear, chronological order. A few will occur simultaneously, but you won't have to juggle too many balls in the air at once. I'll walk you through everything you need to know so it will still seem like you're taking it one step at a time.

THE EIGHT RSS STEPS TO SALE SUCCESS!

1. Identify your selling goals

2. Select your Realtor

3. Execute the five set-to-sell techniques

   a. Save it, store it, sell it, chuck it

   b. Repair to sell

   c. Lifestyle upgrades

   d. Design to sell

   e. Dress to sell

      i. Stage to sell

      ii. Prep to sell

4. Finalize your price and listing agreement

5. Welcome your buyers

6. Negotiate

7. Win the closing escrow

8. Cash out, move out

GETTING READY

Let's sell your house. Right now! Today! But first, let me ask you a few questions. If you were a potential buyer strolling through your home this afternoon, would you fall in love with this house? Does your house evoke the emotional response of a *lifestyle* that would command top dollar? If a caravan of Realtors and potential buyers were knocking on your front door this instant, would you be embarrassed, horrified, or confident that your house is ready to earn you the big bucks that you desire?

I can pretty much guarantee you that your house is *not ready* to sell for its maximum amount right at this moment.

. . . .

So right now you have two choices: You can put your house on the market tomorrow, or you can employ these techniques and make a lot more money when you sell!

. . . .

Are *You* Ready?

The first question you have to ask yourself, though, is whether you are ready to sell at all. And being "ready" includes many factors. For some people, the idea of selling their home with intentions of moving up to a bigger house or relocating to a new town excites them with the adrenaline and inspiration to make the most out of this experience. For others, however, selling their house can draw mixed emotions. After all, you're leaving a place you call home. You might have raised children in this house, shared many fond memories, and never thought about *not* living in it.

Know Your Selling Goals

Before you can devise a selling game plan, you have to understand *why* you are selling. You may be limited by a calendar dictated by life's unavoidable and unchangeable circumstances. That's okay. I wrote this book with you in mind. Knowing why you are selling allows you to set your goals. You can then maximize your house's value, and save as much money as you can by keeping in mind the big picture of your ultimate selling goals.

If you had to give a reason for selling, what would it be? Must sell for financial reasons? Like to sell for profit reasons? Moving up? Moving down? Retiring? Expanding your family?

Some real estate gurus say "never sell unless you have to sell." But that's not always realistic. Life has a way of forcing us to sell when the circumstances necessitate it—notably, death, divorce, or a job transfer.

If you're expanding your family and upgrading your lifestyle, maybe you have the luxury of commanding your own timeline, which allows you to be choosier about buyers and their offers. It may also allow you to take more time for upgrade projects or longer escrows. That extra time and money can really put you in a powerful selling position.

Given your current obligations, you have to decide what your goal should be and how flexible that timeline is in relation to that goal. Don't give yourself unrealistic sale goals. Likewise, don't paint yourself into a corner timewise.

PINPOINT YOUR REASONS FOR SELLING

Job transfer/Moving/Relocation

Marriage/Divorce

Illness/Death

Retirement

Moving up/Moving down

Cashing out

YOUR REASONS FOR SELLING AFFECT
HOW YOU SELL

Most home sellers fall into a category I call "on the move." In fact, according to the CEO of Coldwell Banker, Jim Gillespie, more than 65 percent of all home sellers need to sell quickly due to financial constraints or a relocation. In the must-sell scenario, you'll want to have your house on the market within thirty to sixty days from the time you make a decision to sell. And, of course, once your house is on the market, you will want it to sell as quickly as possible.

Whatever your reason is, it will affect how you price, time, and market the sale of your home. But here's the good news: Regardless of your personal or professional reasons, you can maximize your cash-out. I'll give you all the options you need to choose the best route to take in selling your home on *your* timeline.

Prioritize Your Selling Goals

Let's match up the common reasons for selling with the corresponding timelines typical for most people in these situations:

- **Job transfer/Moving/Relocation:** This usually requires a relatively quick sale, especially if you've already purchased another home elsewhere. If you're being transferred for work, you may need to get your house on the market in thirty days or less and, with luck, sell in thirty days. You will want your home sold before you have to move to your new location. As we will discuss, keeping your home staged and immaculately maintained will be key to getting a big asking price.

- **Marriage/Divorce:** Whether a divorce forces the sale of a home, or a marriage forces one person to sell a home and move in with the other, people in these situations usually want to sell quickly to move on with their lives.

- **Illness/Death:** If you're selling for health reasons or as a result of a death in the family, you will most likely want to get the highest possible price in the shortest amount of time. This usually calls for a quick sale.

- **Retirement:** Depending on your patience and willingness to take your time in preparing your home for sale, home-selling retirees can sometimes make the most out of their selling experience and go for longer escrows, more upgrades, and top-dollar sales.

- **Moving up/Moving down:** If you've already bought another house and are moving up or moving down, you'll also be in a hurry to sell quickly. Carrying costs on two houses can be a big strain on the pocketbook.

- **Cashing out:** If you're selling to make a profit and then move on, you have the luxury of time on your side. You may even have the time to do a full kitchen or master bath upgrade. And if getting top dollar is your priority, then time is probably not that much of an issue.

THE RSS TIMELINE

Regardless of your reason for selling, some typical questions once you've decided to sell are: How long is it all going to take—weeks, months, a year? What is a realistic timeline? How long before I get an offer? If I decide today that I want to sell my house, how long will it take before I'm cashing out and moving out?

While timelines for a house sale vary, there is a basic timeline that serves as our average and our goal. I'm all about goals. I like to set goals and then work toward them. By establishing realistic expectations and a plan to implement them, you *can* make them happen. Setting a goal and timeline also allows—and forces—you to keep on schedule. I know that, even with the best intentions, sometimes we will put off till tomorrow what we really would rather not do today. Well, when it comes to selling your home for top dollar, you can't afford that lazy luxury!

Thirty Days from Today—Are You Kidding?

On average, most home sellers want to have their house on the market thirty days from the day they decide to sell. That means you're going to have *a lot* of work to do in the next month. Several significant RSS steps must be completed in these first thirty days. Selecting a Realtor will be one of your first major decisions. But you're also going to have to start implementing all the set-to-sell techniques *today*, too. Remember, the clock is ticking. Thirty days will go by very quickly.

The Timeline

The RSS timeline shows a basic overview of what you can expect, with a rough estimate of how long each step in the process generally

RSS 90-Day Timeline

Mon	Tues	Wed	Thurs	Fri	Sat / Sun
	1 "I'M SELLING MY HOUSE"	2 BEGIN REALTOR SEARCH	3	4 SAVE IT, STORE IT, SELL IT, CHUCK IT WEEKEND	5/6 REALTOR INTERVIEWS
7 BEGIN REPAIR TO SELL →	8 SELECT YOUR REALTOR	9	10	11 BEGIN LIFESTYLE UPGRADES →	12/13
14 REALTOR PREPARES PHOTOS, BROCHURES	15	16 BEGIN DESIGNED TO SELL →	17	18	19/20
21 BEGIN STAGE TO SELL →	22 COMPLETE SIGN LISTING AGREEMENT	23	24	25	26/27
28 BEGIN PREP TO SELL →	29	30	31 FINAL SET TO SELL SHOW PREP		

Mon	Tues	Wed	Thurs	Fri	Sat / Sun
				1 MLS LISTING GOES ACTIVE	2/3
ON THE MARKET!	5 REALTORS' CARAVAN	6 BEGIN SHOWINGS →	7	8	9/10 OPEN HOUSE
11 SHOWINGS →	12	13	14	15	16/17 OPEN HOUSE
18 SHOWINGS →	19	20	21 INTERESTED BUYER'S SECOND SHOWING	22	23/24
25 BUYER MAKES OFFER	26	27 SELLER COUNTERS	28 BUYER RESPONDS TO OFFER	29	30/31 OFFER ACCEPTED!

Mon	Tues	Wed	Thurs	Fri	Sat / Sun
1 SALE AGREEMENTS SIGNED	2 ESCROW OPENS!	3 BUYER TO SCHEDULE INSPECTION AND APPRAISAL	4 SUBMIT DISCLOSURES, PLOT MAP, PERMITS	5 REQUEST ESTIMATED CLOSING COSTS	6/7
8 BUYER'S INSPECTION	9 BUYER'S APPRAISAL	10	11 INSPECTION CONTINGENCY EXPIRES	12	13/14
15	16	17	18	19	20/21
22 REQUEST ESTIMATED CLOSING COSTS	23 BUYER'S MORTGAGE CONTINGENCY EXPIRES	24 COMPLETE TERMITE OR OTHER BUYER-REQUESTED REPAIRS	25 CALL TO TRANSFER UTILITIES	26 REVIEW ESTIMATED CLOSING COSTS	27/28
29 FINAL WALK-THROUGH OF PROPERTY	ESCROW CLOSES!	CONGRATULATIONS			

As you read through the chapters, refer to this timeline to give you a visual overview of each step of the RSS process.

takes. Granted, some of these steps' timelines will depend on where you live and what the market is doing at the moment, especially the length of time your house is on the market before it sells, but it will give you a ballpark estimate. A timeline helps you envision where you are today and where you want to be on the day you close the front door behind you for the last time . . . with a big cash-out check in your hands.

RSS Sale Success: Combining Sale Strategies—*This seller in Knoxville, Tennessee, faced some tough competition from other houses on the market. The Realtor, Joyce Tapscott, knew that she had to use numerous sale strategies to get her seller top dollar. Tapscott created a brochure that was visual and inviting. She also targeted her buyers, then marketed to them specifically, showcasing all the wonderful elements that would appeal to buyers looking for a family-friendly home. These techniques got the right buyers in the door, and into escrow!*

Two

THE ECONOMICS OF SELLING YOUR HOME

HOME ECONOMICS 101

- How much is your house worth?
- How much money will you walk away with when you sell—your cash-out?

Real estate is a business. It can also be a passion or a hobby, but first and foremost it is a business. Even if you're not a business type and don't like dealing with numbers, you still must approach the house-selling game as a business. As a seller, though, your math homework will be relatively easy.

HOW MUCH MONEY WILL YOU MAKE WHEN YOU SELL?

Of course that's something all home sellers want to know right from the get-go. It becomes all about the cash-out once they recover from the initial emotional shock they experience after they've committed to selling their home. How much money will I get when I sell? That's a fair question and it's understandable that you want the answer *now*.

A Simple Calculation

Obviously, you want to sell your house for the most money possible. In my last book, *Find It, Fix It, Flip It!*, I talked a lot about profit in relation to the cost of finding, fixing, and flipping a house. Specifically, I showed readers how to analyze a potential flip's current value and then estimate what it could eventually sell for after they completed my six levels of fixes, upgrades, and improvements. However, when selling the house you live in, complex calculations and guesswork aren't necessary. Your *cash-out* at closing is merely the difference between your mortgage balance plus closing costs and what your house sells for. These are not numbers that require much speculating, you just need the *cash-out calculator*.

UNDERSTANDING YOUR EQUITY

Again, your cash-out on the sale of your home will be the sale price, minus your mortgage balance, plus your selling costs. This is called your equity. How much equity you have will depend on two main factors:

1. **Amortization**—to what extent you've paid down your mortgage balance

2. **Appreciation**—how much value the house has gained over time

If you sell for *more* than the combination of your mortgage owed and selling costs, you will walk away with a check come closing day. On the other hand, if you sell for *less* than those combined costs, then *you* will be writing a check on closing day. Given the appreciation in houses over the past several years, it's highly unlikely that you'll be owing any money after the sale. But let's find out which it is, and how much it will be.

THE CASH-OUT CALCULATOR

Estimated RSS sale price of your home $_____
   Existing mortgage   – $_____
   Any equity lines/second mortgages   – $_____
   Closing costs   – $_____
     (fees, transfer taxes, Realtor commission;
     approx. 7.25% of selling price)

   Total Cash-Out   = $_____

ESTIMATED RSS SALE PRICE

This is the value that is currently elusive. Of course you don't have a crystal ball. You can't know for sure at what price your house is going to sell. And what makes this even more complicated is that right at this minute, this second, your house is NOT worth as much as it will be once you have completed all the transformational steps in the coming chapters. At this moment even your Realtor is not able to accurately gauge what your house is going to be worth after you have completed all the set-to-sell techniques.

A best guesstimate is as good as you are going to get right now. *What your house is worth today and what it will be worth after you complete the set-to-sell techniques are two very different numbers.* So, let's take a look at one way that allows you to come up with a pretty good educated guess for the purposes of completing a rough cash-out calculation.

It's All About the Comps

You can't just put any price on your home and wait to see what happens. One of the trickiest parts to selling a home is selecting the right price to get the right buyer given the current market conditions. This is when you need to think like a buyer and scope out other homes that are on the market or have recently been sold in your neighborhood. Spy on a few open houses . . . ask around . . . pick up brochures . . . and work with a Realtor to analyze the other comparable houses, or "the comps."

As you begin to interview Realtors, every Realtor will do a cost analysis of your home and give you a ballpark idea of what he or she thinks your house is worth at this moment. But how does your Realtor come up with a price? You are going to work as a team to find out.

The only way to know what your house is basically worth is by knowing what all the comps for sale in your neighborhood are worth. Contrary to what our parents taught us, this is one of those cases where our true value *doesn't* come from within—it's actually based on those around us.

Analyzing your comps does entail some detective work. Obviously, your house isn't exactly like every other. It can be far better or far worse. You have to wade through those comps and pick out the ones that truly come close to yours.

Compare:

- square footage
- bedrooms/bathrooms
- room count, including den, home office, etc.
- land and landscaping
- privacy
- street traffic
- amenities, including gourmet kitchen, walk-in closets, pool/spa, outdoor living space, two- or three-car garage

RSS Pricing Tip: Don't Look Back!

The price of your home today can't be compared to the selling price of your next-door neighbor's identical home two years ago. Prices change as do the markets. If you're looking at comps older than six months old, dump them. Your house could be worth a heck of a lot more—or less. In a superhot market, like the one we saw in 2005,

(continued)

some cities around the country, such as New York, Miami, or San Diego, saw homes move so fast that when sellers priced them they couldn't look at what had sold even sixty days earlier. They had to base prices on what had just gone into contract within the previous thirty days. The reverse applies in a rapidly softening market.

Check Out the Competition in Person

Don't analyze your comps on paper alone. Get moving! Ask your Realtor to recommend homes you should drive by or open houses you should attend. It's important for you as a home seller to know what's out there. Know what other homes have that yours doesn't—or does. It will help you immensely as you set to sell your home.

Go Online and Check Prices

The face of real estate has changed quite a bit in the past five years. Much of the information about homes for sale used to be under the exclusive domain of the Realtor. Now, with the advent of the Internet and onslaught of the dozen new realty Web sites, a wealth of information is available online and accessible at the click of a mouse.

How does access to this online information change the way you price your house? Not very much. You still need to price your home based on the competition. The difference now is that you have even more information and it's literally at your fingertips. It helps you to be better educated, and thus manage your pricing determinations—both high and low. Just go online to any one of the many sites that list homes for sale (i.e., Realtor.com, RealEstate.com, Homes.com, etc.) to view a list of comps in your area.

Online Home Pricing Is Not Always On the Nose

There is a downside to online pricing that I want to mention. It's not always 100 percent accurate. For example, a fun new Web site to check out is www.zillow.com, where you can enter any address and it will give you a satellite photo of the house and its neighborhood with its current market worth—according to its own internal calculations and assessment.

I did a report about the site for the Fox News Channel, and was asked to do an on-air investigative report to compare the actual prices of homes to the values listed on the site. In my research I found that online pricing sites were *not* always entirely accurate. While some homes were priced for what they were actually worth, others were 10 percent or more over or below their value. The point is, mouse clickers beware: Do not leave the pricing of your home *solely* to what you read on the Internet. However, I would recommend that everyone check it out, just to get a ballpark idea of what is happening in your neighborhood in general. The Internet is one of many tools available to help you and your Realtor determine that ballpark figure for your cash-out calculator.

THE 411 ON REAL ESTATE WEB SITES

www.cyberhomes.com

www.homeadvisor.com

www.homepages.com

www.homeroute.com

www.homes.com

www.homesdatabase.com

www.homeseekers.com

www.iown.com

www.owners.com

www.realestate.com

www.realestatebook.com

www.realtor.com

www.revillage.com

www.zillow.com

EXISTING MORTGAGE

Here comes that second item in the cash-out calculator. Are you still paying off a mortgage? Then locate your latest mortgage statement. That statement will give you a current balance of what you still owe. You can even call the mortgage company and request a "payoff amount" for a more exact figure. Now, plug that number into the calculation.

EQUITY LINES AND OTHER LOANS OR LIENS

Do you have an equity line of credit that you've tapped? If you have borrowed against this equity line, then it will have to be paid off before you receive any monies at cash-out. Your escrow company or real estate lawyer will handle this just as they do the existing payoff balance on your mortgage.

Equity lines are sometimes called second mortgages. There can also be second mortgages that aren't necessarily home equity lines. Home equity lines of credit and home equity loans are both types of second mortgages because the loans are secured by the home's value. You may have purchased the property using a second smaller loan or you may have taken out more money on the house at a later date. All those loans must be paid off before you receive any proceeds from the sale of your house. So make sure you include them in your cash-out calculator.

CLOSING AND SELLING COSTS

As a seller, the costs you have to bear are minimal, and I'll go into greater detail about them in Part Three: *Sold!*, including how to understand the Estimate Closing Costs Statements otherwise known as the "HUD Settlement Statements." You'll want to know how to avoid paying more fees than you have to, as well as how to spot charges that either should be on your buyer's side of the table, or that you should request to have taken off.

However, I have a very simple formula for estimating closing costs any time you sell a home: 7.25 percent × the estimated RSS sale price of the house. This formula takes into consideration all of the closing costs and fees that are incurred at sale time, including the 6 percent commission that goes to the Realtors involved.

· ·

Closing Costs = 7.25% × Estimated RSS Sale Price

· ·

An Example of a Cash-Out Check

Let's do an example using the cash-out calculator. Cheryl is about to get her home ready for sale. It needs some minor repairs and fixes, but she thinks she can get a good idea about what her asking price can be from considering the comps in the neighborhood. Two homes very similar to hers are up for sale and a third one just sold. The one that recently sold went for $450,000. One that is up for sale is priced at $475,000, and the other is at $460,000. Because her house is in better shape than the one that just sold for $450,000, and although hers doesn't have a finished basement like the one priced at $475,000, she and her Realtor settle on $465,000 as a reasonable guesstimate. This is when she smiles because she bought it for $220,000 six years ago.

Second, Cheryl looks up her existing mortgage balance. According to her latest bank statement, she still owes $174,072 on the house. She also took out an equity line of credit a few years back that she used and that must get factored in; this totaled $40,000. Then, all she has to do is calculate her estimated closing costs by multiplying her estimated RSS sale price by 7.25 percent and presto!—she can arrive at a rough cash-out figure.

CHERYL'S CASH-OUT CALCULATION

Estimated RSS sale price of Cheryl's home	**$465,000**
Existing mortgage	− $174,072
Any equity lines/second mortgages	− $40,000
Closing costs	− $43,128
(fees, transfer taxes, Realtor commission; approx. 7.25% of selling price)	
Total Cash-Out	= $207,800

Whoa! For Cheryl, $207,800 is a great sum of money. She's excited. But then another question suddenly hits. Does she have to pay taxes on this money? She's realizing a huge gain, so isn't there something called capital gains taxes?

Yes, there is. But as you're about to find out in the next chapter, most sellers are safe from having to owe Uncle Sam any money from their real estate profits. I am going to give you the scoop on all you need to know about timing your sale to avoid taxes. And of course I'll briefly outline what happens when you sell a home for so much that you awaken the taxman.

RSS Sale Success: Understanding Your Equity—*The sellers of this northern California home had lived in it for more than twenty years. They were ready to retire and downsize. Using the cash-out calculator formula, their Realtor, Rick Geha, determined their potential equity. Estimating what their cash-out would be ahead of time allowed them to shop around while their house was still on the market. They found a home that was less expensive than the one they were selling, yet bigger and with more amenities. They sold their home in record time and were able to purchase the new one with cash only.*

Three

SUCCESSFUL SELLING IN AN UP OR DOWN MARKET—TAXES AND TIMING

Real estate over the past thirty years has appreciated at an annual average of approximately 4.5 percent. That seems low, as we've seen many homes increase in value at 10, 20, 30, and even 40 or more percent in recent years, especially in growth areas such as major cities and oceanfront property, and in states such as Florida and California. But regardless of which way the market is heading, up or down, you still can sell your home for top dollar for your market.

When you follow the RSS steps to success, not only do you benefit from the appreciation and equity you've gained over the years, you also stand to be a comp-breaking winner. By adding both tangible and perceived value to your house, you surpass the comps, or get a significantly higher price for what, on paper, may seem to be the same house . . . no matter what the market is doing!

RSS TECHNIQUES ARE BENEFICIAL IN ANY MARKET

In an ideal world, you would time the sale of your house perfectly so you could get a record-breaking market price, right? But, as I've already indicated, sometimes we don't have the time to wait for the bullish real estate market to bring us those amazingly high prices. We have to work with what the market is doing at any given moment.

Can you say "bubble"? Is there a chill in the real estate air? Or is a renewed red-hot market just around the corner? In any market there are keys to getting the most you can out of your sale. Understanding the market and which way it's headed helps you know what to realistically expect, how to price, and how to negotiate.

RSS set-to-sell techniques are what every home seller absolutely must implement in any market. Using these techniques and ideas, you're going to be able to ask for top dollar *for your market*. If you're in a fiery market, lucky you. You can beat out the comps and break records. If you're in a downward or cooling market, you can also rest assured that you'll come out a winner because you'll be able to maximize the value of your home and sell for the most the market will allow.

· ·

RSS set-to-sell techniques are what every home seller absolutely must implement in any market.

· ·

IS TIMING A FACTOR?

Is there a perfect time to sell a house? Here's the fast answer: not really. Actually, timing the sale of a house isn't as important as the steps you take in the sale process. When it comes to *annual* home-sales cycles, the slowest months of the year are typically January and February, as fewer deals are made over the holidays and those months are generally the coldest. A peak in June reflects the fact that many people want to move in between school years, and the weather is typically good. But those patterns have eased, and some say those trends are at an end. There may no longer be any seasonality to home selling. The best time to sell is *when you're ready*. Likewise, the best time to wait is when *you're not ready*—or when your *house* isn't ready. If you play dice with the market and wait, thinking that you can snag a higher price next month even though you're all set today, you just might lose in the end and have to sell when it's less convenient for you.

I've had one Realtor tell me that he always does very well placing houses on the market between Thanksgiving and New Year's. His theory is that there is far less competition and inventory. He gets all of the traffic to himself as there are fewer new homes on the market to preview.

That said, different parts of the country do have periods when sellers can be most aggressive with their pricing. Yet warm climates like Florida, Southern California, Las Vegas, and Arizona don't see much of a difference between selling in one season over another. If you're living in North Dakota or Maine, however, it may be more difficult to sell high when you're buried under five feet of snow.

THE BEST TIMES TO SELL IN SELECT CITIES

Atlanta: end of January
Aspen: late summer
Boston: spring
Chicago suburbs: end of February
Los Angeles: anytime, but not between Christmas and New Year's
New York: winter months the toughest, spring and fall the best
Palm Beach: November
Santa Fe: late spring and summer
Scottsdale: November through May

(Source: Forbes.com, 2006)

RSS Timing Tip: Happy New Year!

Avoid putting your home on the market the first two weeks of January. Everyone has waited until after the holidays, and a boatload of properties will appear during those first weeks of the year. Your house will get lost in the shuffle.

PAY NO TAXES—LEGALLY!

When you sell your house—actually, when you sell anything—there is one person who gets his share: Uncle Sam. So you have to keep in mind that your cash-out may be the amount on the check that is handed to you at closing or wired into your account, but it's not the total amount of money you get to keep. The amount you may have to pay in capital gains tax can range anywhere from 0 to 27 percent. Hey, 0 percent is ideal, and yes, there are ways to have that be your percentage—legally. Talk about a savings! That's ten, twenty, thirty, or even a hundred thousand dollars in savings in one big chunk!

Most of you are probably selling homes you've owned for more than one year, so the issue of short-term versus long-term capital gains taxes isn't a big deal. Uncle Sam always wants a piece of your profit, but several new tax laws have in recent years actually benefited sellers rather than the government. I'll review the basics of these laws here, but I urge you to discuss them with your accountant. Everyone's situation will be different. Tax rules can get complicated, and they seem to change as quickly as the weather. You never know what new loophole will be created or closed up just when you need to rely on those laws for successful selling.

What Are Capital Gains?

Before we can determine how to save money on capital gains, let's first discuss what the heck they are. We've all heard the term, but we probably wouldn't pass a tax test on them.

Simply put, *capital gains* are profits realized from the sale of an asset that has increased in value since its purchase. The word "capital" refers simply to the investment or asset itself, which in this case is your house. And *capital gains taxes* are what you owe on that asset to the government as a result of your profit upon its sale. And thus, your gain must be claimed on income taxes. A capital gain may be *short term*—one year or less—or *long term*—at least 366 days. How much you pay in taxes, or what percentage, can depend on a variety of factors, including the timing of your sale, whether the house is your primary residence or just an investment property, and your general income bracket. Obviously, you want to minimize how much of your cash-out check goes to the U.S. Treasury, if any. And that's where the beauty of current tax laws comes into play.

THREE SIGNIFICANT WAYS TO MINIMIZE TAXES—IN A NUTSHELL

The issue of taxes boils down to this question: How long have you lived in your house?

- **If you've lived in your home for two years or more** and it's been your primary residence, you can pocket up to $500,000 tax-free upon the sale of your home. This assumes you have a spouse or partner with whom you file a joint return. If you are single, then you can exempt half of that, or $250,000, from taxes.

- **If you sell in less than two years** but move more than fifty miles away because of work relocation, health reasons, or certain unforeseen circumstances, you can prorate the taxes on your profit. That means you can keep 25, 50, or 75 percent of your profit tax-free depending on how long you have owned your house—as long as it has been your primary residence.

- **If you sell one year and one day after buying,** you pay significantly less capital gains tax than if you sell on day 365. That's because at the one-year, one-day point your profit is subject to long-term capital gains—not short-term. Uncle Sam rewards those who hold on to their investments for at least one year by lowering the percentage you have to pay in tax. If you sell within a year, you're taxed at a much higher rate.

The Two-Year Primary Residence Tax Breaks

Today, the cornerstone of the tax-break tax laws for homeowners is the primary residence capital gains rule. When the Taxpayer Relief Act of 1997 became law and went into effect on May 7, 1997, it completely changed the face of real estate. It made it even more lucrative to sell houses. In layman's terms, the rule is: If you have owned your primary residence for more than two years, when you sell you can keep tax-free up to $500,000 in profit if you are married, $250,000 if you are single.

RSS Tax-Saving Tip: Hang in There

According to Brian Hatch of Sotheby's International in Palm Springs, California, if you have to sell a house you've owned for less than a year, try to wait until that one-year, one-day mark to take advantage of the long-term capital gains. You can put the property on the market after ten months, but insist on a sixty-day escrow so you close after one full year. Remember, it's a year from the date you take possession of the property to the date you sell it, not the date you list it for sale.

If this sounds confusing, ask a tax advisor for help in understanding your tax obligations upon the sale of your home. But basically, unless you sell and have a capital gains equal to or greater than $250,000 (for a single person) or $500,000 (for a couple), then you don't have much to worry about. If you can exclude all the gain, then you owe no taxes. You fall within the safety net the government gives us now to protect your profit!

CALCULATING YOUR GAINS

I know some of you will want to figure out your gain without asking for help right away. I'll give you the quick overview of how this calculation works. First, you must figure out your *basis* in the home. This is what you paid for the house originally plus the costs of all the capital improvements you've made, such as adding a room, installing new plumbing and wiring, paving the driveway, or finishing the basement. And because improvements increase your basis, a smaller portion of your selling price would be viewed as gain.

Get it? I know it's complicated and there are lots of terms for all these things . . . but in very simple terms, to get a ballpark idea of what your capital gains could be, here's how to do it:

Take your RSS sale price and subtract three things:

- What you originally paid for the house

- The cost of the capital improvements you've made to the house over the years

- Your upcoming sale closing costs (the RSS sale price × 7.25 percent)

EXAMPLE OF CAPITAL GAINS CALCULATION

Estimated RSS sale price of your home	**$850,000**
Original price paid for the house	− $251,000
(your cost basis)	
Cost of capital improvements	− $35,000
Closing costs	− $65,000
(fees, transfer taxes, Realtor commission; approx. 7.25% selling price)	

Total Capital Gains	= $499,000
Taxes owed by homeowners John and Sarah Perkins	$ 0

According to the above example of John and Sarah, a married couple who file jointly, their capital gains tally is just under the primary residence two-year exemption limit. Therefore, they don't pay any capital gains tax.

. . . .

Most people are not going to have a tax obligation unless their gain is huge.

—Bob Trinz, tax specialist and editor of tax publisher RIA's Federal Taxes Weekly Alert

. . . .

What Counts as Capital Improvements?— Save Your Receipts

When you do the calculation I described above, does the number you come up with exceed the $250,000 or $500,000 thresholds, depending on your tax-filing status? Any overage is taxable at the applicable rate.

So, if your gain is more than the limits, it could be time to start digging through your records to find documentation that could help you increase your adjusted basis. Keep in mind that the IRS doesn't consider maintenance and simple repairs to your home as tax-deductible improvements. The improvements must add value to your home, prolong your home's useful life, or adapt your house to new uses. The biggest key ingredient to claiming these improvements, however, is having documentation of your expenses. Have your home improvement center receipts and contractor invoices at hand!

RSS Tax-Saving Tip: What Counts Toward Capital Improvements?

The IRS does provide an elegant chart on page 8 of its Publication 523, "Selling Your Home," and you can check it out online at www.irs.gov. This IRS publication can take you through the process of figuring out your cost basis and ultimately your gain, if any. It also includes worksheets and loads of information on exclusions, exceptions, rules, special circumstances, and so on.

TAX DEDUCTIONS FOR MOVING

Here's another tax-time money-saving tip: moving costs. If you're on the move because of a job transfer, you may be able to write off the moving company's entire bill, including packing and boxing costs and any charges for storing household goods within thirty days of relocation. The IRS rules for deducting moving expenses, however, are complex, so you'll need the help of a professional to guide you through the paperwork. You may also qualify for writing off some travel expenses, too, such as one-way trips to your new home. Because travel expenses can add up quickly, getting a tax break for them could be a huge relief.

RSS Sale Success: Taxes and Timing—*The owner of this San Diego beachfront property had this home for only eighteen months. He decided to hold off the sale for an extra few months to accommodate the timing of the two-year home-ownership tax exemption, which would allow him to avoid paying capital gains on the first $250,000. It also permitted him to avoid the rainy season, and thus show his gorgeous home with all doors and windows wide open, taking advantage of the beautiful ocean breezes. The right timing saved tens of thousands in taxes.*

Four

FOR SALE BY OWNER VS. FOR SALE BY REALTOR

For sale by owner or for sale by Realtor? For many home sellers, this is probably one of the most important questions you'll ask yourself when you consider selling your home: Let me answer this for you before you go much further.

THE REAL TRUTH

I have found that much of my success in real estate has come from knowing one thing—that I don't know everything! I realize I am not a contractor, a designer, a Realtor, or a lawyer. Nor do I want to be. But where my expertise lies is in knowing how to surround myself with experts in their fields. Realtors are experts in their field. Their job is selling houses. I would never represent myself in a murder trial, so why would I sell my own house? I always work with a Realtor when I sell a house. So I say, "Leave it to the experts!"

Put simply, you don't have the time, the expertise, or the market access to market, show, negotiate, and close the deal. The money you *think* you'll save on commissions is easily equal to the higher price you can get with the added experience and access a Realtor can provide. Leave the selling of your house to a pro and you'll benefit. They have the resources to get top dollar for you and it's in their best interest to do so.

Why Do I Recommend Working with a Realtor?

The first thing I want to ask here is: "My goal in writing this book is what?" Okay, say the answer with me: *To help you make more money when you sell!* I have no agenda to endorse Realtors merely for the sake of endorsing them. I simply believe that if you sell your house yourself, *you will not make as much money when you sell.* I recommend that you work with a real estate professional, a Realtor. I agree that a Realtor's 6 percent commission seems like a lot of money, but it's worth every penny.

THE SUCCESS AND FAILURES OF
"FOR SALE BY OWNER"

I have listed selling your home "For Sale by Owner" as one of the Top Ten Sins of Selling. According to the National Association of Realtors, success rates of For Sale by Owner (FSBO) are fewer than 1 in 5.

Statistically, a home on the market For Sale by Owner takes longer to sell and eventually sells for less than its Realtor-represented counterparts, and any buyer worth his or her salt is going to be represented by an agent of his or her own. So you are going to have to pay that buyer's agent 3 percent. Thus, if you think you are saving 6 percent, you're really saving only 3 percent. And your chances of getting into multiple offers For Sale by Owner are pretty slim. You may never even come close to getting over-asking offers. Combining just these reasons alone, the scales tip heavily away from FSBO and toward For Sale by Realtor.

· ·

The percentage of owners who sell without a Realtor has been trending down and hit a record low in 2005, when only 13 percent of home sellers sold their home without professional help. When asked if they would do it again, only half said yes.

—2005 NAR Profile of Home Buyers and Sellers

· ·

WHAT A REALTOR CAN DO THAT YOU CAN'T

Realtors know the business inside and out. Technically, a Realtor is an agent who belongs to the National Association of Realtors and adheres to its code of ethics. They have experience with each and every step of the home-buying and -selling process. They are the experts in a number of areas critical to the selling process, including:

- Knowledge of neighborhoods

- Knowledge of recent comps—what has sold and for how much

- Access to the Multiple Listing Service (MLS)

- Inside-track access to properties that have not yet hit the market

- How to price and justify that price of your home

- How to market your home using proper selling procedures

- How to create excitement with other agents in their home office

- How to structure your deal

- The methods of screening buyers

- The way to work the sale process efficiently so you don't waste or lose time

- How to step in when there are buyers' financing problems

- Experience dealing directly with buyers' objections and complaints (including shielding you from personal interaction with the buyers)

- Methods to deal with the buyers' agents directly and professionally

- Skills at negotiating any concession requests from the buyers

- Motivation to keep buyers on their closing timeline

- The best ways to keep the closing on track

- How to push the escrow, contracts, or closing to a successful close

Now that you realize what a Realtor can do that you can't, let's find the *right* one. Why? Because not all Realtors are created equal. You'll need to find the person who's the right fit for your needs. And you had better get to it; identifying the Realtor who will become your partner for the next 120 days is now your top priority.

BROKERS, REALTORS, AND AGENTS

To be honest, it took me a long time to get these distinctions straight. It was not until I wrote my first book that I was able to figure them out. But now I've got it down pat. So let me explain them to you. In selecting a Realtor you'll need to know the difference between a broker, agent, and a Realtor. The difference varies from state to state, but in most places, you must be a licensed broker in order to list a property for sale. Brokers usually own the realty company and can hire agents and Realtors to work for and with them. Brokers are the "bosses" in the real estate business.

Agent vs. Realtor

Up to now, I've been using both the terms "agent" and "Realtor" loosely, and you probably thought they mean the same thing. However, there is a difference that's simple but important. An *agent* can only be called a *Realtor* if he or she belongs to an association of Realtors or a realty board. By doing this, he or she signs a code of ethics and is bound by it. A big advantage of working with a Realtor is that if an issue arises between your Realtor and the other party's Realtor, not only can you take their broker—their boss—to task, you also can have disputes settled by the local realty board. Also, to qualify as a Realtor, an agent must participate in additional training and certification. You can choose to work with any of them but I generally recommend that you try to work with a licensed Realtor. And for purposes of this book, when I say agent, let's assume that I'm talking about a bona fide licensed Realtor.

HOW TO FIND THE PERFECT REALTOR

Some Realtors specialize in representing buyers, some work best with sellers, some handle mostly condos, and some specialize in extremely high-end luxury properties. In many communities, you might already be familiar with the local real estate agencies and their Realtors.

There are *a lot* of Realtors out there today. Chances are you may already know of one from within your own social circle. You can get referrals from neighbors, friends, and family members, but one word of caution is this: Don't pick someone close to you with whom you can't have a serious "straight talk" business conversation. And don't pick a Realtor based on emotion, either. Instead of picking a friend, choose the most qualified person for the job.

* *

Take the emotion out of business decisions. Remember that real estate is a business. Save your emotions for your friends and family.

—Donald Trump

* *

Look for Marketing Materials That Stand Out

I am always watching for Realtors who market themselves and their properties well. Pick up the local paper. Which Realtors advertise extensively? Who has great-looking ads and photos for their listings? Who seems to be doing an aggressive job of marketing their properties in the Sunday Home section? Look at your mail. Does one Realtor in particular send eye-catching, consistent mailings? These are all signs of a Realtor with marketing savvy who is hardworking and aggressive.

Look for Someone Who Is Internet Savvy

According to Realtor Curt Truman of Coldwell Banker Beverly Hills, at least 70 percent of all buyers will start their search on the Internet even before they contact a Realtor. Make sure your Realtor has a Web site and Internet presence. The Internet is also a great way to check your Realtor candidates' marketing skills and style.

Investigate the Company Before Picking the Individual

If you find a potential Realtor or broker, tell him or her that you are thinking of listing your house but need information about their entire local office first. You want to first seek out the right broker and realty company, and then find the Realtor. Ask how many listings the company currently has, because you want to list with an office that's active. Once the company passes that test, inquire how many of its own listings its Realtors have sold in the past six months.

Go Straight to the Top

Jim Gillespie, president and CEO of Coldwell Banker Real Estate Corporation, suggests that when looking for a Realtor, go straight to the manager of your local realty office. Tell him or her you want a Realtor with extensive experience in your neighborhood, someone who has been actively selling homes for a long time. The manager will have a vested interest in your satisfaction and in keeping your business. He or she has an overview of all the Realtors' skills and will suggest the one best for you. If he or she doesn't offer one particular person, simply ask who is the best seller in that office in terms of home sales—not listings. Look around, too. You just might find a "wall of fame" close by that honors the office's top agents. Pay attention!

Interview More Than One—At Home!

So how does the Realtor interview process work? Well, usually when you tell Realtors you're interested in listing your home, they will set up *listing appointments* with you. They should then come to your home armed with their Realtor materials, which should include their research and market analysis of your neighborhood. These will also include a market analysis of your home and what they believe your home is worth.

Listing appointments are an amazing resource for you. You should interview at least two Realtors this way—but no more than three. Don't waste everyone's time. You will learn a lot of valuable information, the least of which includes these very important items:

- You'll get to see your potential Realtor in action.

- The Realtor will give you his or her current valuation of your house's worth and what he or she believes your sale price should be.

- Your Realtor candidate will preview your house and give you his or her on-the-spot recommendations regarding its condition.

- He or she will give you an overview of what's going on with the competition and other homes on the market in the neighborhood. This might include an analysis of list versus sale prices for recently sold comparable homes; how long inventory lasts; and how long it generally takes to sell a home in the current market.

TOP TEN QUESTIONS TO ASK
A POTENTIAL REALTOR

☐ How many properties have you sold in the last six months?

☐ How many properties have you listed in the last six months? (Obviously, a great Realtor will be delighted to show you his or her success at selling homes. Walk away if the agent hems and haws over handing over that proof. In particular, you want to see the agent's list-to-sale ratio—the number of homes the agent attempted to sell in comparison to the number of homes actually sold. This ratio should be 70 percent or greater.)

☐ How long have you been in this business? (Hopefully, at least five years.)

☐ Are you fully licensed?

☐ What kind of additional certifications or credentials do you have?

☐ Can I view your MLS (Multiple Listing Service) printout for your last couple of listings? I'd like to see the list price, sale price, and how many days on the market.

(continued)

☐ What professional organizations do you belong to? (He or she should at least be a member of the local real estate board and Multiple Listing Service, as well as the National Association of Realtors [NAR] and its equivalent in your state.)

☐ How long will you list my house if I pick you? (Watch out if his or her reply is more than three to four months.)

☐ What is your typical plan of action from the moment I choose to list with you?

☐ What can I expect of you in terms of marketing, advertising, and open houses?

A Word for the New Guy

I'm a big believer in supporting the underdog, the new guy, the novice. Listen, we all started somewhere. Were it not for the wonderful people in my life who took a chance on me when I was green in acting or producing, I never would have accomplished my goals and dreams. I remember when I got my first TV acting role on *Ryan's Hope*. I was a total novice. I had never been on television before. But the casting director saw that I had the confidence and the drive to give it 100 percent, and they had faith in me. I starred on daytime television for fifteen years after that—all beginning with someone recognizing my potential. In return, I did a great job for them.

Similarly, when I joined *Extra,* I had never hosted or produced before, but executive producer Lisa Gregorisch-Dempsey took a chance on me. Five years later, *Extra's Mansions & Millionaires* is going strong and I now host the show and am the senior supervising producer as well.

That's why I also believe that, yes, a Realtor needs a few years of experience under his or her belt, but I am also willing to give a promising starter a shot, too. A neophyte's inexperience can be balanced by his or her drive, hunger, fresh approach, and enthusiasm. So even though I recommend someone with at least five years' experience in selling, don't overlook a hardworking fresh face.

Avoid the Part-Time Realtor

Avoid anyone who isn't serious about the real estate business as a career. You want someone who has sold homes like yours many times, and who makes it a full-time job. Anyone who dabbles in real estate for supplemental income or as a part-time job is a no-no.

Select a Realtor You Like

If you don't like the Realtor, then chances are no one else will, either. But you say, "I may not like him, but he's a real bulldog and will fight for a deal."

Okay, here's the way I look at business. *Life is too short*. You are going to be spending a lot of time with your Realtor, so his or her style had better be compatible with yours. Do you need someone easygoing or someone aggressive? Personally, I am a self-proclaimed overachiever and I like working with someone similar, as long as he or she has an easygoing personality and a great sense of humor. It pays to be both serious and business-minded in spirit but also able to show a good bedside manner. Make sure you *like* your Realtor. You are going to want the people you are negotiating with to feel the same way.

Dirty Little Secrets—Real Estate Insider Workings Revealed!

Dirty Little Secret #1: They Don't Always Want You to "Set Your House for Sale"

Before you pick up the phone and call your local real estate agents for their expert opinion and market analysis, let me warn you about what you might hear so you won't be surprised. It's very possible that a Realtor who has only his or her own interests in mind will say, "Your house is perfect, you'll get top dollar. Let's put it on the market right now!" Or, "You don't need to fix a thing. It won't make you any more money, and this is the time to sell. Something just sold for X up the street, but I am sure we should ask for more."

Why would a Realtor say these things? Because some Realtors really want the listing this very instant! They won't make money till you sell.

The time you take to get your house ready to sell by making the improvements that maximize your equity and profit will delay his or her receiving a commission check.

Some Realtors, especially ones who'll put their *fast dollar* before *your maximum cash-out,* don't really care whether you properly *set* your home. An additional $25,000 that you make on the sale means only about $650 more to the Realtor. The $25,000 higher sales price times 6 percent commission equals $1,500. Your Realtor's share after splitting it with the buyer's Realtor and his or her own agency leaves him or her only about $650. That's right: You would make an additional $25,000; however, the Realtor is going to make only an additional $650. Do you think the Realtor going to encourage you to take the time to work on your house and make that extra money for you? He or she is not inspired to wait for his share of your increased profit. He or she wants the listing *now* so he can sell it *now*! This is not the Realtor you want to work with.

Dirty Little Secret #2: They Don't Always Do as They Say

The authors of the book *Freakonomics*, mentioned earlier, do an excellent job of describing how the Internet and our access to information today have closed the gap between "experts" and amateurs. The real estate business is no exception to this trend. In their analysis of studies, they state that real estate agents get higher prices for their own homes than comparable homes owned by their clients because they use more patience to find the perfect buyer. In other words, they keep their homes on the market an average of ten extra days so they can get that better offer. They then sell for greater than 3 percent more than their clients do. That translates to about $10,000 more on a $300,000 house.

The point of my mentioning this is that Realtors sometimes employ different strategies when selling their own houses than when selling yours. Ask your Realtor these questions: If this were *your* house, would you do anything differently? Would you price it differently? Would you hold out for a better offer? Would you negotiate differently? You might be surprised at the answers.

NATIONAL REALTY COMPANY OR
INDEPENDENT—WHICH IS RIGHT FOR YOU?

Big Guys vs. the Little Guy

Long ago, most realty agencies were independent. Nowadays, when you think about Realtors, the big chains come to mind—Century 21, Coldwell Banker, Prudential, RE/MAX, and so on. Does it matter whether your Realtor is part of a chain? The short answer is no. The quality of service you get doesn't necessarily correspond to your using a chain or an independent. If you find a great Realtor, go with that person whether or not he or she is part of a bigger real estate company. Usually both the independents and the chains belong to the same listing service.

Your local real estate office that's part of a larger chain is like a good restaurant franchise. It offers a certain quality level and maintains industry standards. You know what you're going to get and you can typically rely on it to guarantee you a predictable degree of performance.

Pros of the Independent Realty Company

The perceived value of a chain may be a reason to take your business there, but keep in mind that an independent might work harder because he may not have as much strength in name recognition and advertising. According to Mike O'Riley, the broker at the independent agency Mossler Doe Realtors in Los Angeles, working with a boutique or independent agency has several advantages that sellers often overlook. One important difference is that independent Realtors usually are not under pressure to meet monthly quotas, unlike some of their chain counterparts. This can mean more attention and time focused on you, rather than on other clients.

Discount Brokerages

Okay, what about the discount brokerage that we hear so much about all the time? Somewhere in between the For Sale by Owner and full-service Realtor sits this type of company—the discount brokerage. Popularized in recent years with the help of the Internet and aggressive real estate outfits trying to carve out a market for themselves, they're popping up everywhere. The discount brokerage presents an interesting alternative—especially if the market is hot and you think you can sell your home quickly. Going this route bears some notes of caution, however. I do believe in the old adage "you get what you pay for." You might find yourself disappointed when a discount brokerage doesn't meet your expectations. For less commission, you get less service. Imagine using a discount brokerage, failing to sell your home in a reasonable time frame, and then having to subsequently hire a full-service brokerage. By then, it's a triple whammy; you've lost *time, money,* and *effort.*

But not all discount brokerages are the same. At one end of the spectrum there are brokerages willing to accept 1 or 2 percent less commission while at the same time offering a full menu of services. At the other end of the spectrum, there are brokerages that charge a flat fee of $500 to $1,000 basically just to get your house on the MLS. You then do the rest of the work yourself: marketing, handling potential buyers, negotiating contracts, and closing the deal.

Do I Recommend a Discount Brokerage?

In writing this book, I'm taking some responsibility to give you recommendations based on my own experience. I say . . . go for a full-service, traditional realty company. Sorry, discount guys, but I don't want to do all that work. I don't believe it's worth the commission saved. And I believe that the more exposure and expertise involved in the sale of your home, the better. I have even heard that some Realtors will not show their clients' homes represented by discount brokerages. So sellers may miss out on a big portion of potential buyers. After all, let's not forget, you want to make more money when you sell!

DON'T FORGET YOUR ATTORNEY

In some states, attorneys are regularly part of the selling game. They can oversee the transfer of title from one party to another, just as a licensed Realtor can. Be careful, however, when using an attorney who's not in the real estate business day in and day out.

Michael Lario, one of New Jersey's top real estate attorneys, says, "Having a good real estate attorney on your side is key for selling homes—more so than if you were the buyer. An attorney, especially one well versed in real estate contracts, gives you legal leverage if your buyer starts to miss deadlines." Plus, you can have your attorney review any documents that you have to sign, starting with the Realtor's listing agreement.

In Part Three: *Sold!*, I'll give you an overview of how real estate transactions typically work state by state. It varies as to who the main players are—attorneys, title companies, escrow companies, lenders, and realty companies with closing departments. Your Realtor will be able to tell you exactly how it works in your area and what you can expect.

922 MASSELIN AVENUE $1,595,000

1926 country English perched above the street and framed by beautiful trees. The covered entry opens to a dramatic vaulted ceiling living room with fireplace and hardwood floors. Formal dining room and a new gourmet kitchen with breakfast room. Four bedrooms and two beautifully remodeled baths. The center hall, as well as French doors from two of the bedrooms, lead to the newly landscaped grassy yard with patios and a two-car garage.

RSS Sale Success: Show Me the Goods—*There are many ways to identify the right Realtor for you. I always ask to see the marketing material or one-sheets that the Realtor has created for his previously sold properties. This is an example of a one-sheet that would inspire me to work with the Realtor who put it together. It's eye-catching, informative, and well thought out, and it contains all the important marketing information.*

Part Two

SET

Five

SET YOUR HOUSE FOR SALE!

I have titled this book *Ready, Set, Sold!* for a reason. And I'm happy to announce that *you* are now Ready . . . Ready to Set! Ready to set your house to sell!

By this section of the book, you now understand your timing and your selling goals. You have lined up a Realtor and you have a fair idea of what your house is worth right now. You've been learning how the selling process works with the timelines involved and how you can save money through all the Ready steps we just discussed. So, it's time to sell your house, right?

YOUR HOUSE IS *NOT* READY TO SELL

Getting your house set to sell first starts with a cold hard look at your house. How would you rate its wear and tear? As you walk through it, what would jump out at you—good *and* bad? If a caravan of Realtors and potential buyers were knocking on your front door this instant, would you be embarrassed, horrified, or confident that your house is ready to earn you the big bucks that you desire?

I will guarantee you that your house is *not* ready to sell for its maximum amount right at this moment. And trust me, if you think it is . . . you are mistaken. But, hey, I don't want to insult your judgment; I'm just basing this on my own expertise.

· ·

I will guarantee you that your house is **not** *ready to sell for its maximum amount right at this moment. And trust me, if you think it is . . . you are mistaken.*

· ·

IT'S A STEP-BY-STEP PROCESS

Okay, now the fun begins. Now it's time to make your house *worth more money*. If every home seller were to read just this section, they would make thousands more dollars at sale time. I'm always so shocked when I see homes go on the market without any thought to setting their house for sale. It truly is money thrown away.

It's not difficult, it's not nuclear physics. If you just follow the information in these chapters and implement the set-to-sell techniques, you will transform your *house* into a *home* that will attract more attention, more buyers, and higher-priced offers . . . which equals more money for you!

THE FIVE SET-TO-SELL TECHNIQUES

1. Save It, Store It, Sell It, Chuck It

2. Repair to Sell

3. Lifestyle Upgrades

4. Design to Sell

5. Dress to Sell: Stage to Sell & Prep to Sell

Each Step Inspires the Next

I'm sure you're thinking, "What!?! I have no idea where to start—what to repair, replace, or upgrade, or how to dress my home for sale." But I promise you that once you begin the first steps, you'll watch your house morph into a buyer's dream home. Your house's transformation will take on a life of its own. One improvement will inspire you to do improvements elsewhere. One repair will suggest others. One organized and uncluttered room will encourage you to do another.

Hopefully, within thirty days, after all the set-to-sell steps have been completed, you'll walk into your house and say, "Wow! Do I really live here? Is this really *my* home?" Believe me, I have worked through this set-to-sell process of repairing, upgrading, organizing, clearing out, and cleaning up with many people. I can't tell you how many times the seller says, "I had no idea there was such a great house under all that. Maybe I don't want to sell after all!" *That* is the kind of transformation that will get you the bigger offers and more money when you sell.

From mansions to modest, a visible transformation takes place and the value of every home is instantly increased when set-to-sell techniques are applied.

BUT WHY NOT SELL IT THE WAY IT IS?

Of course you can choose to *not* set your house for sale. But let me ask you a question first: Have you ever sold a car, or know someone who has? Well, people understand that to get top dollar for a used car, they will spend hours cleaning, waxing, and detailing every square inch. They will get it tuned up and running in perfect shape. The windows will sparkle and the interior will look, feel, and even smell great. We all realize that detailing your car before the sale increases its value.

So why would it be any different when selling your house? Not only should the process of selling a house be similar to selling a car, but the incentives to put more time and effort into selling your home should be greater. We're talking about a significant asset here! Just think, if you expect to get 10 to 15 percent more for your $15,000 car after it has been meticulously detailed, that's an added return of $1,500 to $2,250. Nice! That cash will come in handy, I'm sure. But with an expected return of 10 to 15 percent more for your set-to-sell home that was worth $500,000 *before* you improved it, that's an added potential return of $50,000 to $75,000. *Even nicer!*

Allowances Won't Help You

Okay, now you might be thinking, "Well, if I just give my buyer a little discount for doing the paint job and update himself, then I don't have to bother with it and the buyer will love rolling up his sleeves and adding in some TLC." *Wrong!* What happens when you avoid doing the work and give your buyer an allowance instead? You will corner yourself into accepting a lower offer because your house doesn't look "buyer perfect"—*and* you'll still pay the allowance! C'mon, don't give up your negotiating room before you've even *started* to negotiate with a buyer. This is why I'm devoting so much time to teaching you how to set your house for sale. It's essential. It's required. It's the only way to get top dollar and a top-of-the-market price tag for your home.

RSS Selling Gone Wrong—$25,000 in One Weekend

A Realtor whom I have worked with, Toby Wolter of the Carson Realty Group in Miami, called me one day and said, "Michael, you need to come look at a condo I have just previewed. This is something for your next book!" Indeed it was. It was the classic example of money thrown away.

The two-bedroom condo, unit number 30, was for sale at $195,000. However, the identical condo next door, number 31, had just sold for $210,000. Even though both condos were exactly the same, the Realtor was forced to offer unit number 30 for $15,000 less because it was so packed full of the owner's DVDs, movie paraphernalia, and stacks of magazines. There were boxes of unopened mail and even two bicycles sitting in the living room. And to make matters worse, the drapes were broken and could not be pulled open in the perpetually dark living room. The carpets were stained and filthy.

Despite the Realtor's pleas to have the unit cleaned and set to sell, the owner refused. The condo sat on the market for more than two months and finally sold to a low-ball offer of $185,000. That condo could have been set to sell in one weekend. The owner's laziness and indifference cost him $25,000—the difference between what he sold for and what the identical set-to-sell condo next door sold for.

TOP TEN REASONS TO SET TO SELL YOUR HOUSE

1. You'll uncover the hidden money in your house's equity.

2. When you start packing up your personal belongings before you go on the market, you'll not only make your house more valuable, but you'll also save time and money later when you move.

3. You'll eliminate any distracting negatives in your house and allow buyers to have a positive experience as they preview your home.

(continued)

4. You can avoid costly price reductions by making repairs before the house goes on the market. Any money you spend now to set your house for sale will be far less than the cost of that first price reduction if it sits on the market.

5. You'll avoid giving credits back for problems discovered during the buyer's inspection.

6. You'll increase the *perceived value* of your home by staging it.

7. You'll turn your house into a *home* and *lifestyle* for which buyers will offer top dollar.

AND THE THREE BEST REASONS ARE . . .
(DRUM ROLL, PLEASE)

8. Realtors will love to show your house.

9. You'll sell an average 50 percent *faster*.

10. You'll sell for an average 10 percent *higher price*.

Selling Today vs. Selling Tomorrow

If you sold your house today and bailed on putting any effort into making some fixes and upgrades, you'll lose the race against someone who invests a little time, effort, and money into repairs and renovations—even minor ones.

Why? Well, first of all you won't be able to sell your home as quickly. It will sit on the market longer and you'll become shackled to a price tag lower than you ever intended. Then, once you think you've landed your buyer, guess what? He'll hit you with all sorts of complaints and allowances for items you didn't fix. He'll want credits for that leaky roof, questionable water heater, and rotted tree in the backyard that should have been removed years ago. He'll corner you into making at least *some* repairs, but also get you to accept his lower offer and nod your head yes to a few credits back. That's like being a three-time loser. And that means you are *throwing away money* three times over!

If, on the other hand, you sold your house "tomorrow" after having cleared up any obvious problems and applied a few of my lifestyle upgrades, which you'll soon learn, then you literally set your *home* and *yourself* up for a win-win situation. You'll unveil a house with all of its equity potential shining. You minimize your carrying costs and maximize your profit. You can sell quickly and at the price you want. You reduce the haggling of endless negotiations, and basically keep the ball in your court.

The Set-to-sell Cost vs. the Cost of a House That Doesn't Sell

The cost you bear in applying these techniques pales in comparison to the financial rewards associated with selling quickly at your asking—or even above-asking—price!

For example, let's say you decide to allocate $5,000 toward repairs, upgrades, and set-to-sell techniques. And let's say your ideal price tag is $720,000. That $5,000 is less than 0.7 percent of your price tag. Now let's say you don't do the work and you can't get that price. As your house sits on the market, desperation sinks in and you decide that you must start ticking down on your price to generate more interest. Instead of $720,000, you're stuck accepting $690,000. You've lost $30,000—more than 4 percent of your price! I don't know about you, but I'd like to have that extra $30,000 in my pocket come closing day.

. . . .

The cost of any repairs and upgrades you will make is far less than the cost of your first price reduction when your house doesn't sell right away.

. . . .

SET TO-SELL FOR BUYERS AND REALTORS

You need to keep in mind that not only are you trying to impress, excite, and seduce your *buyers,* you're also trying to win over the *Realtors.* Yes, your buyer may be the one writing the check, but if the real estate agents who preview your house aren't knocked out, they ain't gonna bring the buyers there to see it!

When your house goes on the market, it's thrown into an existing pool of properties for sale. All the Realtors in town will look through the MLS and find that your house is new on the market. They will then head out to see your home and every other newly listed home. Realtors want to walk into a home and be blown away, impressed, excited . . . because they know their buyers will be, too. It makes their job easier. They don't want to have to do a hard sell. The house will sell itself. And, I promise you, once you set to sell your house, it will be the one about which the Realtors say, "Thank you, Lord . . . I can't wait to bring over my buyers!"

If the real estate agents who preview your house aren't knocked out, they ain't gonna bring the buyers there to see it!

CHANGE THE WAY YOU THINK ABOUT YOUR HOME

Yes, I know that this place—this *home*—has been your protection in a storm for many years, with all of your memories and your precious moments with family and friends. But now is not the time to think of this place as your *home*. Start to call it a *house,* at least in your mind. Yes, your house, but not your *home*. Your home is the place you will be moving to in a few months. Your house is now a product to package, dress, market, and sell—hopefully, for a lot of money. Once it's packaged to sell, it's *someone else's* home. It's your ideal buyer's home. You can't think of this home objectively as a commodity until you change your attitude toward it.

Your house is now a product to package, dress, market, and sell . . . hopefully, for a lot of money.

INSIDER SECRETS OF THE REAL ESTATE PROS

What is it that the pros know that you don't? I work with some of the most successful real estate agents in the country. I've seen some of the most beautifully presented homes for sale. And I've seen some of the worst! I've seen what sells in a day for over-asking price, and I've seen homes that languish on the market for weeks and months. Here is the simple yet powerful secret:

. . . .

Purchasing a home is not a logical or intellectual experience for the buyer—it's an emotional one!

. . . .

Once you embrace this basic principle, setting your home for sale will be a breeze.

Buyers sometimes look at dozens of houses. Sometimes they need to see only a few. But what is it about the *one* that they pick to purchase? It's the *one* not because it meets all the requirements on paper or it had just the right square footage. No, it's the one that *feels* like home.

Make It FEEL Like Home to Your Buyers

Your goal is to create an environment for your potential buyers that makes them feel good, feel welcomed, and feel as if they want to come back to your home, because it could possibly *feel* like *their* home. You want your potential buyers to be so transfixed by the plusses about your home that they don't notice any minuses. That's why it's crucial to tackle any fixes and problems long before the For Sale sign goes up. You're also going to implement all the ways to emotionally tug at your buyers' hearts. Once you've done that, you win! You get the quick sale . . . and you get top dollar for your house—the very same house that only thirty or sixty days earlier would have languished on the market, attracting less attention and lower offers.

GETTING STARTED

You've probably seen some or all of those home improvement shows. *Extreme Makeover—Home Edition*, *Trading Spaces*, or my friend Doug Wilson's show *Moving Up*. Well, think of your house as an extreme makeover project. By doing the necessary repairs, upgrading the elements that can be improved quickly and easily, and clearing out your "stuff" to create a clean slate, you can craft your buyer's dream home. You'll use my design-to-sell decorating techniques, learn how to stage your home to create maximum buyer appeal, set the stage with my dress-to-sell essentials, and learn how to stir up an emotional experience for your buyers that will have them making offers.

KNOW YOUR BUYER

Who is your buyer, and why is it important to know who they are? Well, just like in the business of television advertising commercials, you need to know who your target audience is. To get a clear image of your buyer, talk with your Realtor and ask the question, "Who are we planning to sell this house to?" His first response may be, "Anyone with the money!" That would be great, but the reality is that certain types of buyers look for certain types of houses. But what all buyers have in common is that they are emotional creatures, looking for a house that they can call home. They will buy the house that evokes the strongest positive emotional reaction and emotional bond.

Types of Buyers

The amenities you add to your home are always based on what the neighborhood will bear, that is, whether you are setting to sell a low-end home or about to sell your medium- to high-end house. By knowing the four most common kinds of buyers and what they look for, you invest in features your buyers want and expect, and you save money by avoiding the amenities they don't.

A Single First-Time Buyer

This type of buyer is usually a renter moving up into home ownership, and wants a perfectly presented home. Since a huge percentage of renters are women, it's no surprise that they represent a large percentage of first-time buyers. The house needs to be spotless, have great curb appeal, and evoke a warm and welcoming feeling with a few amenities. At the same time it must be basic enough to be affordable.

A Working Couple

Working couples are looking for a slightly larger, well-maintained home with an extra private/working space for each individual, his-and-her sinks, a well-outfitted closet, and neighborhood-appropriate upgrades.

A Family

Buyers with more than one child want a fabulous house with the extras for the way they live, such as a great room or open-plan kitchen/dining room, ample storage space in each of the bedrooms, an upgraded laundry room, and a separate master suite or area for the parents.

Retirees or Empty Nesters

These buyers are a growing portion of the population. After cashing out of their longtime family homes, they are often looking for a simpler lifestyle in a home with lots of amenities, such as a gourmet kitchen. They also look for smaller, more manageable backyards and low-maintenance landscaping. Upgraded security systems are also in demand. If you are selling in Florida, Arizona, or Southern California, these buyers will be plentiful.

RSS REALITY CHECK: THE HUSBAND MAY WRITE THE CHECK, BUT THE WIFE DECIDES!

As out of step with the times as this may seem, the above adage is still true more often than not. Keep the wife in mind as you set to sell. Give special attention to your kitchen, master bath, and laundry room. Sell her first, and the husband is bound to follow.

The Buying Power of Single Women

While I was writing my first book, *Find It, Fix It, Flip It!*, Jim Gillespie, president of Coldwell Banker Real Estate Corporation, gave me some very valuable information: During the past several years, one in five new home and condo purchases has been made by single women. The same held true during 2005, when single women snapped up one of every five homes sold. That's nearly 1.5 million, if you're counting—more than twice as many as single men bought, according to the National Association of Realtors.

This trend is striking, because in 1981, the number of single male and female home buyers was virtually the same. Since then, the percentage of buyers who are single women has almost doubled, while the percentage of single men buyers slipped one percentage point to 9 percent in 2005. That's 20 percent of the market. Give these important potential buyers careful consideration.

KNOW YOUR MARKET! HOW DOES YOUR HOUSE STACK UP?

You did the house comparison in Chapter 2 to determine a ballpark price point, so you now have a pretty good idea of how your house stacks up against the competition. And when I say competition, I mean the other houses currently on the market in your area that are comparable to yours. All those competing houses will give you a sense of what you need to do to get your house up to speed and up to top price. If buyers are going to be looking at similar houses in the neighborhood that are well manicured, beautifully maintained, and well dressed, then you better match their level of quality to compete. You won't be able to command top dollar if your house looks a notch or two below a neighbor's.

Knowing your price range is critical, too. Are you in a $200,000-home neighborhood or an $800,000-home neighborhood? You don't want to over-improve and try selling the only house with a newly added hot tub. You want your RSS house to be just slightly better than the best house that has sold in your neighborhood.

What Does the House Down the Street Have That Yours Doesn't?

I've always been smart enough to know what I don't know. When it comes to upgrading and adding just the right amenities to get top dollar, I continually seek the help and advice of others. Your real estate agent is always a good source for ideas about what needs to be repaired, improved, and upgraded. Ask him or her: What do the houses in this neighborhood that have sold for more money have that my house doesn't have? Is there any amenity that the average buyer in this neighborhood will expect that my house doesn't have? Whatever his or her answers, include them in your set-to-sell plans.

You may be surprised by the answers. There may be certain things about your home that your Realtor will insist you do, yet other things he or she will say are overkill for your particular neighborhood. But you'd be shocked at how many sellers don't do this market analysis first. They just redo or upgrade randomly . . . or do nothing at all. They act blindly with no consideration of their market competition.

Keeping Up with the Joneses

Okay, so now you've seen what the neighbors' homes are like, you've seen what's on the market in your neighborhood, and you know what buyers are looking for. You've heard of "keeping up with the Joneses," right? Well, now you are going to take it two steps further. You're going to kick some butt and leave the Joneses in the dust! Why? Not out of pride or because you don't like the Joneses. You want your house to be the hot commodity in the neighborhood when you put it up for sale, because that means you'll *make more money when you sell your house*. And now that you have a clear understanding of exactly what the Joneses have, you're able to go that two steps better, but not three. Being just *slightly* better is the key. That way you hold the decided edge in capturing buyers, and you expend just enough time, energy, and resources— but not a minute or penny more than you need to.

YOUR HOUSE'S FLAWS ARE INVISIBLE TO YOU

You no longer notice that little stain in the ceiling in the upstairs hall. Everything that needs to be fixed, repaired, replaced, or upgraded is officially invisible to you. Your lovely home, no matter how perfect you think it may be, is *not* ready to be put on the market. Your home is completely personalized and full of the items that most people feel make a house a home. The closets are packed with stuff, the garage is stacked with boxes, and the backyard is full of projects that are half finished, but look "fine" to you.

But where do you even begin to change the invisible to the obvious? It's time to pretend you're a buyer.

SEE YOUR HOUSE WITH A BUYER'S EYES

I know how hard it is to look at your house—your *home*—like a prospective buyer would. So many memories. Over there is where Peter and Leah planted their first Christmas tree twenty years ago. Oh, here in the door trim in the hallway are the marks where we measured Michael and Victor's height every birthday. And oops, that's where Dad dented the aluminum siding by the front door while carrying in the new recliner.

Donald Trump gave some invaluable advice to me while we were both speaking at the Real Estate & Wealth Expo. He said, "Learn to keep the emotion out of business!" I highlighted this advice in the first part of the book already, but it bears repeating. Why? Because selling a house and getting top dollar is business. So, get over your emotional attachments, at least for a few weeks. Even if it's just long enough to analyze and determine what needs to be fixed, upgraded, or made the most of!

Your *buyers* will see that your twenty-year-old Christmas tree is now thirty feet tall and blocking the pathway up to the house. The trim in the hallway with all the marker and crayon lines looks like a mess, and the only feeling that the dent in the front door will conjure up for your potential buyer is, "Crap! How much will *that* cost to fix?"

You now must let go of all your subjective homeowner's thoughts wrapped around your house, and become an objective buyer.

THREE TECHNIQUES TO SEEING YOUR HOME THROUGH A BUYER'S EYES

- Move Out Emotionally
- Develop Your Buyer's Critical Eye
- Take a Photo, Why Don't Ya!

Move Out Emotionally

Once you understand that it's imperative for you to see your house objectively through a buyer's eyes, it's not hard to detach emotionally. Step one: You have to *move out!* Okay, not physically . . . yet . . . but mentally and emotionally. You have to "leave" in order to arrive at your house as if you were seeing it for the first time. You need to be a buyer before you can become the seller!

Go away for a few days, or even a few hours if you are short on time. But when you return, "arrive" as a prospective buyer. Approach your house from a different direction than you normally do. Take different streets. Look at your house as you drive up, try to see it as if for the first time. Shake things up. Don't park in your garage. Park on the street, just as if you were there to preview the house. Walk up to the front door, and ring the doorbell.

Go through the entire house this way. Observe the interior for the first time. Sit in the living room for a moment, but *not* in your favorite chair. Use the powder room. You have probably never been in there except on cleaning days. Continue through each room and end in the backyard.

Turn around and look back at your home. Take just one minute to thank that home for all of the time it sheltered you and served as a gathering place for you and yours. Now say good-bye to your home . . . and say hello to the house you are going to set to sell. For the next thirty to sixty days, commit to seeing it and living in it in a new, fresh way . . . just as your buyers will.

. . . .

Now say good-bye to your home . . . and say hello to the house you are going to set to sell. For the next thirty to sixty days, commit to seeing your house and living in it in a new, fresh way . . . just as your buyers will.

. . . .

Develop Your Buyer's Critical Eye

Here is another great technique for seeing your house through your buyer's eyes. This one really helps to identify problems and drawbacks about your house. As the homeowner, you don't notice them, but as the home buyer, you sure will!

Again, pretend you are seeing your house for the first time. Take note of the first three negative feelings or impressions that come to you as you look at the house. For example, your first three reactions might be:

Negative #1. The house feels so bare.

Negative #2. It looks cheap and really tacky.

Negative #3. The neighbors are too close.

Once you have identified your first impressions, quickly analyze the problems that create that first impression:

Problem #1. The house feels bare because there is almost no landscaping.

Problem #2. It looks cheap and tacky because the front door is cheesy, and the front window frames are aluminum and don't match the original wooden ones on the upper floor.

Problem #3. Nothing separates it from the house next door or defines yard lines.

Now, decide on a solution for each problem:

Solution #1. I could plant flowering bushes next to the house, put white roses along the walkway, and plant a green lawn.

Solution #2. I could install a new solid-looking front door and give it a good glossy paint color. I could replace the aluminum window frames with some substantial wooden ones in the original architectural style.

Solution #3. I could put in fencing or hedges along the sides of the house to help block out the neighbors and take command of the property lines.

Congratulations! You have just learned how to see your home exactly as a critical buyer would. You identified your negative feelings about a house, analyzed the problems that created them, and found practical solutions. Now do the same thing throughout your property and go room by room!

Take a Photo, Why Don't Ya!

In the entertainment business, when an opportunity arises for a great photo, it's called a photo op. Well, here's your photo op! The third great technique to seeing your home with a buyer's eyes is to photograph it. By looking at photographs of your home—from the street to the entranceway, backyard, driveway, garage, and every room throughout the house—you are able to see your home right now exactly as a buyer would see it. It allows you to be one step removed from your house—an essential step in helping you decide what you need to upgrade or replace to make your house worth top dollar.

HAVE CONFIDENCE: YOU CAN DO THIS!

As you can tell by now while reading this book, I have a very linear thought process. I like everything to be laid out and explained in a step by-step process. I also believe that no task is insurmountable. So if you are thinking, "I can never get this entire house together in only thirty to sixty days," you'll never even begin. Doubting yourself or selling yourself short doesn't support you in accomplishing any task. I'll admit, I find it hard to get started on a variety of projects—writing being one of them. I have to really force myself to stay focused on the chapter or specific topic at hand to get through it. But once I sit down and tell myself that I'm going to do just this one section, everything seems to flow. I've been very fortunate to have worked with acclaimed life coach and business intellectual Anthony Robbins, whose philosophy and motivational techniques I truly admire. When he endorsed my first book, he underscored the value in offering an "effective strategy and empowering psychology for turning passion into profit." This is the heart of my RSS technique.

In addition to approaching any task as a step-by-step process, I'm also a big believer that there are three invaluable techniques to achieving any goal.

THREE GOAL-ACHIEVING TECHNIQUES

1. Before you start, do some positive visualizations. See the task in your mind's eye as already completed.

2. Experience the sensation and feeling of accomplishment that this finished task brings.

3. Move through the task one step at a time, focusing only on the step in front of you at the moment. Don't get overwhelmed at the long-term prospects. Just focus on taking small steps one after the other, always keeping your final goal in mind.

These three motivating techniques are so valuable. Once you are able to visualize what your house will look like after you set it to sell, you can begin the first few steps and your enthusiasm will grow as the process takes on a life of its own. You'll watch your house transform before your eyes. And you'll be ready to put your house on the market in no time at all!

RSS Sale Success: My Eyes, My Eyes!—*I want to impress on you how critical it is to review your house objectively with "buyers' eyes." When I was getting this house ready for sale after having lived in it for almost two years, I forced myself to use my "buyers' eyes" techniques. Even though I excel in keeping a house looking great, I was shocked to discover all the small repairs and upgrades that I still needed to do. They had magically become invisible to me while I was living there.*

Six

SAVE IT, STORE IT, SELL IT, CHUCK IT!

SAVE IT, STORE IT, SELL IT, CHUCK IT

Repair to Sell

Lifestyle Upgrades

Design to Sell

Dress to Sell: Stage to Sell & Prep to Sell

So, are you all ready and excited to get those leaky faucets repaired, make those luxurious upgrades, add in those designer touches, and start dressing your house for sale? Well, forget it! You have some other more serious work to do first. Yep, it's payback time!

Payback for all the times you tossed those empty computer packing boxes in the attic rather then throwing them out. It's now time to make amends for the pleated pants, Nehru jackets, and flouncy blouses that went out of style years ago—the things that you just refused to part with and stashed in the back of your closet. How about those long lonely nights you spent ordering dozens of frightening lifelike plastic children from the "Marie Osmond Doll Collection" on the Home Shopping Network? Or your refusal to empty that junk drawer in the kitchen that you now have to force closed by using your hip?

Call them collectibles, call them family heirlooms, memorabilia, or even little bits of your life. Well, when it comes to getting you more money for the sale of your home, these things are called *stuff to get out of the house!*

· ·

When it comes to getting you more money for the sale of your home, these things are called* stuff *to get out of the house!

· ·

GET THE STUFF OUT

Okay, we agree, your house is probably packed to the rafters with your personal stuff. Before you even think about doing repairs, upgrading, designing, or *dressing* your house for sale, you have to *undress* it first! As a very good friend of mine always says, "You have to see it before you can repair it!" And right now, there is so much clutter—furniture, photos, accessories, and junk—in your house that it's hard to even identify the areas to repair. Think of this process as a way to start from a clean slate . . . from which we will create your dream home.

- Save It, Store It, Sell It, Chuck It
- Clutter Eats Equity
- Pack It Up
- Depersonalize
- Creating Space
- Organize Your Home, and You Organize Your Life

Peel Back the Layers

I usually hate it when authors use food analogies, but this one really seems to apply, so bear with me. Think of each one of the set-to-sell steps as peeling away the leaves from an artichoke. Every leaf you remove from the artichoke brings you that much closer to the prized heart hidden inside.

Well, that's what a well-lived-in home is like. Over the years, it has accumulated layers of wear and tear, neglected repairs, deferred maintenance, knickknacks, worn-out pieces of furniture, kitchens decorated with rooster wallpaper, and closets full of unworn clothes. When you repair a dripping faucet, upgrade the security system, replace the hardware on the kitchen cabinets, empty out that junk drawer, repaint the master bath . . . you're peeling away leaves on that artichoke that will uncover the dream house underneath.

SAVE IT, STORE IT, SELL IT, CHUCK IT

The concept of *less is more*—clutter removal creates more space—is at the heart of the save it, store it, sell it, chuck it! process. Living space is an extremely precious commodity nowadays. Having a little extra breathing room and a sense of expansiveness in your home feels luxurious, rich, calming, and uplifting. And as obvious as this seems, a buyer will naturally be drawn to and pay more for a home that feels like it has extra space rather than one chock-full to the ceiling with stuff. Clearing out the clutter is not only cathartic, it's also one of the simplest ways to increase the value of your home. Just by removing clutter and creating space you instantly make more money when you sell! And more important, it's an essential step in preparing your home for the next set-to-sell chapters.

· ·

Less is more—clutter removal creates more space— is at the heart of the save it, store it, sell it, chuck it! process.

· ·

Letting Go Without Guilt

We are taught "waste not, want not." C'mon, let's face it. We've become a generation of pack rats as we stuff our homes and garages with old, unusable decorations, vases, grandmother's old sewing machine, and that decorative plate from cousin Shelly. We have to realize that we're not "bad" or "ungrateful" if we give away or sell grandma's wicker chair with the broken back leg.

You will be rewarded twofold when you start to de-clutter:

1. You will make money when you sell your old items.

2. You will make *more* money by selling a streamlined home!

So, I hereby give you permission to let go of all that stuff . . . and all that guilt!

CLUTTER EATS EQUITY

If walking into your garage, basement, or utility closet makes you cringe because all that clutter suffocates you visually, imagine what your potential buyers will think!

Barb Schwarz, author of *Home Staging* and founder and president of the International Association of Home Staging Professionals, often says: "Clutter eats equity." And I agree—big-time. Schwarz has seen her fair share of poorly organized and cluttered homes. The more clutter you have in your home, the less your home is worth. It's that simple. Clutter, or *stuff*, as I like to call it, can be the biggest obstacle of all when it comes to selling a home—even a great home. It shouts *disorder, confusion, chaos*. None of these are feelings you want your potential buyers to walk away with.

Making a home visually inviting and emotionally appealing entails creating order and breathing space. It needs to exude feelings of opportunity and even freedom. So let's just bite the bullet and start room by room to save it, store it, sell it, or chuck it!

Pack It Up

As of this moment, according to your timeline, you may have only 90 to 120 days until sale day and that moving truck arrives—or less! So keep in mind that you're not going to need many of the extra space-gobbling items that are currently packing your rooms and your closets over the next few months.

So, if it's May and you live in Pennsylvania, you are not going to need those winter clothes. Pack them up. If it's November and you live in Chicago, chances are you can safely box up all the pool floaties and barbecue equipment. Wow, just the seasonal items alone can start to put a dent in your clutter! The secret to getting a house clutter-free is to remove the things you can live without while your home is on the market. That's the mind-set you'll have to have as you go through each room and closet.

FOUR OPTIONS FOR EVERY ITEM IN YOUR HOUSE

- **Save it:** These are items that will remain in your home during the sale process. These had better be ones that either add a decorative value to your home, or ones that you won't be able to live without over the next few months.

- **Store it:** These are all the personal items, photos, mementos, extra clothes, and extra pieces of furniture that you will want to move to the next house. You are going to be packing these items ahead of the move so that they are out of the house while it is on the market.

- **Sell it:** Can you say "yard sale"? These are all the items in your home that are marginally valuable—*to somebody else!* One big sale can actually generate a surprisingly large wad of cash. And you have the opportunity to rid your home of space-devouring "stuff."

- **Chuck it:** These are the items that you are going to throw out or give away. If you are anything like me, once you get started allocating items to this pile, the process becomes cleansing and cathartic—that pile is going to get pretty big!

This condo in Claremont, California, was in desperate need of a save it, store it, sell it, chuck it makeover. The process took the homeowner only a few hours, but the house sold that week for more than the asking price!

> ### RSS Space Tip: Don't Create a Vacuum!
>
> Keep in mind that you aren't trying to remove *everything* from your home. An empty home doesn't sell quickly or profitably. An empty home feels just like that—empty. There's no life or heart in it. You want to depersonalize, de-clutter, and create space—not create an empty shell.

Depersonalize

I guarantee there is far too much of "you" in your house. It's time to depersonalize your home. Get rid of what you're not using, then edit and organize the rest. Start in one room and systematically go through every drawer, every closet, every shelf. Throw or give away what you haven't used in more than a year. Your first reaction is going to be, "Oh, dear God, I don't have the time to do that." Believe me, you don't have the time *not* to.

THE WEEKEND MAKEOVER THAT CAN MAKE YOU $10,000!

A makeover may sound like a lot of work, but if you could make at least $10,000 in one weekend, you'd jump at the chance. Well, devoting just one weekend to de-cluttering your house and applying the save it, store it, sell it, chuck it principles can add $10,000 or more to your home's value. So grab the trash cans and work gloves, and load up the SUV!

CREATING SPACE

Next time you enter a room jammed with furnishings, accessories, and knickknacks, take a moment to notice how you feel. No matter how expensive or well arranged they are I'll bet you'll feel a little closed in, tight, and constricted. Then, next time you find yourself in an open, bright, airy, minimally furnished space, such as a museum or a well-designed and organized shop, stop and check yourself out. Chances are you'll feel more relaxed, more open, and lighter. This is how you want your *buyers* to feel when they enter your home. To get that feeling, you have to create space.

Three Steps to Creating Space

Step 1. Give Yourself a Two-Day Space Break

This may sound odd, but it really works. Select a particularly cluttered corner of the room, or a wall on which there are too many hanging photos or other objects. Remove them! Put them in another room or, better yet, in the garage. You're going to hate it. Don't worry—this is only for forty-eight hours. By the next day, it will start to look more normal. And, by day two, when you try to put all the items back, you won't be happy. It will feel too crowded. Congratulations! You have just learned how to edit. You are on your way.

All the things that comfortably fit back in the room, you *save*. With everything else you need to decide what you are going to *store*, what you are going to *sell*, and what you are just simply going to *chuck* or give away.

Step 2. Take on the Whole Room

Now, use this same technique with that whole room. Remove the accessories on the coffee and end tables, along with bric-a-brac and photos. Next, pull out anything broken or in need of repair, especially any furniture that you've been promising yourself you would re-cover or clean. This is the time to strip the room to the bare minimum of furniture.

I can hear you mumbling, "Oh my God, I can't live like this for two days!" You may even feel a bit naked. But hang in there; that feeling will pass.

In forty-eight hours you're allowed to put things back—but only half of the items you took out. In fact, I'd prefer you put back only one quarter of the furnishings.

Step 3. Take on the Whole House

Go room by room and do this same process. This includes the baths and, of course, the kitchen. Promise me you'll get rid of all those plastic figurines and bottles of decorative fruits and vegetables sealed in oil.

Honestly, I have some of those decorative bottles, too, but I put them away at sale time. Clean them out, sell them off, or chuck them.

This is the time for your house to take center stage, not your 182 framed family photos or the Murano glass cat collection you brought back from Italy.

. . . .

Remember, a lot of your stuff is good for living, but not for selling.

—Barb Schwarz, home staging professional

. . . .

CLOSETS AND CUPBOARDS AND DRAWERS . . . OH MY!

When you get to the closets and cupboards, you've got to do more than just save, store, sell, or chuck. You're going to have to completely organize and stage the interior of closets, cupboards, and drawers. These interiors are just as important as the interior of each room. Don't think you can just shove your stuff in there as you move room to room cleaning, staging, and dressing.

All your closets and drawers need this overhaul. Every item of clothing in the closets needs to be strategically placed, color-coordinated, and perfectly hung or neatly folded. You are creating a feeling of order and space. The same goes for kitchen cabinets and bathroom medicine cabinets. You are setting a stage and creating a *feeling* of ample storage and a well-organized life.

Your Clothes Should Look Like They're Right Off the Rack

Look critically at all those clothes, shoes, and closet hangers. What do you really need to get through your next month or two? What will you really want to wear again in six months? This is your chance to do a little proverbial spring cleaning—as well as lighten the load to take to your next residence. If you're having a hard time deciding what you should keep and what you should chuck, get a friend to help out. Someone else can probably pinpoint all the junk—excuse me, *stuff*—that you shouldn't think twice about hanging on to. Pack it all up and donate it to charity. Then save more money by using the contribution as a tax write-off!

Everything in your closet needs to be coordinated. Go to Costco, Target, K-Mart, Wal-Mart, Ikea, or any home improvement store and buy six dozen hangers all of the same type. Make sure they are the new "flat hangers," not the curved crescent-shaped hangers. Flat hangers take up much less space. It will cost you about $49. Throw out all of your mismatched hangers: it will transform your closets. First, group your clothes together by category: shirts, pants, skirts, short dresses, long dresses, suits, and so on. Then group each category by color. You will never again want to have your closets organized any other way. I do this now with my own closets all the time, and not because I am obsessive about my belongings, but because it saves me so much time each morning finding what I want to wear.

Now, once you have completely overhauled your closet, I want you to pack up 20 percent *more* of your clothes to make those closets look spacious. And don't worry, you can live without those extra clothes for a few months. But you want your buyers to open the closets and see lots of space! Even the tiniest closets will seem bigger.

Organize Kitchen and Bathroom Cabinets

This may seem silly, but I promise that you will be shocked at what a remarkable change it makes. Organize your food cabinets by similar items. All cereal boxes together, all cans together, all coffees together, etc., then *face* them. Huh? What does that mean? Go to a grocery store and look at how things are arranged on the shelves. All the labels face forward, making everything look neat and organized. That's *facing*. Do the same for medicine cabinets. It's a set-to-sell must-do!

Not only do you want to organize and face your cupboards and pantry, you will want to make sure there is lots of empty shelf area as well to imply spaciousness and plenty of storage.

Edit Plates, Glasses, Pots, and Pans

Go through all your cabinets and throw out all those mismatched single glasses, coffee cups, and plates. Don't forget to organize your pots and

Organizing, then "facing" all your cupboards and pantries makes them look more spacious, and implies a well-maintained home.

pans, too. Throw out that skillet with the burnt bottom, or the lids to saucepans that went missing two years ago. Also, you should have only your nicest matching tableware in view from now on. This does not mean your good china. It means your everyday wear. But lose the Scooby-Doo promotional plastic cups that have been on the second shelf since 1989. Stack all your cups with the handles facing the same direction. And if you have cookbooks, make sure they look as if they're on a bookstore shelf!

Clean Out the Kitchen Junk Drawer

Everyone has one. I certainly do. It's the one drawer where you throw everything without an obvious place to call home. Used nails, tape measure, old hinges, and other items that probably belong in the garage. Strange kitchen tools or duplicates you never use. Rubber bands. Matches. Magnets. Who-knows-what. I can guarantee that 75 percent of everything in there is ready to be chucked. Give it a new home—the trash. And organize what's left.

Sheets and Towels in Line

Empty your linen closet. Get rid of all the mismatched sheets and towels that have been accumulating for years. Just leave the sets that you will need over the next two months—period. Group sheets and towels by color, throw out all the mismatched ones, then neatly fold and stack the rest. Always have the fold side facing out. Place the floppy edges of the linens toward the back.

WORKING THROUGH THE STUFF—ITEM BY ITEM

As you work through the house, sorting, packing, and tossing, here are a few items you will need to target.

Family Photos: Store Them!

Box them up in a watertight plastic bin, and bubble-wrap them as well. Try giving some away to family members. You will not want to have any family or personal photos around when you go on the market. These are a distraction to the buyer. Remember, you want them to see themselves—not you—in your house.

. . . .

Family photos in every room are like a dog marking its territory. You want buyers to view each room in your home as their own. Personal photos stamp each room with you.

—Michael Maloney, designer, and owner of Castle Keepers

. . . .

House Plants: Chuck Them!

You know that ficus tree with five remaining leaves is never going to bounce back . . . and even if it did, you are *not* going to move it with you to the next house! And get rid of all those gnarly ferns and vine plants in the kitchen. Just chuck them. Got fake plants collecting dust? Don't dust them—chuck them!

Throw Pillows: Chuck Them!

Got seven throw pillows on each sofa? Throw them out or give them away. But I can tell you that even Goodwill may not want all those used ones.

Collectibles: Store Them!

Pack up that Barbie collection, or those stacks of vintage 1950s LPs and 45s.

Trophies and Children's Keepsakes: Store or Chuck Them!

For all you empty nesters, this one is going to be hard, but go into Amy's or Victor's old bedroom and pack up all of their childhood and teenage memorabilia. Get it out of the house. Trophies, diplomas, high school photos, a sixth-grade decoupage project—it all has to go! Save yourself some work and have the kids come over immediately and take what they want, and then dispose of the rest.

Valuables and Family Heirlooms: Store Them!

Clean out that china cabinet and start packing up now. Or is it a good time to give some away to other family members? Only leave a few items to use for staging later.

Files and Stacks of Important Papers: Chuck or Store Them!

Buy a shredder and go through all your papers. This is a great time to or-ganize those files and the past ten years of receipts that are still lying

This room made me a lot of money. The home seller left his son's room looking like this when he put the house up for sale. Obviously it was a strategically bad move and other buyers couldn't see around all the junk in the house, including in this room. The house sat on the market. I made a low-ball offer and got it!

around. If they are stacked up in the basement, go through each box and start chucking!

Christmas or Holiday Ornaments: Store or Chuck Them!

I know some of you may think this is not even worth mentioning. But I have been to homes where one half of an attic or garage is filled with boxes of holiday decorations. Most haven't been used in five years. Well, ho ho ho, this is the year of the Grinch. Either give them away, chuck them, or send them off to storage.

Remove Anything "Polarizing"

When clearing out the house, remove any polarizing elements— anything with religious or political significance. Everyone has strong emotional reactions to religious artifacts and political mementos or statements. Don't give your buyer a chance to prejudge your home because of your political or religious beliefs.

Clean Up the Outdoors

Don't think you can get away with clearing out the house and organizing it meticulously, yet ignoring the outside. Oh, no. The same technique applies to the front, back, and side yards. Throw out those old hoses, that rusty rake, those piles of old wood scraps, your worn-out tools, and all those terra-cotta pots that you mean to reuse someday.

The Garage Is Not the Dumping Ground

Get that garage cleared out, too. Don't make the mistake of permanently storing everything there as you clear out each room, either. You are eventually going to have to store the garage's contents as well. If something is meant to be chucked, throw it out. If it's meant to be given away, mark the boxes accordingly and set up a charity pick-up date a week or two in advance.

Use Offsite Storage

My favorite trick is to use a company here in California called U-Store-It. They bring a giant eight-foot-tall storage "room" to your door, which you can neatly fill with all your newly marked boxes and extra clothing and furniture. You lock it up and they come and take it away. This way, it's held indefinitely for you, and after you have moved, they deliver the box to the door of your new home! (Go to www.u-store-it.com to find one in your area.) It's incredibly easy. And the cost of the storage will be offset by the profit you make at sale time. Other companies to check out include Public Storage (www.publicstorage.com), and Door to Door (www.doortodoor.com).

ORGANIZE YOUR HOME, AND YOU
ORGANIZE YOUR LIFE!

There is something so empowering about working your way through a house and throwing away unused, unwanted, and old items, from papers to clothes to accessories to old furniture.

Here is the wonderful added benefit to this clearing-out process: *When you organize your home, you organize your life.*

Not only are you getting your house ready for sale, but when you create space in your home you also *create space in your life*! Remember, your home is a mirror of you and how your life works, so *as you simplify your home, you simplify your life*. By investing the time needed to clean out, edit your possessions, and organize your entire house, you will give yourself more time for your life. Plus, you are on the road to creating a home and lifestyle that not only functions better, but looks more appealing and valuable to your potential buyers. In essence, you are increasing the value of your home and simplifying your life. Talk about a win-win!

· ·

Remember, your home is a mirror of you and how your life works, so as you simplify your home, you simplify your life.

· ·

I have moved dozens of times. So, no kidding, I have gone through the save it, store it, sell it, chuck it process dozens of times over. Whenever my set-to-sell time approaches, I dread knowing I have to start the cleaning process. But then I remind myself of how fantastic the results can be once I trudge through all that stuff. I focus on the payoff, which is not only financial but emotional.

If you don't know what I'm talking about, you certainly will very soon. Once you have worked through your home, garage, and attic and removed the shocking amount of stuff that you thought you could never live without, you realize . . . you *can* live without it. And you know what? You live *better* without it. There is real spiritual freedom in letting go of all that "stuff."

You Won't Be Left Naked

Not to worry, you aren't going to be left with one chair in the middle of an empty, echoing living room. There won't be one suit or dress hanging in your closet. You'll simply be peeling away some of the leaves from that artichoke that hid the heart of a more valuable house. Now you can move to the next set-to-sell step. Plus, you will have a huge sense of accomplishment and empowerment, along with a more valuable, better organized, and more manageable house—and life—to show for it!

Art Museum Area
Luxury Townhouse

Priced at $485,000
Call Julie Welker
for more details.

This fabulous architect-designed brick townhouse has a one car garage and an additional parking space. The first floor is open and spacious with oak floors, a separate dining area, a living room with a ten foot ceiling, fireplace and a French door to the decked rear garden.

Oak stairs lead to the second floor, with two spacious bedrooms with tall windows and a full tile bathroom, a laundry area and lots of closets. The third floor has a spacious master bedroom with its own deck with city views and a bank of closets in the private hallway and a master bath with shower.

This wonderfully designed home has it all and a very bright and airy feel along with lots of space and lots of storage.

**COLDWELL
BANKER** 🅱

Welker
Real Estate, Inc.

Each Office Is Independently
Owned And Operated

Coldwell-Banker Welker Real Estate, Inc.
2311 Fairmount Avenue, Philadelphia, PA 19130

RSS Sale Success: Save, Store, Sell, Chuck = Top Dollar—*In Philadelphia, Realtor Julie Welker took her seller to task. Before listing the house, she worked with the seller to remove the clutter in the house—all the stacks of books piled around the home, on the floors, tables, and chairs. She insisted the seller sell off the long-abandoned exercise equipment in the guest bedroom. The final frontier was the kitchen countertop, loaded with knickknacks. After a single weekend of getting rid of the stuff, the newly de-cluttered house sold within ten days!*

Seven

REPAIR IT BEFORE YOU SELL IT!

Save It, Store It, Sell It, Chuck It

REPAIR TO SELL

Lifestyle Upgrades

Design to Sell

Dress to Sell: Stage to Sell & Prep to Sell

Wow, the clutter is gone. You have some extra space in which to maneuver. But, oops, now that all those half-used bottles of dishwashing detergent and old stinky sponges have been pulled out from under the kitchen sink, you have discovered a leak. It's probably been leaking for months, maybe years. But now you can see it and so will your buyer . . . and his or her inspector!

It's time to strap on the tool belt and get to work. Let's start with making all the repairs that you *must* complete before you sell.

THE REPAIRS YOU MUST MAKE

Repairs, renovations, and upgrades are a must-do before you put your house on the market. All existing systems, including windows, doors, plumbing, and electrical must be in perfect working order. You may not have to replace or upgrade every item. But you need to know that buyers in this marketplace expect that the home they purchase is in perfect working order. The benefit for you is that these buyers pay you top dollar for a home that is "toothbrush ready." That's a real estate expression that agents often use to signify a house that is in move-in condition without any further preparation—that is, "Just bring your toothbrush."

Ignoring Repairs Costs You Money!

You want to make the big bucks when you sell? You want to sell quickly? Then you are just going to have to bite the bullet and do all the needed repairs. It's important to complete these repairs *before* the sale because you are going to have to do them eventually. Yes, that's right, somehow and at some point these repairs will cost you! And if you don't do them before sale day, you're going to be selling your house for a lot less than the price of these fixes. And here's the real bottom line: Fixing them now is the most cost-effective way to take care of them. The longer you wait, the more you'll spend on them. Simple as that. So just do them!

Saving Money on Repairs

The least expensive way to deal with problems and repairs is to address them before you sell. Waiting to have the buyer inspect and then ask for a credit or price reduction always results in the cost of the repair being overestimated—*costing you money*. It also forces the negotiations to drag out longer—*costing you money*. It can force you to reduce the price of your house—*costing you money*. But most important, even the littlest repair or problem will distract your buyers as they walk though your house, trying to decide whether they want to buy and how much they want to offer. It takes them out of their positive emotional experience and forces them to focus on problems, not positive aspects. Again—and big-time—*costing you money!*

> ## FOUR REASONS WHY REPAIRING *BEFORE* YOU SELL SAVES YOU MONEY
>
> 1. Your potential buyers won't be distracted by problems and repair items; they will focus on your home's positive, not negative, features.
>
> *(continued)*

2. Your actual cost to fix items will always be less than a buyer's estimate.

3. Your purchase negotiations won't drag on and on over minor repair issues.

4. You won't have to do a price reduction to reflect the estimated (and inflated) cost of repairs.

INSPECT YOUR HOUSE LIKE AN INSPECTOR

The house-selling process requires you to wear many hats. You are the house seller, yet you need to think like a buyer. You need to become a handyman, a set designer, a janitor/cleaner, and a gardener. But now it's time to put on your inspector's hat.

Here's a system to identify all the repairs you will need to make: It's my repair-to-sell hit list. This list walks you though the house and identifies most of the areas and items that the inspector will target. Starting with the repair-to-sell hit list in hand, you're going to analyze your house, room by room, and from the curb to the backyard fence. Remember, every item you overlook *now* will cost you more *later*!

THE REPAIR-TO-SELL HIT LIST

Item	Repair	Replace	Completed
SYSTEMS			
Electrical System			
Panel			
Fuses			
Amperage			
Plumbing			
Main line			
Sewage line			
Septic tank			
Main line clean out			

Item	Repair	Replace	Completed
Copper lines			
Hot water heater			
Heating and Cooling			
Central air			
Forced air			
Heating and air			
Thermostats			
Foundation			
Sagging			
Shifting			
Cracks in the cement slab			
INTERIOR			
Kitchen			
Plumbing			
Sink			
Faucets			
Garbage disposal			
Soap dispensers			
Countertops			
Cabinets			
Doors			
Drawers			
Hardware Appliances			
Refrigerator			
Oven			
Range			
Dishwasher			
Freezer			
Hood			
Ice maker			
Built-in microwave			
Trash compactor			
Electrical			
Lighting			

(*continued*)

Item	Repair	Replace	Completed
Under-counter lights			
GFIs			
Outlets			
Switches/dimmers			
Flooring			
Carpet			
Vinyl			
Tile			
Hardwood			
Sub floor			
Windows			
Skylight			
Master Bath			
Vanity/cabinets			
Countertops			
Plumbing			
Sink			
Shower pans			
Shower head			
Bathtub			
Jacuzzi			
Toilet			
Bathtub enclosure			
Shower doors			
Wall tile			
Floor tile			
Caulking			
Repair sub floor			
Accessories (towel racks, etc.)			
Medicine cabinet			
Electrical			
GFIs			
Switches/dimmers			
Light fixtures			

Item	Repair	Replace	Completed
Mirrors			
Windows			
Bathroom 2			
Vanity/cabinets			
Countertops			
Plumbing			
Sink			
Shower pans			
Shower head			
Bathtub			
Jacuzzi			
Toilet			
Bathtub enclosure			
Shower doors			
Wall tile			
Floor tile			
Repair sub floor			
Accessories (towel racks, etc.)			
Medicine cabinet			
Electrical			
GFIs			
Switches/dimmers			
Light fixtures			
Mirrors			
Windows			
Walls			
Ceilings			
Powder Room			
Sink			
Cabinet/pedestal			
Toilet			
Electrical			
Lighting			
GFIs			

(continued)

Item	Repair	Replace	Completed
Accessories			
Tiling			
Flooring			
Living Room, Dining Room, Den, Hallways			
Fireplace mantel			
Electrical			
Lighting fixtures			
Recessed lighting			
Outlets			
Dimmers			
Skylights			
Light fixtures			
Crown molding			
Windows			
Flooring			
Hardwood			
Tile			
Carpet			
Master Bedroom			
Flooring			
Hardwood			
Carpet			
Lighting			
Closet organizer			
Bedrooms			
Flooring			
Hardwood			
Carpet			
Lighting			
Closet organizer			
Laundry			
Plumbing			
Sink			
Faucet			

Item	Repair	Replace	Completed
Cabinets			
Countertops			
Washer/dryer			
Laundry chute			
Attic			
Insulation			
Structural reinforcement			
Vents			
Basement			
Sump pump			
Windows			
Moisture issues			
Lighting			
Storage/shelving			
EXTERIOR			
Exterior General			
Roof			
Gutters			
Chimney			
Aluminum siding			
Stucco walls			
Wood siding			
Windows			
Screens			
Exterior doors			
French			
Sliding			
Glass			
Wood			
Pool			
Spa			
Pool/spa pump equipment			
Front Entrance			
Front door			

(continued)

Item	Repair	Replace	Completed
Mailbox			
House numbers			
Front porch			
Doorbell			
Landscape			
Sprinkler system			
Trees			
Shrubs			
Lawn			
Hedging			
Fences			
Site drainage			
Hardscape			
Driveway			
Pathways			
Decks			
Patios			
Stone paving			
Brick paving			
Masonry			
Garage			
Garage doors			
Garage floor			
Shelving			

While you walk through the house inside and out using your repair-to-sell hit list, here are some repair hot spots on which to focus.

INTERIOR REPAIR HOT SPOTS

Electrical Panel

Check the electrical panel. At this stage prior to sale, you are not going to be doing any major upgrading on your electrical system. But you will need to locate your main electrical panel. Chances are it will need a good cleaning. Brush out all the cobwebs, dead spiders, and dust. Try to wipe off rust or mildew, if there is any. Make it look well maintained.

Plumbing and Sewage

Check each and every sink and tub in the house to make sure they are draining properly and that the drain lines are clear. Flush them all, but don't stop there. Your buyer's inspector won't. He or she will run water in several sinks and flush several toilets at the same time. This is a great test of the house's main drain line. So, if your house doesn't flow with the flush, get that plumber over now!

Water Pressure

All at once: Another revealing plumbing trick is to run the dishwasher and washing machine along with a sink and shower. How's the water pressure? Do you need a bigger hot-water tank? Is it big enough to handle the needs of a small family? You better find out now. You can bet an inspector and buyer will want to know why they may have to settle for wimpy showers. Plan on doing some re-piping if necessary.

Hot-Water Heater

Get a flashlight and a handheld makeup mirror. No, it's not time for a Hollywood touch-up. You need to look under the water heater to check for rust or leaks. If you find any, you must have the water heater replaced. A rusty or leaking water heater will be an immediate request for replacement to your buyers from their inspector. Replace now, and save some money and negotiating.

Septic Tank

If your house is on a septic tank system, make sure you schedule it to be emptied at least two weeks before the sale. With the added traffic through your house during the week before your sale and while the house is on the market, the last thing you want is to empty that tank during showings: a smelly way to sour a potential buyer.

Leaks

Most pipe and faucet leaks are an easy and inexpensive fix, but a real turn-off for your buyers. Inspect each and every faucet and hose bib inside and outside the house—both above and below countertops.

RSS Tip: What's Hiding Back There?

Check the connections behind your washing machine as well. It may be hard to get back there, but make sure there isn't an unnoticed slow leak that has been rotting the floorboards for the past several months. Oh yeah, while you are back there, clean up all the lint, dirt, and missing socks that have accumulated.

Heating and Cooling

Crank them up! Test both your heating and air-conditioning systems. How old are the systems? Any rooms missing vents or ducts? If the systems are eight years of age or older there may be a problem about to happen, or you may have to replace something before you sell.

If it's summer, you may not have had that heater on for six to nine months. You had better make sure it's working properly. Do the same if you have central air. It's a big expense to replace, and sometimes buyers don't care how small the problem is; often they will ask for a credit for a whole new system. So make sure yours works. Also, this is the time to change your filters, and make sure the units and visible ducts are spanking clean. Get out the vacuum or Shop-Vac, and get to work.

Thermostats

Test your thermostats. If they are broken, replace them now!

RSS Tip: Go Digital!

Replace your old thermostats with digital ones. Even if the heating/air system isn't new, it will seem like it is!

Foundation

First of all, what kind of foundation are you dealing with? Is it built on wood footings with a cement base, a stone foundation with a basement, or a cement slab, or is it a raised foundation with a crawl space? The East Coast and Northeast tend to have basements. Coastal areas and hurricane-prone states, such as Florida, and earthquake-prone states, such as California, rarely do.

If there is any sagging or shifting in your foundation, you have probably lived with it for years. It may not have crossed your mind even when the kids' marbles always rolled toward the same wall! Or it no longer bothers you that one end of the porch is lower than the rest and feels like the deck of a slowly sinking ship. Well, now is the time to get a contractor or foundation expert in there to check it out. It may be a very minor problem that can be corrected quickly and inexpensively. If so, this is the time to do it. Sagging or shifting flooring is a huge red flag to buyers and inspectors, and can cost you big bucks later.

RSS SELLING SUCCESS STORY: THE SAG THAT MADE ME MONEY

A sagging foundation is so significant that I was able to profit handsomely from one seller's oversight. One of my best "buyer's bargains" was a house whose front wall had sunken to one side. Even the front door would not open. Many unknowledgeable buyers tried to push through that crooked doorframe and went running back out. I, however, called a foundation expert and got an estimate for the work

(continued)

before I made the offer. He quoted me only $2,500. Yet, I made an offer that was $50,000 below the asking price of $400,000. I got the house at $350,000. By the way, I fixed it and flipped it four months later for $749,000. Had the seller done his homework before putting the home on the market and meeting me, he could have saved himself the $47,500 it cost him to "fix" the problem for me.

This is the sinking-foundation house. Had the seller spent $2,500 to have it fixed prior to sale he would have been able to get his asking price, which was $50,000 more than the price at which he eventually sold.

Kitchen

The kitchen is probably the most important room in your house when it comes to getting top dollar. Because it is such a focal point for buyers, it's crucial that you spend some time deciding exactly how much time, energy, and renovation you are able and willing to do in the kitchen. I will review in detail how you can upgrade your kitchen in Chapter 9, on lifestyle upgrades. In that chapter I'll cover all the repairs that go hand in hand with the upgrading that must be made on your existing items.

Because if you are planning to put in a new upgraded faucet, there's no need to repair your existing leaking one!

Windows

Do your windows work? Do they go up and down or are they painted shut? Do they stay open when you want them to? Does the window hardware work? All of these problems are fixable, and will definitely make a difference. Your inspector will nail you on this. And you will also want the option to have windows open just prior to or during showings as well, weather permitting. So get them fixed now.

Exterior Doors

Do they open? Sounds silly, but if you need a little shoulder push to get in or out the back door . . . that ain't good. Check all your exterior doors to make sure they open, close, and latch easily. Doors can swell and warp over time. You may not notice it anymore, but I promise you that your buyers will. It may be as simple as shaving down a bit of the edge or even using some WD-40 on the hinges and locks.

Living Room, Dining Room, Den, Hallways

Hardwood

Are your hardwood floors scraped, scratched, and dull? Did you know that you can give your hardwood floors a quick and easy refinish merely with a coat of urethane, rather than having to sand and completely refinish (which is a monstrous mess)? If you go that route, you'll find hardwood dust in places you didn't realize you had. This quick and easy process involves adding a new layer of urethane to seal the floor, fill scratches, and bring back the shine. *Warning:* Hire only a professional hardwood-floor refinisher to do this.

Do you have hardwood floors hidden underneath your favorite carpet? This could be a selling point for buyers who'd want to rip out the carpet and feature the hardwood. If there's a showcase hardwood floor underneath carpet that you need to replace, consider dumping the carpet and giving the hardwood some face time.

RSS Repair Tip: Give It a Shine!

Always have the floor finisher use high-gloss finish. When I redo a floor I like it to look as shiny as a basketball court! It reflects more light, gives a crisp new feeling to the room, and will tone down eventually over time.

Carpet

Carpet really is an easy and value-enhancing fix. If the carpet is dirty but salvageable, have a professional carpet-cleaning company do the job. If you've got wall-to-wall carpet that's coming up in corners, tack it back down. If it's beyond cleaning and fixing, then order new carpet. Trust me, this is money well spent. The look of fresh new carpeting is a welcome sight to buyers and an essential part of creating a dream-home feeling to get you that top-dollar asking price.

If you are replacing the carpet, go for neutral tones in brown or beige. It may seem boring, but apart from paint, nothing gives you more bang for your buck. Choose a half-inch pad and please, select a carpet with 27-ounce density. Anything less will feel cheap and tacky—and it's not much more money to be cushy underfoot!

Fireplaces

Is your fireplace working? If you have a wood-burning fireplace, does the flue work? If it's gas, does it light properly? If not, get it fixed ASAP. If it's at all chilly or cold when you put your house on the market, you're going to want to have the fireplace lit. It's an amazing addition to the ambiance and emotional experience for your buyers. And please clean it out as well if there are three winter seasons of ash at the bottom of the fireplace. Shop-Vac or sweep out the embers.

Attic

Got a big one? Your buyer may look at your attic as a potential guest room, and this can be a great selling point for you. Ask your Realtor for information on the local codes and height requirements for attic conversions.

If any sections of insulation have fallen down or come loose, make sure to tack them back into place. Look for signs of roof leaks in stains on the floor. Examine any visible heating and air ducts.

Basement

Moisture, Mold, and Toxins

Check to make sure that your basement—or any below-ground-level area—is free of moisture and mildew. If it is not, find out why. This can be an enormous problem when selling your house. You will want your basement to be dry when the brokers, buyers, and their inspectors arrive. Any moisture will send up a huge red flag. No one will ever believe that there is not a major structural problem. Even the most insignificant or one-time moisture problem will kill a house sale. Trust me, I know.

Selling Gone Wrong—A Moldy Moment

In 2005, I set my mom's house for sale. It was a nice 1940s-style ranch in Collingswood, New Jersey. The house had a finished basement complete with wood paneling and carpet that was installed more than forty years ago by my dad. It was the home to many Ping-Pong games and semi-successful pizza parties throughout my childhood. A sump pump was installed to keep the basement dry, and it remained so for four decades. As luck would have it, the month before I put the house on the market, a big rainstorm hit. One of the basement windows had been left open and I had stupidly *un-plugged* the sump pump while I was cleaning it. Well, the basement flooded with about an inch of water, staining the bottom of all the paneling.

Moisture in basements is such a huge issue that 50 percent of the potential buyers walked away immediately because they wouldn't believe that this was truly a once-in-forty-years event.

So make sure you deal with any moisture issue immediately. It can cause a buyer to completely disregard every other amenity and upgrade in your home and run from your house mumbling mold, mold, mold!

EXTERIOR REPAIR HOT SPOTS

Roof

Roofing is a major issue and can be a major expense. If there are existing leaks, you must have them repaired to prevent further damage. If you have the time and the finances, you should replace the roof if it is nearing the end of its life expectancy. However, if you are planning to go on the market within thirty days, and time and money are issues, the upcoming section "When to Fix and When to Call It a Day and Adjust Your Price," will give you some "repair disclosure" options.

Gutters

Clean them out now. One rainfall with clogged gutters during the time you are on the market and you will have a big mess on your hands. If any are loose, hanging down, or clogged, repair them now as well.

Aluminum Siding

A power washer is a great way to give new life and a fresh look to old siding. Quick and easy, power-washing should only take an hour or two, and will tremendously enhance your curb appeal. And while you have the power washer, whether you rent it or hire a company to do the job, power-wash your walkways, driveway, and anything that isn't tied down.

Pathways and Driveway

Repair or build a welcoming pathway to the front door. Repair or replace broken or cracked cement, or consider lining the existing pathway with brick, a row of flowers, or low shrubs. Remember, everything the buyer sees as he or she approaches your house must look inviting and perfectly maintained. The same holds true for the driveway. It's part of the first impression, and cracks and oil stains won't do. A water power washer can often take care of the oil stains. Cracks require re-cementing or putting on a new coat of tar if it's an asphalt driveway.

Steam or pressure-wash the sidewalks and driveways. Eradicate any oil and rust stains. Replace damaged concrete.

Garage Door

Make sure it looks great, especially if the garage door is visible from the street. When you are selling a lifestyle, there is no such thing as "just a garage." Replace the existing door, if need be, and repair or replace automatic openers. Give it a fresh coat of glossy paint in an accent color for architectural detail. Add a garage-door opener if you don't already have one. It's around a $250 investment, but a real value adder for your buyers.

PUNCH LIST!

By making notations on your repair-to-sell hit list, you have now created what we in the business call a *punch list*. It's a simple way to keep track of all the repairs needed. By now you should have all of the necessary repairs noted on your list. You will check off the ones that you finish in the "completed" column. This is the list you will use for yourself and for your handyman, if you are hiring one to help get your house prepared.

WHEN TO HIRE AN INSPECTOR BEFORE YOU SELL

You might wonder whether you should go ahead and hire your own inspector now at your expense—before your house is on the market. Well, the jury is still out on that one. But as I always say when I teach or lecture about real estate, I can only teach you what *I* do.

I encourage you to first work through the repair-to-sell hit list and then make that decision. Also, if your Realtor urges you to get an inspection based on his or her concerns with your house, then listen and follow through. But discuss the option thoroughly and determine whether it's just a blanket recommendation he or she normally gives all clients or if he or she has specific concerns.

So here's my ruling: If you're confident in the condition of your home and don't think you've got any serious problems, wait until your buyer brings in the inspector. If you think you've got a gas line leaking from the basement or there's any kind of problem with the chimney or sewer line, for example, get an inspector to come in *before* any offers start arriving. The same holds true if you come across a potential problem in your repair-to-sell process that merits hiring an inspector to either confirm your hunch or get you the information you need to decide how to fix or otherwise address the problem. That way, you can evaluate the cost of the fixes, and figure out what's worth fixing and what's not.

WHEN TO FIX AND WHEN TO CALL IT A DAY
AND ADJUST YOUR PRICE

What happens when you come across a *major* problem as you course through your repair-to-sell hit list? Or what if you do hire an inspector and he or she identifies a significant problem? If you discover serious problems, say, with the foundation or roof, or you're faced with asbestos, mold, or geological issues, you have three options:

1. Disclose the problem in the listing and hope to still get your asking price.

2. Be prepared to give the buyer a credit for the cost of the problem.

3. Be prepared to drop the price of the house to accommodate the repair.

Have this discussion with your Realtor. He or she will be able to help you determine what you should fix no matter what, and which problems might be too costly to address even though they mean you come down in price or face more negotiations with a buyer. Your Realtor should be able to evaluate the cost versus return in your specific situation so you can make an educated decision.

RSS Sale Success: Take the Heat Off—*This home in Palm Springs had problems with the air-conditioning system, and whenever buyers came by, it was an uncomfortable sweatbox. They wouldn't stick around. Realtor Brian Hatch of Pacific Union/Christies Great Estates insisted that the sellers make the repairs before any more time was wasted with the house sitting on the market. Once the air system was fixed, the very next potential buyers felt right at home, and comfortable enough to write a nice cool offer!*

Eight

LIFESTYLE UPGRADES—PART 1

Save It, Store It, Sell It, Chuck It

Repair to Sell

LIFESTYLE UPGRADES

Design to Sell

Dress to Sell: Stage to Sell & Prep to Sell

Now that you've made all the repairs you *had* to make, it's time to think about the upgrades that you will *want* to make! These are the *lifestyle upgrades*—the improvements and enhancements that are going to turn your house into your buyer's dream home. Trust me, I have counseled people to do these, and after they are done, their house has been so transformed, they have second thoughts about selling!

THE POWER OF LIFESTYLE UPGRADES

They are called *lifestyle upgrades* because not only are you improving and upgrading your house, you're upgrading specific elements in the house that are also enhancing the *lifestyle* that your home has to offer.

Lifestyle upgrades are the creative, emotional, intangible improvements that return huge profits compared to their cost. They do nothing less than transform your *house* into a *home!* To you, your house will not appear to be in bad condition, but it may have no *appeal*. So often,

Buyers are drawn to homes that elicit a positive emotional response. This home was put on the market by Steve Wilder of Laguna Staging and Design. It had buyers in multi-offers!

homeowners don't realize that their home doesn't look like a place anyone would want to live in because it lacks emotional appeal or "livability." Lifestyle upgrades, along with the other set-to-sell techniques, create the emotional response and feeling of livability that buyers are irresistibly drawn to.

COMBINING SET-TO-SELL TECHNIQUES—A POWERFUL SYNERGY

Something magical happens when all set-to-sell techniques are combined. Individually, yes, each level of set-to-sell improvement adds value. But a synergy occurs when you put them all together. The whole really is greater than the sum of its parts! The result is a home that looks great and, more important, *feels* great. You are going to take your house and create much more than a home. You will create an emotionally appealing *lifestyle*. And the value of that is, well . . . priceless!

You will create an emotionally appealing lifestyle. And the value of that is, well . . . priceless!

YOUR SAFEGUARD AGAINST A DOWN MARKET

When a housing market becomes softer and average home buyers become more savvy, you need to have something more to offer your potential buyers. Lifestyle upgrades are the improvements that make the difference between a low-ball offer and an offer that gets you your asking price or more. These upgrades give your house the winning edge no matter which way the market is moving. Without them, your house will be nice, but ordinary. With them, your home becomes extraordinary . . . and so does your sale potential.

Lifestyle upgrades give your house the winning edge, no matter which way the market is moving.

LIFESTYLE UPGRADES = TOP-DOLLAR SALES

Lifestyle upgrades are born out of problems that can't be fixed with a simple replacement part. They take creative thinking, insider knowledge, and vision. You will have to think like both a buyer and a seller as you walk through your own house, looking for lifestyle-upgrade opportunities.

Lifestyle upgrades make the space feel livable and always inspire an emotional response. They are the special touches buyers see in the shelter magazines and want in their own homes because they make life better or simpler or more pleasing. They include creating an inviting backyard patio and seating area; adding a custom master closet with shelving and space to spare; built-in, charming touches such as a window seat in the living room; and safety features such as a full house alarm system. These are upgrades that will make a buyer walk through the door and say, "I can see myself living here," and write an offer for your price or more.

Sharing the Insider Secrets That the Pros Use

I've had years of experience finding, fixing, and flipping houses. When flipping a house, lifestyle upgrades are the cornerstone of generating the big profit. In every class I teach on how to find, fix, and flip houses, I stress how important it is to incorporate lifestyle upgrades into a flip property to get top dollar when you sell. The same applies to selling your house. Every home seller should incorporate them into their homes prior to selling. Why shouldn't you benefit the same way as the real estate insiders do? I am a big believer in sharing the knowledge . . . and the wealth!

MAKING THE MOST OF WHAT YOU'VE GOT IN THE TIME YOU'VE GOT

When time is of the essence and you need to get your house on the market to do a quick sale, chances are you may also have some financial constraints and you may not have thousands of dollars to undertake major renovations. In fact, I asked the very wise and successful real estate broker Aaron Leider, owner of the Keller Williams real estate agency in Los Angeles, the million-dollar question: When you list a property for sale, how do you advise your sellers on the level of repairs or renovations? If a house needs some serious updating, what do you suggest? How do you decide? Here's what he said: *Make the most of what you've got.* He went on to observe that 75 percent of all home sellers are ready to move once they decide to sell. "They will only have the next thirty, forty, or sixty days to maximize their house's potential." Using the set-to-sell techniques allows you to maximize your home's potential by learning how *to make the most of what you've got!*

*Using the set-to-sell techniques allows you to maxi-
mize your home's potential by learning how to make
the most of what you've got!*

THE TOP THREE HOUSE-SELLING HOT SPOTS

1. CURB APPEAL

2. THE KITCHEN

3. THE MASTER BATH

When it comes to creating an emotional experience and a buyer-
grabbing, offer-writing response, there are three major hot spots: the
front entrance, the kitchen, and the master bath. These three locations
offer huge opportunities for you to get the buyer excited, motivated, and
in that "I could live here mood." And they are areas ripe with attention-
getting possibilities. If you take advantage of all of the possibilities by
using the lifestyle-upgrade techniques in this chapter, I guarantee that
you'll increase the value of your home, enhance your home's appeal, and
make more money when you sell!

UPGRADE THE OUTSIDE TO UPGRADE
YOUR PRICE TAG

The Appeal of Curb Appeal

First impressions are everything. As superficial as this may sound, most
people shop for homes the same way they date. A pretty face will get them
in the front door. The first impression potential buyers have of your
house will prompt them to explore further or drive away. And you
never get a second chance to make a first impression. That's why curb
appeal—the way your house looks from the street—is so critical. Curb
appeal is the single most important component to your *Ready, Set, Sold!*

strategy. Here's why: 80 percent of your qualified potential buyers will make their decision to preview your house based solely on the look of the front of the house in a drive-by or from a photo. Your curb appeal is your most powerful marketing tool!

A Grand Entrance

If you grab buyers' interest and emotions at the front door, you've got a better shot at keeping them entranced as they tour the rest of the house!

To that end, dressing up the front door is essential. The individual items listed below may seem obvious, but taken together these small, inexpensive changes and often overlooked details give a captivating welcome.

THE FRONT ENTRANCE CHECKLIST

☐ Paint the front door in an accent color.

☐ Replace old door handles and locks with shiny new ones. It's often much easier to replace the door handles and any brasswork than to polish them!

☐ Install a new brass kick plate at the bottom of the door.

☐ Add new decorative light fixtures that match the style of the house.

☐ Add classic house numbers.

☐ Add a lovely welcome mat to match the style of the house.

☐ Add a shiny new mailbox.

☐ Add a new doorbell and doorbell plate.

☐ A flowering potted plant on either side of the door is also a must.

Four examples of clean and inviting front entrances. Each one makes you want to walk right through that front door!

Even if you're selling your condo, work within your condo guidelines and make your front entrance look as inviting and special as possible.

Doorbell

There are many wonderful decorative new doorbells on the market today. Replace your old one immediately. A fresh, clean, expensive-looking doorbell makes any entrance a welcome one. If your doorbell is hard-wired, get a new one that lights up as well. If it's not hard-wired, there are some very good designer-style wireless ones at most home improvement stores.

Take a Seat at the Door

One other lifestyle upgrade you can add is a comfortable sitting area on your front porch. Add a bench or outdoor rockers, a place where your buyers can go to sit comfortably after viewing your home. Remember, the longer potential buyers stay at your house, the more they become attached emotionally. Enhance the setting by adding some lovely potted flowers. I always recommend this technique when teaching my real estate classes and I find it highly successful.

About a month after a class I taught this past year, one of my students called to tell me that when he followed all of my techniques, he sold his 2,100-square-foot house in Los Angeles for the whopping price of $1.8 million! He said, "Michael, it was just as you predicted; I created an outdoor seating area on the front porch. Each time potential buyers finished their tour, they would sit on the porch and reflect while they discussed the house. They all eventually made offers. That is the spot where they decided to buy the house and write offers for over asking!"

. . . .

Remember, the longer potential buyers stay at your house, the more they become attached emotionally.

. . . .

RSS Selling Tip: Get in the Door Easily!

Not only should the front door look perfect and newly painted, but it also must work! Does the door stick? Is the lock fickle? Does the key jam? All those little snags will keep your buyers standing there as the agent fights to get them in the door, thinking, "Hmmm, what else doesn't work in this house?" You have now lost all your goodwill, and your potential buyers' positive expectations. Remember, selling a home is not a logical experience, it's an *emotional* one. And you want to establish a positive experience for your buyers in those first few minutes as they enter the property.

This outdoor seating area allowed my student's buyers to sit and reflect after their tour of his home. It was in this lovely front porch setting that they became emotionally attached to the house and wrote an offer for $1.8 million.

Landscaping

Landscaping is transformational. When done properly it can make an ugly house inviting and a beautiful home even more spectacular. It can dress up any property and distract from or hide a multitude of sins. A lush and inviting front yard with lots of green works wonders. And make sure to plant any bushes or flowers as soon as you decide to sell to give them a few weeks to take root and flower. This gives the landscaping a more mature look, and the more established your front yard looks, the better.

RSS Landscape Tip: Go Bigger!

Spend the extra few dollars to plant more mature trees, shrubs, and flowers. If you were going to buy a few five-gallon shrubs, buy a fifteen-gallon one instead. It's a little more money but the result is well worth it, especially if there's not much time left to sale day, and certainly not enough time for any noticeable growth. Many home sellers overlook this valuable opportunity to create instant curb appeal, but it is the best money you can spend and it is never lost on a buyer.

If You Can't See It, You Can't Sell It

When I was comparing notes on the common pitfalls home sellers make with home stager Barb Schwarz, we shared our frustrations about how many home sellers unwittingly *hide* the front of their houses. They often don't realize the damaging effect of an overgrown front yard to the profitable and timely sale of their house. And apropos to outdoor clutter, "If you can't see it you can't sell it."

You need to stand at the curb or across the street and look at your house. Can you see the front door? Is more than two thirds of the house obscured by overgrown landscape? Are there trees in the front yard that eclipse the house? Have the foundation bushes under the windows grown well above the windowsills? Foundation bushes are what landscapers call the shrubbery that is planted close to the house and under windows as a "foundation" for the overall landscaping theme.

To peel back those "artichoke leaves" from the front of your house, grab the hedge shears and branch trimmers. Trim your trees from the bottom up and the plants from the top down!

Barb Schwarz was working with a house in Seattle, priced at $1.4 million. The house, as you can see in the photos on the next page, was invisible from the street. It sat on the market for months without a single offer. She stepped in and took control of the front yard. By trimming the trees

This house in Seattle languished on the market for months. "Uncovering" it by trimming the trees from the bottom up and the bushes from the top down snagged this home seller an additional $500,000 over asking in multiple offers.

Here is another great example of "If you can't see it you can't sell it." This home in San Diego sat on the market for months. Home renovation specialist Alan Sklar came to the rescue and trimmed the landscape, which instantly gave it curb appeal by revealing the house's nice architectural details. It sold five days later!

from the bottom up and the plants from the top down, a gorgeous house with a beautiful fountain was unveiled that previously had been hidden from view. The house sold within twenty days for $1.9 million! Yes, that's right: it got multiple offers for half a million over asking! That was quite a profitable trim!

RSS Curb Appeal Tip: Right Under Your Window

Trim foundation plants below windows to just below the windowsill height—approximately 40 to 44 inches. Trim the privet hedges down to about 42 inches. Don't have trees and plants blocking the front view of the house.

Got a Sprinkler System?

If you do, get it working! If not, consider installing one as an added feature to your home. If you don't want to go to great lengths and cost to have a professional landscaper do the work, home improvement stores now carry a variety of different kinds of watering systems that make it easier than hauling out a hose.

Flowers

A bed of colorful petunias, impatiens, or tulips in the front yard is a must for spring, summer, and fall house sales. I love consistency, so I like to choose one color and stick with it. For the design-challenged (like yours truly), go with all white. It always looks good, really pops out against the green, and is a sophisticated look.

I Hate Dirt, Don't You? So Will Your Buyer

I never like seeing any areas of dirt in and around the plants and flower beds. I like to fill in around those areas with a wood chip ground cover. It's very inexpensive and comes in large bags from any home improvement center. What you get is a well-maintained and manicured look for about $25.

Sod It!

You must have a lush green lawn. If you're really down to the wire or it's not prime season for growing grass seeds, simply sod it! Sod is a very inexpensive way to get a lush-looking lawn quickly. It costs a few dollars more than grass seed, but it is a *must* to get your lawn looking top-dollar worthy!

Exterior Painting

Painting is a set-to-sell upgrade that can create one of the greatest values with the least expense. Every surface that is not in good condition should be patched, prepped, and then painted. The paint job must be perfect. All walls and wood trim need to be updated. If your siding is made of brick, vinyl, or aluminum, pressure-wash with mild detergent and replace any damaged sections. Paint any faded trim and siding.

Understanding and utilizing color is the best and most beneficial way to increase the value of your home. Picking colors and creating a price-grabbing color palette is daunting, but completely doable. I'll teach you my three-color technique for perfect exterior painting and color schemes in Chapter 10: Design to Sell.

Garage Storage

Garages are not just for cars, they're an extension of the living space. Neat and clean is just the beginning. Get a hanging wall starter kit with hooks, a wire basket, and a shelf. For $200 you'll give buyers the idea that your garage has storage capacity and style.

Outdoor Lighting

Make the house look fantastic at night! Once a buyer is interested, he or she will usually drive by multiple times to review the house or show friends and family. Accent lighting will really dress up the house at night. Look for new low-voltage lighting kits that give a dramatic finished look, are easy to install, and are very inexpensive. Don't miss this "brilliant" opportunity to entice your buyers!

RSS Upgrade Tip: Light It Up!

Use up-light, low-voltage lighting at the base of your new land-scaping to create wonderful light-and-shadow patterns. It's very dramatic and creates an instant designer look for the cost of some low-voltage lights (approximately $39–$89).

To improve the look of these two different homes of mine, I spent $39 for the lights and $35 each for the two plants in front of the wall—a total of $109 apiece for priceless nighttime buyer-snagging curb appeal!

Take Possession of Your Front Yard

With real estate so expensive and land at a premium, I like to do better than to landscape the front yard just for the neighbor's dogs. Add value by defining and separating the front yard from the hustle and bustle of the neighborhood. For instance, a lovely low wooden fence wrapped with wisteria vines creates a barrier and adds visual appeal to the property. It also helps to expand the impression of scale and depth of the property, adding a significant sense of value to the house for very little money. It can be added quickly and easily, and is a big boon to the buyers. If you do add a decorative fence, low hedge, or low stone wall, make sure it is in the same architectural style as the house. Don't add a white picket fence to an old Spanish-style hacienda or a river-rock wall to a modern-style home. And don't you dare go for a tacky chain-link fence.

Undefined Property Lines

Are there no fences or hedges separating the house from its neighbors? Are there no physical property line delineations? Well, it's not too late. Houses with completely exposed backyards are unsettling for most buyers. All you have to do is fence in and hedge your backyard to make it feel "safe," a priceless selling point in these times. Not only are you creating top-dollar-grabbing beauty but you are adding value by creating privacy—an increasingly hard commodity to come by today.

Upgrading the Neighborhood

It may not have even crossed your mind to look beyond your own front yard. You may not think it's valuable to worry about anything next door or across the street. But this is an aspect where home sellers can add value to their home by adding value to their neighborhood.

Every neighborhood could use a little upgrading, and the more you help it along, the more your property value rises. Granted, there are limitations to your upgrading the neighborhood. Some projects may entail a timeline you just can't accommodate, but you can target the easy problems and get a few things accomplished to spruce up your block.

For example, if a neighbor is bringing down your property values because he's turned his front yard into a junk yard, then it's time to bury the hatchet and try to work it out with him. Offer to clean up his yard and plant a few flowers. Or, if your block looks "tree bare," talk to a few of your neighbors about planting street trees by the sidewalks.

LA MEETS THE HAMPTONS

JUST LISTED!

922 S Cloverdale Ave · Offered at $1,649,000

- No expense spared on this 4-bed, 3.5-bath, 2-story remodeled, just completed home
- Incredible master suite includes fireplace, wall to wall closet and beautiful brick balcony
- Gourmet kitchen incl. center island, new cabinetry, Viking appliances & granite countertops
- Extra large living room with wood beamed ceilings and restored Carrera marble fireplace
- New electrical and recessed lighting with designer fixtures
- Beautiful ebony hardwood floors, crown moldings, high ceilings and central air
- Exterior painted with designer colors and lush landscaping in front and rear
- Fantastic quiet tree-lined Miracle Mile location, close to museums & The Grove
- Discriminating buyers wanted, come fall in love!

RSS Sale Success: Setting Your Boundaries—*This home seller was smart and creative. By simply adding a lovely picket fence to this property on a busy Los Angeles street, he was able to create a lifestyle upgrade and a perceived sense of separation between the house and the well-traveled thoroughfare. This house sold for top dollar despite its urban location.*

Nine

LIFESTYLE UPGRADES—PART 2

Save It, Store It, Sell It, Chuck It

Repair to Sell

LIFESTYLE UPGRADES

Design to Sell

Dress to Sell: Stage to Sell & Prep to Sell

You have repaired and upgraded the outside of your house. And now that you've focused on the curb appeal and the other exterior upgrades, it's time to move inside!

HOUSE-SELLING HOT SPOTS

1. CURB APPEAL

2. THE KITCHEN

3. THE MASTER BATH

Now is the time to work your way through the house room by room, adding lifestyle upgrades wherever time and finances permit. And there are lots of ways to add value to your home from the inside out. The two interior selling hot spots are the kitchen and master bath; these are your biggest value-adding areas.

GO AHEAD AND JUDGE YOUR NEIGHBOR—BEFORE YOU UPGRADE

Before you start planning any interior upgrades, you must consider your neighborhood and your target buyer. If most of the homes in your neighborhood have tidy, neat kitchens with Formica countertops, then you should, too. If granite and flagstone seem to be the local flavor, your kitchen ought to use these as well.

Establishing the quality level of your neighborhood is also crucial to saving you thousands. You do so by knowing when *not* to spend on unnecessary amenities or upgrades. A kitchen upgrade can range from a weekend low-budget brushup, with a paint job and a better grade of appliances for around $2,000, to a $50,000 complete upgrade with granite countertops and luxury appliances. You want to make your home look as fantastic as possible—*by making the most of what you've got*—without wasting money and overcapitalizing.

UPGRADE TO SELL THE INTERIOR

The two most closely inspected and anticipated rooms of a house are the kitchen and bath. They need to look their best. Statistically, as politically incorrect as this is, these are the rooms that women are most interested in—first and last. A dynamic, well-appointed, and well-dressed kitchen will dramatically increase the value of your home. This is the room where you will want to add some extra "brooches," or perks, to really grab attention as well. The same holds true for the bathrooms, especially the master bath.

These lifestyle-upgrading techniques and the design-to-sell and dress-to-sell techniques for your kitchen and baths are crucial to snagging that hungry buyer with the big purchase offer. Let's analyze what needs to be done and what a buyer will expect.

THE KITCHEN

Even if the kitchen isn't in bad condition, things can be improved. Now that you have learned to see your house through buyers' eyes, it's time to take advantage of your newfound vision. You'll also want to line up all the photographs of your kitchen I told you to take, and examine them closely, looking at everything as if you're seeing it for the first time. And for many of you, now that you have saved, stored, sold, and chucked items, you really *might* seeing it for the first time!

IMPROVEMENT OR UPGRADE POSSIBILITIES

☐ Cabinets/cabinet doors

☐ Cabinet hardware

☐ Appliances

☐ Sinks and fixtures

☐ Countertops

☐ Flooring

☐ Lighting

Kitchen Upgrade for Under $3,500

The first question is how much to spend. I believe you can create a very stylish kitchen for a very reasonable amount of money. An economical kitchen mini-makeover can be accomplished for under $3,500. The key is to make the most of what you've got. These are the exact same techniques I use when I'm flipping a house and preparing it for sale, and they will be big value-adders for you as well.

Upgrade Your Existing Cabinets

If the existing cabinets are of good-quality wood and still in good working order, you're in luck. Examine each and every cabinet door and drawer. They need to be working properly. One of the most common problems is the hardware that keeps the doors shut. There may be a magnet latch or a pressure latch. They cost about two dollars each, and are not that difficult to replace. Drawers often stick and are lopsided because they are usually off their inside runners. The runners are often simply missing a screw, so take a look and have them repaired as needed.

Three ways to repurpose old cabinets and save thousands are to:

- Professionally spray-paint them

- Re-laminate them

- Add new doors and drawer fronts

Spray Paint: Have all the cabinets cleaned and lightly sanded, then have a painter come in to spray them. Don't try to do this yourself. This is not about getting a couple of cans of spray paint, either. A good paint spray job can transform ugly cabinets, making them look factory-new. You can't get the same look by painting the cabinets by brush or roller. Spraying is no more expensive when done by a professional painter. And sometimes it's *less* expensive!

I used this cost-cutting technique on a high-end property in Los Angeles that sold for $750,000. I spent about $800 on the cabinets!

Re-laminate: For already laminated older cabinets, a face-lift will work wonders. They can be recovered with a wood or vinyl veneer. There are many companies that specialize in kitchens. Again, it's a great way to get a great look on a budget. Any home improvement center or specialized lamination company will offer this service. It usually takes only a few days, so it could fit into a tight selling schedule.

New Doors and Drawer Fronts: Another trick is to replace the cabinet doors and drawer fronts. This can completely transform old cabinets and drawers, especially if you want to add a little more style to the kitchen. Have the new doors and drawer fronts made and then spray the old frames.

Upper Cabinet Doors: I love glass paneling in the top cabinet doors. It clearly adds an extra dimension and depth to any kitchen. Fit the top cabinet doors for glass panels in the same style as the existing lower cabinet doors to add a very high-end look to even a basic kitchen.

New Hardware

Home remodeling superstores carry a wide selection of cabinet door hardware. Select ones that complement your architectural style. Don't scrimp here. This is another example of what I call a *brooch*, an added touch that makes the whole room work! For existing hardware, take a screwdriver and pliers and make sure all your door handles are tight and screwed in properly. Also, remove and replace all the old painted-over hinges with shiny new ones. It's time-consuming, but very inexpensive. And it makes a huge difference.

This kitchen makeover was an example of a set-to-sell, inexpensive upgrade that created a much higher perceived value. I painted the existing cabinets, replaced the upper cabinet fronts with glass panels, added new cabinet hardware, put in the new appliances, and painted!

Appliances

A great trick if you are not replacing your appliances is to order new replacement parts where needed—parts for the stove, such as the burners. I did this with a property that had relatively new appliances; however, the stove grates looked worn, scraped, and dull. So for a few bucks I ordered new ones from the manufacturer and the stove looked brand-new. Make sure all the other appliances (ice maker, dishwasher, etc.) and their working parts are functioning.

All the same, when selling your house you want your appliances to be as new as possible. If a stove or built-in oven looks tired and worn-out, spend the money to have it replaced. Keep your quality level in mind. Stoves can range from as little as $399 to several thousands of dollars. But a new range, oven and/or stove, regardless of the price, is a substantial upgrade to your kitchen. You always want to replace the built-in appliances, but you also want to replace the refrigerator and the washer/dryer. If you're worried about the expense of buying new appliances that you'll never have the joy of using, not to worry. Here's the good news. You are moving. So, you'll have the option to take the refrigerator and washer/dryer with you. You win on three levels:

1. The new appliances look great and increase the value of the house.

2. The refrigerator and washer/dryer are appliances you can usually take with you.

3. If necessary, you can use these new appliances as bargaining chips in negotiations with your buyer.

A High-End Appliance Look for a Low-End Price

All the new home remodeling and lifestyle shows—including my own, *Extra's Mansions & Millionaires*—have raised the bar of buyer expectations, perhaps a wee bit unrealistically when it comes to kitchens. Fortunately, appliance manufacturers have begun to create great-looking, lower-priced lines. With a little research and some smart shopping, you can find appliances with a high-end look for low-end prices. The GE

Profile line, for example, is well styled, comes in the popular stainless finish, and is moderately priced. It pays to spend a few dollars more on terrific-looking appliances.

Built-in Appliances

Built-in appliances are a cost-effective way to add tremendous value. On a low-end upgrade, for less than $100 over the cost of a regular counter-top model, you can build in a beautiful microwave. And with the custom-framing kits, you can add it into existing cabinet space. On a medium- to high-end property, the new built-in refrigerators or the new "slim-line" models are a must. Because they are not as deep as traditional refrigera-tors, they don't extend into the rooms as much. Until recently, only the most costly appliances, such as Viking and Sub-Zero, did built-ins. But now many manufacturers are creating wonderful moderately priced models. A built-in or slim-line fridge transforms a kitchen, making it feel larger and making your buyer itch to write that offer.

RSS Tip: Don't Mix and Match

When replacing your appliances, try to keep them as similar as possible. Always be consistent. Buy the same color and finish for each of your appliances and have them all be the same brand as well. It helps to create a well-thought-out, designer look.

Sinks and Fixtures

Not just for washing your pots anymore, sinks have become a lifestyle fashion statement! I do like the porcelain ones the best because they don't scratch, the way the stainless steel ones do. Installation style is what makes the difference. With a basic kitchen upgrade, go with a drop-in sink; be-cause it literally drops into the hole in the countertop, the installation costs less. On a higher-end home, install under the counter–mounted sinks. They are sleek and sophisticated, more expensive to install, but worth it, but only if you are replacing the countertops. If not, just drop that baby in and save the money!

Repair, upgrade, or replace any faulty faucet. Spend a little money here and get a great eye-catching faucet—one with a pull-out spray attachment or a gooseneck with detachable head. It's a necessity *and* a brooch. The difference between good and great is only $50 to $75. Stick to one consistent fixture finish for each your faucets throughout the house, as an assortment of finishes can look like patchwork.

Also, make sure the sink stoppers are working. Will this sink hold water? And are there any leaks? But don't stop there. Pull out your flashlight and go under the sink to check for leaks, rust, and mildew. Run that garbage disposal. Is it working properly? Does it sound like a plane landing? If so, get it replaced.

Countertops

How do your countertops look? Replacing countertops is a big job. This is not a quick fix, mainly because it involves several types of tradespeople— the workers to remove the original counters, the plumbers to replace the sinks, the tile or granite or Formica tradespeople to install the new counter materials, and so on. If your countertops are granite, Corian, or travertine, they probably look great. It's pretty hard to ruin those materials.

Older houses, especially those built between 1910 and 1950, often have tile countertops, and frequently the grout is stained and chipped. You'll want to scrape off the top surface of the grout and replace it with a fresh grout topping. It will transform your tired tile into buyer-grabbing new!

Now, if your kitchen has Formica countertops, they probably need to be replaced. There are lots of new looks for this old standby. For a minor investment, you can select from a variety of great new textures and patterns that will really upgrade the look of your kitchen.

Flooring

Is your kitchen floor pitted, ripped, or scraped? As an inexpensive alternative to porcelain tile or hardwood, I've seen some terrific vinyl floorings come on the market lately. Vinyl is inexpensive and can be laid by an

installer for a reasonable fee. I love some of the new textured ones. Head
to your home improvement center or a flooring center and look around.

When replacing the kitchen floor, keep the floor color and tone similar to any adjacent flooring, especially if you have a home with a very
desirable open-kitchen floor plan. Visually, this helps the flow and creates an expansive and open feeling

RSS Kitchen Upgrade Tip: Under Foot, Under Cabinet

If you have damaged or chipped tile floors, you may want to replace the kitchen floor with new porcelain tile. However, before
you run to the tile store for samples, make sure to check whether
the tile was installed *after* the cabinets went in, or whether the cabinetry rests *on top* of the tile work. This will be a consideration for
you in both time and expense. If the cabinets were set into place
and then the floor was laid, you are in luck. It will be easier to remove and replace the entire floor. But if the cabinetry was placed
on top of the tile, it's a messy and costly job and very difficult to
remove just the visible tile. You may want to rethink your upgrade
and try to repair or replace only the cracked or broken tiles.

Lighting: Switches/Dimmers

Make sure all your light switches are in working order. Not just in the
kitchen, but throughout the house. A malfunctioning light switch could
imply a bigger problem, so you don't want buyers to have that negative
impression. Call a handyman or electrician. Don't try to do this yourself.
I myself am very hands-on when doing repairs, but the one area I won't
go near is electrical. Leave that to the pros. It's not worth risking a
shocking experience.

Also aim for a mix of natural and overhead light. Get rid of the fluorescent lighting. I don't mean to offend anyone, but it's just plain ugly,

and no one looks good under it—especially your prospective buyers as they walk through your kitchen.

High-End Lighting Without the High Cost

Under-cabinet lights create drama. They now come in sets of three or six, and are not hard to install. They can be added underneath your existing upper kitchen cabinets and put on a dimmer switch. These thin strips of light are an inexpensive instant lifestyle upgrade with a designer look.

COMPLETE KITCHEN UPGRADE

The difference between a "make the most of what you've got" and a complete kitchen upgrade is time and money! If you have the time and the money, then doing a complete kitchen makeover is always a good investment. If you're reading this book, it's a good bet that you are looking at your calendar and thinking you had better get your junk drawers cleaned out today—not that you intend to rip out all the cabinets and build new ones.

But if you are one of the lucky sellers who has the time and finances, here's step one: Go to Amazon.com or any bookstore right this minute and get my book *Find It, Fix It, Flip It!: Make Millions in Real Estate—One House at a Time!* It will take you step by step through the entire process of what to fix, upgrade, renovate, and redo. Then, once you have completed your full renovation upgrade, pick this book back up and continue reading!

THE MASTER BATH AND BATHROOMS

In order of emotional-lifestyle-buyer-grabbing importance, the master bath ranks a close third behind curb appeal and the kitchen. The mere mention of the words "master bath" should make you take a breath. It is the most challenging room in the house to upgrade because so many different skills for craftspeople or handypeople are needed in the master bath. However, on the positive side, a dramatic, amenity-filled, inviting master bath gives you the emotional edge that will ensure that "Oh, honey, I love it!" buyer reaction. It can be a challenge to schedule and incorporate changes into a very small room in a very short time—and all in the proper order, of course. Here's how to make the most of it.

General Master Bath Upgrades

The key to doing a bathroom upgrade is again making the most of what you've got and saving as much of the existing bath as you can, replacing only what is simply not salvageable. You can add value and make your existing bathrooms look more expensive if you keep several things in mind.

Tiling

Tiling is a costly, time-consuming, and messy job. You must determine how bad your bathroom tiling is and decide to what extent you're going to fix it.

Any loose tiles? Or cracked tiles? If you can find replacements for them, carefully chisel out the broken ones and replace with the new. If they are older tiles that can't be matched, carefully re-cement them down. You can find numerous tile cements at your home improvement center.

RSS Tiling Tip: Floor on the Diagonal

If you have to retile your bathroom floor, it will appear larger if you lay the tile on the diagonal, as opposed to running squarely parallel with the walls.

Caulking/Grouting

Check all the caulking in the bathroom. Older bathrooms especially rely on caulking to seal between sinks and countertops and bathtub and tiles.

If the caulking is stained, chipping, or yellowed, remove it and re-caulk. It is such an inexpensive repair, yet you can transform old bathrooms with clean, shiny white caulking.

Again, if the tile is in salvageable condition but the grout is the problem, consider this alternative: Scrape off the top layer, apply premixed, stain-proof grout directly over existing grout, and call it a day. It's easy to apply new grout, and it can perform like new, too. There is a very inexpensive small tool called Traffic Master Stainproof Grout, that will help you scrape out stained, damaged, or chipping grout. It allows you to simply scrape back the surface of the old grout—about one-eighth of an inch—and apply new grout right over the top to give it a fresh new look.

Cabinets

Just as in the kitchen, keep the existing ones but have them professionally spray-painted and re-laminated, or put on new doors for a fresh, affordable makeover. And, of course, new hardware on the doors and drawers.

There's not that much difference between doing a general upgrade to a basic bathroom, and going all out to create a luxurious, high-end bathroom. What separates the two is cost and quality of the materials. (The size of the room will also make a difference.) The upscale version calls for more expensive materials for countertops, floor coverings, and accessories, as well as higher-end toilets and faucets. This will all become obvious to you when you visit a store that specializes in bathroom improvements.

In a guest bathroom, where space is tight, changing the vanity to a pedestal sink can make a small bathroom feel much more spacious and inviting. Also make sure there is plenty of in-wall cabinet space for toiletries.

Don't Take a Bath

Is your bathtub scratched and pitted? That won't do. No buyer will want to put his or her naked behind into that! Rather than replace the entire tub, there is a cost-effective way to resurface the tub very quickly. For about $350 a professional tile resurfacer will spray an Epoxy-like gloss on it, and transform an old scratched tub into one that looks like new. He or she can do the same to any old tile and sink. Not only does the process work wonders, but it usually comes with a five-year guarantee. For photos of what this process can accomplish, go to www.surfacespecialists.com.

Shower

For a separate shower stall, if the tile is in good condition, re-grout and you are good to go. If it needs replacing, do it when you redo the countertops or floors. Spend the bucks to replace your tired old shower door, the one with the frosted Plexiglas and gold frame, with a frameless glass shower door. It's sleek and sophisticated, and gives your bathroom a high-end look, and removing the frames and the frosted glass makes the bathroom appear larger.

After years of use, shower heads build up calcium. When you turn on your shower head, does it shoot in every direction, or worse, dribble out? The dribble could be misconstrued as low water pressure throughout the house, and you certainly don't want buyers to think that your water pressure is subpar. They are going to want a full, lush shower experience. Change the head!

Sinks and Fixtures

Of course, a smart and inexpensive upgrade for your bathroom is to replace the faucets with newer, more stylish ones. Home improvement centers have a great selection of inexpensive yet stylish faucets. Go to several of them, as different centers carry different lines, providing a plethora of choices. It is often more cost-effective to replace than it is to repair. As with the kitchen, check to see that all of the faucets are leak-free. Make sure the hot and cold water is flowing sufficiently, and that the sink is draining efficiently. Sinks should look fresh and new. You can find attractive porcelain drop-in sinks for around $45.

Lighting

Save money by making the most of your existing light sources. Pull back any curtains and drapes without sacrificing privacy. Allowing extra natural light into even the most modest bath adds luxury. If you have lights in the wall above the sink, then find the wall mount that perfectly matches

Opening up this bathroom to natural light added instant value to the room. It also draws your eye to the window and beyond, making even the tiniest of bathrooms feel larger.

your architectural style. This is good excuse to spend a little extra money. Fluorescent lighting is an instant turn-off, so replace any such fixtures with newer, nonfluorescent ones.

Toilets

Most old toilets are salvageable unless they have to be replaced to conform to local "low flow" standards. Simply get a new toilet seat with new fittings and you are done. Oh, yes, only white toilets, please. This is not an item in the bathroom that should draw focus. You do not want it to stand out!

RSS Tip: Creating Space—Mirror, Mirror

Why do mirrors work so well creating space in tight spaces like bathrooms? To the eye they appear to stretch space by reproducing it. If you hang a mirror on the longer wall of a narrow room, you will change its apparent proportions by making the room seem wider.

Entire walls of mirror, though, are a very dated look. One of the few places you can get away with them and have them work in your favor is in the bathroom. And no smoked or etched glass mirrors, please.

The bathroom is the one place where full-wall mirrors are not only acceptable, but they are a remarkable way to visually double the size of your room. I installed this full-wall mirror into my Bogert, Palm Springs, California, house—a huge space-enhancing, value-adding lifestyle upgrade.

UPGRADES AROUND THE HOUSE

Okay, you've tackled the buyer hot spots of kitchen and bath, now you need to work your way through the rest of the house. This process should be easy because you've already meticulously inspected and repaired most items in need of repair and replacement. But here are a few more upgrades you need to consider.

Adding Brooches

Contractor and design expert Steven Wilder has used the term brooches for many years to describe the eye-catching accessories and special amenities that dress up a house and make buyers take notice. Be creative. As you go to open houses, take notice: What individual items or upgrades catch your eye?

These sample brooches will add untold value to your home:

- Add an attractive fountain as a focal point in the backyard or on a side deck.

- Replace the old thermostats with new digital thermostats.

- Install a hotel-style wall-mounted hairdryer in the bathrooms. At $29 each, it's a small expense, but buyers will talk about them when they go home that night!

- Put ceiling fans in the bedrooms if you're in a warmer climate. Please, use the kind *without* lights and make sure to get a flush mount style so the fan is as unobtrusive as possible. Also, keep it the same color as the ceiling. You want it to blend in—not stand out.

- If you are putting in an intercom, add a video intercom system. Spend a bit more for an eye-catching brooch.

- Customize the master closet in a medium- or high-end house. Steal the ideas from one of the closet stores and have your contractor install the elements.

Master the Closets

No matter what size the master closet is, make it a study in organization. The $300 to $600 it costs to do a basic walk-in closet system with three rods, six shelves, and five drawers is worth every penny. These systems create order out of chaos and make a buyer who has never had one feel like a movie star. Upgrade with jewelry drawers and pull-down shoe racks and your most pampered prospects will be impressed.

Love the Security

Time to add a security system. It's an easy plus to add and, even better, I know how to get this valuable upgrade for *free*! Many companies will install the entire system at no charge if you agree to a one-year contract for monitoring. The installation and equipment are often worth up to $1,000. You will have to disclose to the buyer that they will have a one-year contract for monitoring, usually priced around $19 a month. I have done this every time I have sold and the buyer has always been happy to have the alarm monitoring service.

Out of Every Window

Are any of your windows blocked by overgrowth? Are trees and shrubs obscuring what could be a gorgeous view? Do rooms look out to an ugly backyard or, worse, into the next-door neighbor's bathroom window? By either removing or adding landscaping you can create an emotionally pleasing vista out every window. Also, no matter where you stand in the house you should have privacy. If that means planting a tree directly between the house next door and your living room window, do it.

There's a reason that mansions and estates have walls or hedges. By defining the space in a way that is aesthetically pleasing, you can create the sense of a private oasis. This adds value, regardless of the lot size.

Push the Inside Out: Expanding Your Boundaries

Living space is not defined by the interior walls of your house. Actually, it extends all the way to the sidewalk in front of your house or to the hallway outside your apartment or condo and to the edge of your property. Whether you have a balcony or a backyard, you'll want to push the inside out.

But balconies, backyard patios, porches, and even the front steps are valuable living spaces that are all too often ignored. By developing your condo balcony, the cement patio on the other side of the sliding glass door, the front steps, and the front porch, you create a sense of expansiveness and an emotional appeal.

Take advantage of all of these areas. They are incredibly valuable. Even the ugliest, smallest, and most unlikely outdoor space can be transformed into a value-adding destination. You won't have time at this point to add any square footage to your home, but you do have the time to create additional living space.

Realtor Doug Rago of Rodeo Realty in Los Angeles was putting his condo up for sale. The balcony had never been developed but he is very savvy and knew that any outdoor space in a condo is worth a fortune. A weekend redo of this balcony turned it from dumping ground to destination.

Open Up the Rooms

The perfect home for me is one in which every room has some access to an outside area. Take a walk around the perimeter of the house. Is there is *any* space off a bedroom or kitchen door, or front porch, that you can incorporate into your living space to expand out and bring the outdoors in? It is money and time well spent, capturing a big emotional response from buyers. The perceived value added is enormous.

If you have room on the first floor, replace the windows on first-floor bedrooms that face the side or the back of the house with a set of French doors. The small deck or patio you create will feel like an addition—for a fraction of the cost.

RSS WARNING: NONCONFORMING USE

Watch out: Converted garages, sun porches or add-on bedrooms can increase square footage, but when done without permits, they can also add headaches when it's time to make them legal. You may be better off ripping them down before sale rather than bearing the cost of rebuilding or obtaining new permits.

LIVING THROUGH YOUR REPAIRS AND LIFESTYLE UPGRADES

Let me warn you up front, living in your home through any upgrades and repairs is stressful yet manageable. Plus, you are going to be thinking about moving, so there will be a lot on your plate. But there are ways to minimize the inconvenience.

REPAIR AND UPGRADE SURVIVAL TIPS

- Stay on top of your scheduling. Living without a working kitchen for too long gets very annoying and costly.

- Always have one bathroom totally operational at all times. Stagger the bathroom upgrade jobs.

- Create "safe" areas shielded from the dust and debris. Seal off your bedrooms.

- Lock up or remove your valuables. Tradespeople will be in and out of the house for repairs. Be smart.

- Remember the weather! Don't try to do a new roof in the middle of rainy season, and don't replace windows in the dead of winter.

RSS Sale Success: Learn from Other Sellers' Mistakes—*Talk about keeping up with the Joneses. This was one of my houses that had to be brought up to the standard of the neighborhood. Before putting it on the market, I went to every open house, comparing my home to the ones that were selling, and, more important, to the ones that weren't selling. You can truly learn as much about what to upgrade from what is sitting on the market as you can from what has sold.*

Ten

DESIGN TO SELL

Save It, Store It, Sell It, Chuck It

Repair to Sell

Lifestyle Upgrades

DESIGN TO SELL

Dress to Sell: Stage to Sell & Prep to Sell

I openly admit that I'm not a designer and don't want to be one. But I have learned how to prepare a house for sale to maximize its value. I've learned this by observing which houses sell, which ones don't, and why. I've learned from some of the best designers and real estate professionals in the business, and I've learned from watching buyers as they walk through homes for sale and seeing which elements draw them in and which ones turn them off.

DESIGN-TO-SELL TECHNIQUES

Design-to-sell techniques are the design touches that add value, increase aesthetic appeal, and make a house more profitable because they look so great. These techniques allow you to create the style that has mass appeal and will bring you top dollar. They are emotion-grabbing design secrets that will have buyers' hearts pounding! They are the last-minute upgrades that cost very little but return big profits.

I've seen these easy and affordable design elements used effectively in the homes of the wealthy and the famous. I've also seen them used just as effectively in the homes of the modest and the middle class. And I've used them in each and every one of my homes that I have put on the market to great success.

THREE DESIGN-TO-SELL KEY PRINCIPLES

- Don't personalize
- Stay consistent
- Keep it neutral

THREE KEY PRINCIPLES

Don't Personalize Your Design Scheme—Keep It Simple

When you set to sell your house, you need to appeal to the broadest spectrum of tastes. Don't *personalize*. What that means is that just because *you* like a certain design touch or color on the walls, that doesn't mean that it will appeal to the average buyer. You want to walk that fine line of appealing to all tastes without alienating anyone. You may adore your master bedroom that you have painted chocolate brown with girly pink trim, but many people only want chocolate on their desserts and pink on their cupcakes—not on their walls. You want your house to have a beautiful designed look, yet not be so *style-specific* that potential buyers can't see themselves and their own style in the house as well. Make choices that will elicit that all-important positive emotional response from buyers.

When you set to sell your home, you need to appeal to the broadest spectrum of tastes.

Stay Consistent

Think of your entire house as one whole project that works and flows together. One of the problems with selling a home you have lived in for many years is that it has probably gone through many stages of renovation and many "inspired" phases of redecorating. What that translates to is a house in various stages of design and décor. Many home sellers don't even realize that the living room is designed with faux-Mediterranean finishes, while their dining room, redone years later, looks like an outdated shabby-chic nightmare. Nothing flows. The house seems choppy and compartmentalized. To a buyer, an inconsistent style makes the house look and feel small and unlivable, and that won't translate to more money when you sell.

. . . .

To a buyer, an inconsistent style makes the house look and feel small and unlivable.

. . . .

Do a Set-to-Sell Consistency Sweep

Okay, time to put your buyer's hat on again. Try to see your house as if for the very first time. With a notepad in hand, go around your house taking notes about the design flow that you see from room to room. Where are there obvious inconsistencies? Where can you enhance that flow by addressing any obvious breaks in the flow? Look at styles, paint schemes, and trends. Keep a lookout for entire room style breaks, such as a living room that's circa 1979 and a den that was redecorated in 2006 and looks very up-to-date.

THREE REASONS TO STAY CONSISTENT THROUGHOUT THE HOUSE

1. **It creates a design flow.** Gives the house a sense of order, a well-thought-out design that flows and creates the feeling of

(continued)

space and order. Makes a smaller house feel bigger and a bigger house feel manageable and livable.

2. **It's easier!** Using the same style throughout means fewer design decisions. You never have to worry about which colors and shades will work better in which rooms, because if you are consistent, they will all coordinate.

3. **It saves time and money.** Not only will you be able to get a better price when painting, carpeting, and installing window treatments, but if you have leftovers you can use them in other rooms.

MAKE MATERIALS MATCH THROUGHOUT THE HOUSE

Carpet. Stay with the same style and brand of carpet throughout. All bedrooms should be the same color as well.

Cabinetry. If you are taking the time to replace any cabinets, keep all the cabinets the same. Use the same style or color in the kitchen, laundry room, and pantry as you do in the bathrooms.

Window treatments. Keep them consistent. Use the same style in all the bedrooms.

Hardware. In the bathroom, I use a smaller version of the cabinet handles that I use in the kitchen. All doorknobs and door hinges should be the same throughout the house.

Lighting. If you have recessed lighting, use the same type of recessed lighting throughout. In bedrooms or bathrooms, you may use a smaller version of what you use in the living room, but make sure they are all of a similar style and color trim.

Keep It Neutral

These principles may go against your preferences or your instincts, but remember to remain detached—your house is now a *product to market*. So don't get nervous when you're doing that set-to-sell paint job, or changing the carpets or window treatments prior to sale. The purpose is to achieve a great stylish look—quickly and simply—and make it easy to pull together. The way to have it all—style, color, and ease—is to select your floor coverings and wall colors in neutral tones and styles. That way, when you get ready to do the final "staging" of your furnishings, *everything* else is easy to match and accessorize. Keep the big stuff neutral. Add color with the furnishings and accessories you will use when you dress your house for sale.

Keeping neutral and consistent is very important; making sure all the elements and materials blend together creates the open and spacious feel that every buyer is drawn to.

LIGHT AND LIGHTING

It's all about the lighting. You hear that a lot in Hollywood, but it's just as true when selling a house. And one surefire way to create huge value and a lifestyle upgrade to your house is simply to upgrade your lighting. You can transform the dullest of rooms with the flick of a switch. But before you turn on the electricity, always take full advantage of any available *natural* light.

Let There Be Light

Natural light has been the most transformational design secret since time began, and it's *free*! Go room by room and look for ways that any and all windows can be exposed and window coverings minimized. Any opportunities to open the house to more natural light should be maximized.

If your timeline and finances permit, here's a relatively inexpensive design upgrade that gives a big emotional boost to your house: Any time an exterior door can be replaced with a wood-framed glass door, without sacrificing privacy or security, take advantage of it. And if privacy is an issue, consider white or rippled glass that still lets the light in, yet obscures the view.

A rippled glass or frosted glass door is a great way to bring in more natural light while still maintaining privacy. Before sale day, I had the solid wood doors removed on this house and replaced with these rippled glass ones.

Windows and Window Treatments—Less Is More

The first step toward letting it all in is to pull back those window treatments. I don't like drapes and blinds. I like to use minimal window treatments that still dress a room and make it look warm and inviting. But you never want to block any natural light. Buyers are not just physically warmed by a lovely sunbeam shining through the window, they are also warmed emotionally.

Keep in mind, however, that privacy is also a big value-adding asset, so you need to find that balance of light and airy, yet private. There are products that can create privacy, while allowing light to shine in as well as keeping your window-dressing bill down to nothing. A new technology, for instance, uses tiny pieces of crushed glass molded into paper-thin sheets of plastic to give your glass a frosted look. They literally cling to the window, come in sophisticated patterns, and are removable. I love this stuff. As a matter of fact, I was the company's spokesperson when I sold it for them on the Home Shopping Network. It's called Wallpaper for Windows and can be found at www.wallpaperforwindows.com.

Three Lighting Design-to-Sell Upgrades

1. Dimmers

Installing dimmers is a must! But so many home sellers overlook this simple and inexpensive design upgrade. For as little as five or ten dollars each, dimmers transform your rooms. Not only are they an amenity that buyers look for, but they allow you to create a fantastic mood and designer feeling to each room when your buyers come through the house, especially during those all-important early-evening and night showings. Remember, many working professionals can only house shop or preview houses after work. That's the time to use dimmers; they really set the look of each room.

2. Halogen Bulbs

Changing all the bulbs in your recessed lighting to halogen is an instant lighting makeover. Halogen lights create dramatic looks. All the new track lighting systems also accommodate pin spot bulbs in low-voltage halogen lights that allow you to directionalize and literally "paint" your rooms with light.

3. Replace All Light Switches, Switch Plates, and Electrical Outlets

This may sound like a small detail, but it is very important. Every time buyers walk into a room, where do they have to look first? For the light switch. It's sometimes the first thing they will see in each room. New upgraded switches and plates give the impression of new and state-of-the-art wiring and electrical systems—whether you have them or not.

PAINT AND COLOR

I can't reiterate this enough: A fresh paint job really transforms a home. It makes your house look newer and well maintained, and brings it to life. My advice is to bite the financial bullet and have the painting done professionally, even on a lower-priced house. It may look easy, but what I can do compared to what a professional painting team can do is the difference between night and day. I see it—and buyers do, too.

....

A fresh paint job transforms a home. It makes your house look newer and well maintained, and brings it to life.

....

SELECTING THE RIGHT COLORS

Color is a basic part of design. How you use it is crucial. Color creates energy and brings vibrancy into your home. Starting with the walls, the right color also creates depth and adds character to any existing architectural style. Painting is the quickest, simplest, and least expensive way to jump-start the value of your home. It truly is the biggest bang for your buck. When it is done properly, inside and out, you can instantly upgrade the value of your home.

Interior Colors

The biggest mistake home sellers make when trying to use color is to paint the walls wild and trendy colors. To capture the best buyer with the best offer, keep your wall colors neutral. Limit your color palette. Your walls are the backdrop upon which you will dress your room. You don't want the walls to be the focus of your room. You can make the room pop by adding more intense color later with your furniture, art, or a few well-chosen accessories. Think about it: Why draw attention to your walls? Our goal is to expand the feeling of space in your home, not to remind the potential buyer of its boundaries.

RSS Success Story: Paint Over the Fruit Salad

I worked with a home seller in Ft. Lauderdale who had a lovely cottage-style home. It was not a big home, about 1,600 square feet, but it had lots of charm. He had decorated it in Key West style, which is similar to Caribbean style, with each room painted a different vibrant bright color—aqua, pink, coral, lemon yellow, and mango. Even though the house was set to sell using all my techniques, it remained on the market without a single offer for more than ten weeks. When he was moments away from reducing the price from $460,000 to $425,000, he consulted me.

I advised him to have the entire inside of the house, which now looked like a fruit plate from a Sunday brunch buffet, repainted. I suggested that he paint all the walls a soft sand color and do the trim white. The cost? About $1,500. And then I told him not to *reduce* the price as planned by $35,000, but to *raise* it to $475,000!

Well, the house sold the following week for the new price of $475,000. That $1,500 spent actually made him $48,500 more than if he had reduced the price and (hopefully) sold. That's the power of neutral, consistent colors throughout a house!

Picking the Right Colors

I have developed a very practical and successful formula for taking the worry out of choosing the right color scheme and painting the interior.

MY THREE-COLOR DESIGN-TO-SELL TECHNIQUE FOR INTERIORS

STEP 1: CHOOSE THE ONE

Choose one neutral color to be your overall base color—one found in nature, please! Choose from earth or desert tones like sand, beige, tan, and so on. They are the most neutral and appealing to buyers. Make sure to select one that blends with the majority of your current furnishings and carpeting.

STEP 2: THREE OF A KIND

Now select two *shades* of that color, one a lighter shade and one slightly darker. You should now have three shades total—your original color plus a lighter and a darker version—and three is the magic number.

STEP 3: GET PAINTING

Most walls will be painted with your lightest shade. Paint accent walls and adjoining rooms with one of the two darker shades. For example, try the dining room in the darkest shade, and the kitchen in the medium base.

The result is a beautiful neutral palette and a superb backdrop for you to set and stage your home. It is an instant, picture-perfect look—with slightly different shades in each room blending and complementing one another beautifully. The blend creates consistency and increases the feeling of space throughout the house as your buyers walk from one room to another. It gives your home that sense of flow that makes even the smallest house feel expansive and inviting. Another hugely important payoff is that you have one base color to which you will match all of your existing furniture and accessories. That leaves you free to move them from room to room, giving you more flexibility, when dressing your house for sale.

Now Look UP!

When touching up or completely repainting a room, look up! Ceilings are often forgotten by home sellers, but never go unnoticed by home buyers. Check for stains, cracks, and discoloration, especially around light fixtures. Always paint your ceilings a shade of white. It neutralizes them. Visually it makes them disappear and thus gives a greater sense of height. And a white ceiling also reflects more light around the room. My color of choice for ceilings is never a bright white, but a standard variety known as Swiss Coffee or Ceiling White.

Exterior Colors

Your exterior color choices are extremely important. The front of your home is one of the first things that buyers notice as they pull up to the curb. Not only does the house need to be freshly painted and look crisp, clean, and well maintained, it also has to have an appealing color scheme that's suitable for the kind of home you have.

Using paint to create a dramatic and inviting home is so simple yet so often overlooked by home sellers. Paint can emphasize any architectural detail and help mask any ugly elements. Especially in warmer climates and in southern and western states, one or two years of sun exposure has a fading and dulling effect on high- or semi-gloss wood finishes. Your house will most likely need a touch-up.

. . . .

Before you start your exterior paining, go to my Web site, www.MichaelCorbett.com, to see an instructional video clip of my three-color technique.

. . . .

Design-to-Sell Exterior Three Color Technique

Three is the magic number on the exterior paint scheme as well. Choose three colors to work with: a neutral earth-tone base color for your large surfaces, such as walls; a second contrasting but complementary color for the trim and accent moldings; and a third rich, strong color for some very select accent items, such as the front door.

The good news is that all major paint companies now have brochures and pamphlets that have already done the color combining for you. So head on down to your local home improvement center and grab a handful of color combo ideas.

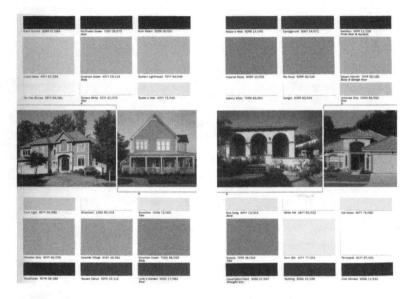

This brochure from Glidden (reproduced here in black and white) lays out numerous color combo choices for you, and makes you an instant design-to-sell expert.

RSS COLOR SELECTION SECRETS

- Dark colors make a house look smaller.

- Light colors make a house look bigger.

- Study sample colors in direct sunlight and in shade before purchasing.

- Watch out for extremely light colors that lose their brightness and color in sunlight.

- Test colors first. Start with a small amount and test it on a section of a wall in an area adjacent to some trim area.

- Colors and color combinations will change throughout the day as the natural light changes, so make sure to check your samples at various times of day.

RSS Exterior Painting Tip: Play by the Rules

Before you paint, make sure your home is not governed by any neighborhood rules to which your exterior appearance must conform. Homes in gated communities often have regulations that detail which colors you are permitted to use. And many older neighborhoods fall under a Historic Preservation Overlay Zone. An HPOZ strictly governs any exterior improvements. If you are not sure whether you are subject to such regulations, ask your Realtor or contact your city's housing board before you put brush to wall!

The Right Finish

Please use the right type of paint finish for the right surface. I have seen so many homes for sale where the sellers have taken the time to get a fresh coat of paint on the house, yet used the wrong finishes. It's such a small detail, but makes a big difference when you're trying to appeal to the buyer's five senses—one of which is "touch." When a buyer opens a door or runs his or her hands along some wood trim and that trim is not painted in a gloss finish, it just feels wrong.

PAINTING FINISHES CHART

Interior

Walls	Flat
Ceiling	Flat
Kitchen walls	Semigloss
Bath walls	Semigloss
Woodwork	Semigloss
Cabinets	Semigloss

Exterior

Stucco	Flat
Cement	Flat or semigloss
Wood siding	Semigloss
Wood trim	Semigloss
Gutters	Semigloss
Doors	Gloss

Hire a Crew, Not an Individual

When getting the house painted, hire a company that employs a painting crew; don't try to save money and hire one single painter. As you are living in the house, the less disruption the better. Painting can be a messy job, so you want it done as quickly and efficiently as possible. I have had entire 3,000-square-foot houses painted in just a few days when using a crew. How? Because they have the manpower and the equipment to do the job right. While some crew members are prepping, others are masking, and still others are starting on the trim. Even with all that manpower, it costs less because they are doing volume work. And the reduction of stress for you is worth every penny.

RSS Painting Tip: Mark Your Can

As you finish painting clearly mark the paint cans. Use a piece of masking tape and identify the rooms and areas painted in each color. Not only will it be a time and money saver for you for the inevitable touch-ups, but your buyers will also appreciate the information and the effort when you leave the cans for them.

RSS Painting Tip: Touch It Up!

Keep a set of sponge-topped shoe polish applicator bottles filled with paint from each color and label them by room. Lowes Home Improvement stores carry these in their paint department. Give scuffs and marks a quick dab, and touch-ups in between showings will be a breeze. Your home will remain paint perfect throughout the sale process.

RSS Sale Success: Keeping It Neutral—*This Las Vegas property languished on the market for four months. The homeowners loved color, and they had allowed their children to select the aqua color for the dining room and the ruby red for the living room walls. Savvy Realtor Russ Grieve took over the listing and advised the homeowners to neutralize the interior with a soft sand color and white woodwork trim. The house sold at the following open house weekend.*

Eleven

DRESS TO SELL: STAGE TO SELL

Save It, Store It, Sell It, Chuck It

Repair to Sell

Lifestyle Upgrades

Design to Sell

DRESS TO SELL: STAGE TO SELL

Dress to Sell: Prep to Sell

Congratulations! You have completed all the set-to-sell steps that have by now whipped your house into buyer-grabbing shape. You have chucked out the clutter, made all the necessary repairs, packed up 50 percent or more of your personal belongings, thrown out a few pieces of furniture, and completed value-adding lifestyle upgrades to your home. Well, I can guarantee that now even *you* are impressed by the transformation of your home at this point.

So, here we go into the final frontier. The final phase. The pièce de résistance. Now it's time to give your home the *emotional edge*. The ineffable quality that turns a mildly interested prospective buyer into an offer-writing bundle of enthusiasm because the place feels like, well . . . *home*. Dressing your house to sell enables prospective buyers to *experience* your home where it counts—emotionally.

. . . .

Dressing your house to sell enables your potential buyers to experience your home—emotionally.

. . . .

TRANSFORM YOUR HOUSE INTO A HOME AND LIFESTYLE

The next essential step transforms a house into an inviting, emotionally engaging home that's irresistible because it personifies a *lifestyle*. This is where you maximize the profit your house can generate by creating the emotional appeal that quickens the pulse of even the most jaded and exhausted house shopper.

Dress-to-sell techniques help create *perceived value*. Perceived value is not a quantifiable improvement like copper piping or a new hot-water heater. It's purely qualitative because it's the price a buyer is willing to pay based entirely on the *emotional appeal* of the house. The more emotionally invested the buyer becomes in the house, the higher the perceived value . . . and your price tag. Dress-to-sell techniques have one goal: to inspire your potential buyers to say the words that are instant cash to any home seller: "I *love* this house. It feels like *home*! I *have* to have it!"

. . . .

Dress-to-sell techniques inspire your potential buyers to say the words "I love this house. It feels like home! I have to have it!"

. . . .

DRESS-TO-SELL COMPONENTS

- Staging
  - Set the stage
  - How much and with what?

- Techniques and tips
- Seduce the senses
  - Lighting
  - Sounds
  - Touch
  - Scents
- Preparing for showtime
  - Squeaky clean
  - Camera-ready
  - Show prep hit list

Your House Becomes a Broadway Show

My background is acting—in theater, television, and film. Twenty years ago, when I began buying houses, fixing them up, and selling them, I was also acting on a soap opera during the day and performing on Broadway at night. So when I think about setting a house for sale, I immediately think of it as a big theatrical production. Just like a Broadway show, you're setting the stage, and creating a mood through lighting, music, even adding the right scents to attract an *emotional buyer*—the buyer who walks through your front door and experiences an emotional reaction, not a rational one. When a buyer's first impression of a house is both emotional or visceral *and* visual, it's more powerful and long-lasting than a visual impression alone. What happens when you put this theatrical magic to work? You have a hit—and a top-dollar sale.

The Pros Bank on a Buyer's Emotions

Working with advertising companies and acting in TV commercials, I have learned a lot about how to grab buyers' attention, hold it, and convince them to purchase a product in under a minute. How do the big advertisers do it? Can we learn to use the same techniques when we want to sell our homes? Of course we can.

HOW THE BIG TV ADVERTISERS CONTROL BUYERS

- Stimulate all their senses

- Grab their emotions

Savvy advertisers and marketers have learned to manipulate consumers by stimulating all their senses and pulling on their heartstrings at the same time. Well, you want to do the same thing when you sell your house. During that first walk-through you want the buyer to *experience* all the beautiful, inviting, and practical elements he or she sees in your home and to connect them to his or her positive, visceral response. If buyers can sense warmth, vitality, tranquillity, and security—all sensations of cherished family moments—they're sold!

I've often heard buyers say things like, "You know, the house was smaller than I had wanted," or "There weren't as many bathrooms as we needed, but I just had such a good feeling about the house that we bought it!" Your job is to create that feeling!

If buyers can sense warmth, vitality, tranquillity, and security—all sensations of cherished family moments—they're sold!

STAGING—THE HOT NEW SELLING TOOL

On *Extra* and *Extra's Mansions & Millionaires* I interview Realtors, big designers, and renovators all the time. One of the hottest trends in real estate is staging, the practice of dressing a house with carefully chosen furnishings and little touches that say *home*. Why? You know what I'm going to say: It's transformational, and taps into the buyers' *emotional experience*.

What *Is* Staging?

Simply put, you treat your house like a stage set, adding furniture, accessories, plants, artwork, and a host of details, right down to carefully organized clothes in the closets.

The actual staging of your house can be as basic as removing some of your existing furniture and then rearranging what you retain. Or, depending on sale price and quality of the home, it can be more elaborate, and involve renting furniture and even consulting with a designer to help you create that dream, top-dollar-fetching home.

This technique has become so valuable to making a profit when selling that there is new breed of professionals in metropolitan areas that specialize in staging. Known as stagers, house fluffers, or property enhancers, they are paid handsomely for their services. What do they know that most home sellers don't know? A staged house sells *faster*, and for *more money*.

. . . .

A staged house sells faster, and for more money.

. . . .

I Was Staging and Didn't Know It!

Staging may be the hot new selling tool, but it seems I have been staging my houses for more than twenty years.

The very first home I ever purchased, a tiny two-bedroom, was next door to my grandmother's house in Collingswood, New Jersey. I did some work to it, improved it, unwittingly incorporating what were later to become my design-to-sell techniques. But I instantly knew it needed something *more*. Not having heard the term staging at the time, I borrowed furniture from both my grandmother's garage and from my parents. I set up a living room seating area with a sofa, coffee table, end tables, and lamps. I also staged the dining room. Yes, it was a crude and rudimentary beginning . . . but the house sold for more than the asking price and the Realtor was astounded. I knew I was on to something.

Hearing About Staging for the First Time

The first time I ever heard the term used was by a very famous designer and pioneer of modern home design. Frequently published in *Architectural Digest* throughout the sixties and seventies, Val Arnold was also renowned for making huge profits when he would sell a home he owned. I had met him in Los Angeles at a fund-raiser back in 1980 and asked him what his secret was. He said, "Staging! Darling, I learned many years ago, never sell a home empty, and never let it look like you are still asleep in the other room!"

Well, more than thirty-three houses later, and having heard lots of great advice from some of the top real estate and design professionals in the world, I consider staging a cornerstone when I sell a house.

Staging Means Different Things to Different Professionals

The most common use of the term *staging* is the dressing and furnishing of an empty home before it goes on the market. Staging can also refer to the entire process of setting your house for sale: de-cluttering; packing up all the personal belongings; doing all the save it, store it, sell it, chuck it arranging I recommend; setting up your furniture to best show off your house; and the final dressing of your house for sale.

In my RSS method, staging is the process of minimizing and rearranging your furniture, creating vignettes, and seducing your buyers' senses. By this point in the *Ready, Set, Sold!* process, you have already *undressed* your home. Well, now it's time to *re-dress* it—but with your buyers in mind.

. . . .

By this point in the **Ready, Set, Sold!** *process, you have already* **undressed** *your home. Well, now it's time to* **re-dress** *it—but with your buyers in mind.*

. . . .

Staging Is Transformational

But why does staging work? No matter what size home, from cottage to mansion, from $100,000 to $3,000,000, your home will benefit from staging for the following reasons.

SIX MAJOR STAGING BENEFITS

- Gives buyers a visual blueprint of what life will be like in the home

- Allows potential buyers to experience your home

- Makes an empty home feel warm and more inviting

- Creates proportion in a big room through furniture groupings

- Makes a tiny room feel larger with customized furnishings

- Showcases positive features and downplays negative features

Buyers are not able to visualize what a room *could* look like. They only observe and judge what a room looks like *right now*. You have to make it a visually and emotionally stirring experience for them in that limited time. Because as buyers walk through your home, the clock is ticking. You have to show buyers how to *live* in your space. And you want them to be inspired to live there. You want them to think about entertaining their friends and family in that home during the next holiday season or at the next Fourth of July barbecue.

Buyers are not able to visualize what a room could look like. They can only observe and judge what a room looks like right now.

These unfurnished rooms felt barren and hollow, and left the buyers feeling the same way. The furnishings brought life into these rooms and transformed them into spaces that buyers could experience. The houses sold within a week of their staging makeovers.

Buyers May Never Set Foot in Your Rooms

As they tour your house, buyers are making visual snap judgments of every room they walk through. But they also see a room from only one angle. That's right, 80 percent of your potential buyers will *never set foot* in many of your rooms their first time through. Remember that I pointed out how much first impressions count as buyers approach your front door? Well, the same is true for each room in your house, especially the kitchen, living room, dining room, and master bedroom. You need to set the stage for these rooms, so as buyers walk past the doorway of each one, it looks well arranged, uncluttered, spacious, and inviting.

Of course you still must stage the entire room, because once you have impressed those buyers, they will be back! Back to look at the house a second and sometimes a third time. So don't think you can design, dress, stage, and clean only the most visible places. Every square inch of every room must be set to sell. The buyers who come back the second time are the ones you have been waiting for, the prime target buyers. Because, by the second time through, they are one enticing vignette away from writing you a top-dollar offer!

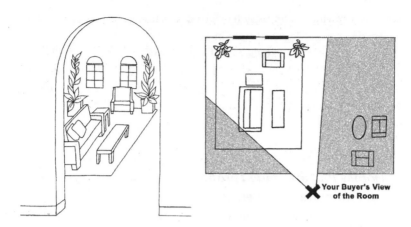

Your Buyer's View
of the Room

Keep in mind that your buyer may never set foot in some rooms their first time through, so make sure their view from the hall is a memorable one.

HOW MUCH AND WITH WHAT?

But I Can't Afford to Stage My House!

You can't afford not to! It can actually cost you next to nothing to stage your house. Keep in mind that so often home sellers are penny-wise and pound-foolish. The cost of most of the repairs, lifestyle upgrades, a new carpet, and a few new furnishings is far *less* than the amount of a price reduction when your house does not sell straight out of the gate. And the money lost by not investing the time and money to set your house for sale can be ten or twenty times the amount spent on staging.

* * *

The cost of most of the repairs, lifestyle upgrades, and a few new furnishings is far* less *than the amount of a price reduction if your house does not sell right away.

* * *

Stage and Reap a Double-Good Whammy!

Robert Crawford, CEO and founder of Brook Furniture Rental, has been helping home sellers stage homes for twenty years in all parts of the country. Crawford's company has found that homes staged properly sell for an average of *10 percent more* in *50 percent less time.*

Let's do the math, shall we? If your house is on the market for $650,000 and you can sell for 10 percent more . . . that's an extra $65,000 in your pocket! Then add in the money you save on carrying costs when you sell quickly, and you've got a nice wad of extra cash for your staging troubles.

. . . .

Homes that are staged properly sell for an average of 10 percent more in 50 percent less time.
—Robert Crawford, CEO of Brook Furniture Rental

. . . .

But I Don't Have the Right Furnishings

Now that you have removed the clutter and packed up all of your small personal belongings, how do you dress the house? Where would the appropriate furniture and accessories come from? Anywhere you can get them!

- Make the most of what you've got

- Borrow certain furniture items from friends and family

- Rent furniture

- Combination of all of the above

Make the Most of What You've Got

You have plenty of furniture to choose from already. More than plenty. The trick will be forcing yourself to edit and get rid of much of what you have. Go through your sorted belongings and "cherry-pick" from them.

Borrowing Furniture

I have often borrowed from Peter to pay Paul when staging a house for sale. Literally. I have a friend, Peter, on whom I have called many times to borrow a few furnishings in order to stage a home. If perchance there are a few pieces you think you really need to complete a living room or bedroom setting, then call Aunt Marie, cousin Shelly, or a friend, and borrow them!

Remember, you are going to need the furniture for only thirty to sixty days. Once the house is on the market and you have an accepted offer with the contingencies removed, you can begin to remove your furnishings. Best of all, you don't have to furnish the entire house. You just have to give a suggestion of a furnished home. Of course the more you do, the better, but go easy on yourself. Do the best you can. For example, if you can only furnish one bedroom, then do the one. But make it look terrific!

Renting Furniture

Pop quiz: Is renting furniture expensive and reserved only for the biggest of mansions and deepest of pockets? No, not at all! With the proven success of marketing your home once it has been staged, it's truly an investment that will reap big rewards. And the higher priced the home, the bigger the rewards will be.

There are many staging and furniture rental companies that specialize in helping home sellers stage and prepare their homes for sale. Brook Furniture Rental (www.BFR.com) is a national rental furniture company with branches found in most metropolitan cities, specializing in staging homes. They can provide the materials to stage a home, from furniture and accessories to plants, for about $1 per square foot per month. Using a furniture rental company that specializes in staging is like having a designer and furniture store rolled into one. It makes the process so simple.

Combination of All of the Above

It's perfectly fine to do a combination of using what you've got, borrowing, and renting. In fact, it's what most people do. Designer Diana Ezerins, who specializes in redesigning spaces, is a fan of this combo technique. Her Chicago-based company, Diana Ezerins Interiors, uses both an owner's existing possessions and furniture, and any additional pieces that can be borrowed or rented to create the desired setting. In doing so she maximizes function, flow, and aesthetics without forcing the owner to start from scratch or spend needlessly. And that's your goal as well.

SET-TO-SELL STAGING TECHNIQUES AND TIPS

You've got five to ten minutes to captivate potential buyers from the moment they approach your house. You want them to feel "at home," so each room should elicit a specific emotional response. Living rooms must be inviting and gracious. Bedrooms should exude a sense of relaxation and comfort. Kitchens should be so clean, spacious, and organized that the buyer can practically hear their friends offer to chop carrots while you clean the lettuce.

Staging your home for sale is more about the feeling and flow it creates than the individual pieces of furniture creating a decorated look. Michael Maloney of Castle Keepers is one of the top designer/stagers in the country. He has a long list of clients ranging from modest home sellers to very big celebrities. His secret to sale success is to stage homes so that they feel like a good hotel. "I want to create for buyers that same feeling you get, even subconsciously, when you first walk into a very good hotel room. The feeling is that each room is ready and waiting for *you*." It's furnished in a way that is elegant and simple, yet comfortable and welcoming. It's not overdone or overfurnished. There's room to walk around and room to sit and unwind. Just as in fine hotels, furniture tones are warm beiges and neutral colors. The rooms are impersonal yet inviting. *Everyone* feels welcome and at home.

. . . .

Create for buyers the same feeling you get, even subconsciously, when you first walk into a very good hotel room.

—Michael Maloney, top designer and stager

. . . .

Create Space—Don't Fill It

When staging, and rearranging, keep in mind that *less is more*. It's far more valuable to *create* space than to *fill* it. Learn to think of space as an actual, tangible entity. Think of space as a huge piece of furniture—and make room for it.

Here's a sampling of several rooms that have been staged very modestly, yet effectively. The transformation is exactly enough to allow the buyer to experience that room. These newly staged rooms feel like home.

. . . .

Think of space as a huge piece of furniture—and make room for it!

. . . .

You'll always want at least two or three "pieces of space" in each room you stage. So make sure you allow for it. It's the cheapest piece of "furniture" you can buy, and it will truly enhance the value of your home.

Don't forget to avoid personalizing when you choose which items and pieces of furniture to include. If you keep the grand piano in the living room, for instance, lose the family photographs that will distract your buyers and show too much of *you* in the room. Consider instead a fresh bouquet of flowers or nothing at all.

Staging Defines the Spaces

Professional designers and stagers have a variety of techniques that showcase the best features of the house's layout. What might be merely an extra room off the living room becomes a cozy den when dressed with a sofa and a leather club chair. That funny alcove under the stairs staged with a small writing desk and some shelving becomes a home office area. With a small glass-topped table and four café chairs, the odd leftover space off the kitchen becomes a breakfast nook. And that slab of cement off the slider from the guest room, when furnished with an outdoor lounge chair and side table, becomes a private sun patio for houseguests.

Step It Up One Quality Level

One of the best insider secrets that I will pass on to you in this book is this: Stage your home for sale *one quality level better* than the house itself. Having furnishings and accessories that are a bit higher in quality can actually subconsciously elevate your house's overall level of quality and sophistication. Buyers won't realize that they are responding to the upgraded furnishings—not the house itself. Upgrading the quality makes the house seem more expensive and more elegant, and gives it a much higher perceived value. And we know that this immediately translates into more money when you sell! It also puts you ahead of the competition. Even with an identical house on the market, buyers will feel that your house is more valuable and thus you can command a higher price. In other words, you'll sell *first* and for *more money*!

* *

Stage your home for sale one quality level better *than the house itself.*

* *

STAGING ROOM BY ROOM

Go through the house and identify places where you can elicit positive emotional responses. Create what I call "living still lifes," three-dimensional snapshots of a heart-filled home. Set up vignettes or small lifestyle areas that fit your target buyer. You want your buyer to feel like spending a little time in your home. You want your buyer to feel welcome and comfortable. If you can create at least one dozen vignettes throughout the house you are certain to grab your buyer where he lives!

Entryway

The entryway must be inviting yet simple. Place a side table or parson's table along the wall inside the front door. Dress it with an attractive tray and a live orchid. Hang a good-sized mirror above it, and you have the perfect first and last impression for your buyer!

RSS Staging Tip: Stage Your Condo Front Door

Play on buyers' emotions the minute they walk down the hallway from your front door. In a condo, have a handsome wreath hanging on the front door. Spend $5 for a wreath hook placed over the top of the door. Run over to a store like Pottery Barn or Crate & Barrel and get an all-season wreath for around $39. It will make a huge difference. Your front door should be ready to receive and seduce your buyer.

This is a simple and elegant entryway that I created in one of my homes in Los Angeles. A simple staging technique like this one creates a welcoming way to greet your buyer.

Living Room

The living room is, of course, a main staging area. Your setting arrangements should be simplified and rearranged. If there is a fireplace, center the furnishings around it as your focal point. Furniture pushed up against the walls is not very appealing. So, group your furniture into settings and seating areas.

Never sacrifice accessibility in and out of a room for furniture. It's more important to create a sense of flow and space than to overcrowd with furniture.

It's always wonderful and welcoming to light your fireplaces for showings if the weather permits. In colder climates, a staged lit fireplace

This is such a simple staging fix. Pull your existing furniture pieces away from the wall and group them to focus toward the fireplace. It gives the room an immediate sense of design and comfort. It makes the room feel well-thought-out and welcoming to your buyer.

is a must. Use either gas logs or real logs and stack fresh logs for an invit-ing and cozy outdoor scent. The reading chair with the open book is a classic touch. And I love to keep a short stack of *Architectural Digest* magazines on a coffee table to add panache. Oh, by the way, if you hap-pen to have a giant old-style projection screen television sitting on the floor and eating up a third of your living room space, store it. Snagging a faster, higher price for your home is worth missing a bit of TV time.

This home was staged to sell by one of my real estate students. He did an amazing job of putting all the senses into play. The fireplace and the lovely vignettes of stacked books and candles made buyers want to move in that same day!

Dining Room

Never set up a vignette of a full dinner service in the dining room. It's okay to do a table setup in a breakfast room or outdoor patio, but the dining room will be overkill. Yes, there should be a nice vase, tray, flower arrangement, or a set of matching candlesticks, but no table setting.

Keeping the dining room simple is the key. Dress the table with a vase, tray, elegant centerpiece, or flower arrangement.

Kitchen

The kitchen is one of the easiest rooms to stage. If you have removed all the extraneous decorative items and have cleared your countertops, you are pretty well done.

Put an open cookbook on a book stand next to the stove. Prop it with a nice butcher block knife set. Have a bowl of fresh fruit. I like apples, lemons, and grapes for a good color combination and a great stacking/draping effect. It sends a subtle and clean citrus fragrance wafting through the kitchen.

Bedrooms

Simplify the bedroom and the furnishings. A bed with a head- and footboard is essential. Include great bedside tables with complementary bedside lamps. If a television is sitting on a dresser or stand, remove it. If there's room, you need a relaxing club chair and ottoman. Also, don't forget to depersonalize. Remove all your family photos from the night stands and around the room.

A bed with fluffy white pillows and a white duvet cover is a classic look that inspires tranquillity and security. Go to a linen outlet and buy fresh new white sheets. It can cost you as little as $59 for a new set per bed. Hotels use all white sheets and towels for a reason. White always looks crisp and reflects more light, and can be used over and over again no matter what the decor or house. Give your bedroom the five-star hotel treatment.

Flowers or an orchid by the bed is a nice touch. If the bedroom has a window seat or a reading chair, place an opened hardcover book and a pair of reading glasses there. No magazines please. The hardcover book implies value.

This is a simple yet elegant staging of one of my homes. Great white hotel-like sheets, some reading material on the table, and a comfortable lounging chair. It all suggests to your buyer a welcoming, tranquil oasis.

Master Bathroom

You want your bathroom to look like a sophisticated hotel bathroom or spa. Fold a set of fluffy white towels. Add a white terry cloth robe on a hook or a small basket of rolled-up hand towels. Keep it simple.

Breakfast Room or Eat-in Kitchen

Keep the number of chairs to a minimum. Make the breakfast room look spacious, even if it can hold more. Place only four chairs around the breakfast table.

Create an inviting table setting at the breakfast table with white plates, polished silverware, and colorful napkins. A house whose target buyer is a couple with a child might like a cheerful breakfast table with cereal bowls at each setting, a bowl of oranges in the center, and a morning newspaper ready to read at the head of the table.

This is so inviting, your buyers will want to stay for coffee. Hopefully they will write that big check for full price that will allow them to do so every morning!

Powder Room or Guest Bath

Make sure you always keep your powder room or guest bath stocked with toilet paper and some nice fresh hand towels. Some of your prospective buyers will need to use the facilities, and you want them to feel right at home.

Laundry Room

Staging the laundry room is extremely important. Make sure all bottles, detergent boxes, and soaps are out of sight. A stack of neatly folded white towels on the washer does the trick.

Backyards

If weather permits and there is an outdoor dining area, stage an outdoor table setting. If you have a separate barbecue, stage a nice set of barbecue mitts and grilling tools next to it. Be creative. I have seen a backyard staged with a croquet set—as if there were a game in progress. Or if there is a pool or spa, include rolled white towels and a terry cloth bathrobe draped by a Jacuzzi.

Dressing this outdoor setting creates an emotionally engaging moment. Buyers can visualize themselves having a relaxed Sunday brunch by the pool. This will be a feeling that they take with them as they go home to discuss their purchase decision.

Open Floor Plans Are a Challenge

Everyone wants open floor plans today. If not staged to show them off to their best advantage, they can be very scary to buyers because most buyers just don't know how to make them work. They love the space that an open floor plan provides but are intimidated as to what to do with it. Simply by laying down a few rugs that define the areas and adding a grouping of club chairs and a love seat, you give the buyer both an idea and a *visual blueprint* of how an open floor plan can work.

RSS Dress-to-Sell Tips

Create Focal Points in Every Room. Draw the buyer's eye to the farthest point in the room and create a sense of space. See for yourself: Put a brightly colored flower on the bedside table farthest from the door, and voilà! It instantly draws your eye to that point, making the room appear larger.

Face It! Don't Turn Your Back On It. To create a visual focal point that extends well beyond your interior walls and creates a feeling of space, orient some of the furniture in your room to face a window or sliding glass door. Chances are you already have a configuration oriented toward the fireplace or television. Add two comfy chairs and a side table that face an outside space as well.

Color Your World. An inexpensive and dramatic way to add color to your space is to use accent pillows and simple accessories. They make a plain room pop.

Mirror, Mirror on the Floor. Lean a tall, oversized mirror against the wall and resting on the floor opposite a window or sliding glass doors. This reflects the outdoors as you walk into a room. It also creates the illusion of an additional wall of windows. Not only does it do its job of bringing more of the outdoors indoors and visually expanding your interior space, it now also becomes a piece of accent furniture.

Bring in Fresh Plants. Just ask the Home Boys of Los Angeles how important greenery can be in staging a home. The Home Boys, a successful realty partnership of a Realtor and a designer (www.thelahomeboys.com), will not only take on the task of selling your home for you, but will also first evaluate your home and then execute all the set-to-sell techniques for you. It's a wonderful service and very cost-effective. The expense of setting to sell is more than returned by the higher sale price of the house.

(*continued*)

The Home Boys have a signature staging technique. They insist that every home be a *living* home. They stage their properties with lots of lush indoor plants. They believe that wonderfully staged greenery gives your home life, grounds the energy, and helps to connect buyers emotionally to each room.

RSS Sale Success: Star Staging—*I recently shot a segment on* Extra! *with the lovely Jane Seymour, who had been working on her amazing Malibu mansion prior to putting it on the market. She gave me the personal presale tour. She had completely redone her home, but when I asked her what she believed were the elements that would snag her the $18 million price tag, she waved her arms and said that she had the main rooms in the house staged to make buyers feel the house.*

Twelve

DRESS TO SELL: PREP TO SELL

Save It, Store It, Sell It, Chuck It

Repair to Sell

Lifestyle Upgrades

Design to Sell

Dress to Sell: Stage to Sell

DRESS TO SELL: PREP TO SELL

Okay, this is the final piece of the puzzle. The last little insider technique that will get you the big bucks when you sell. Most home buyers make a yea or nay decision on your house in the first few minutes. They do it that quickly because it is a subconscious and sensory response. That's how long it takes to formulate a "sense" of your home. And because this is not a logical thought process, you must immediately grab them by seducing their senses.

* *

Most home buyers make a yea or nay decision on your house in the first few minutes.

* *

SEDUCING THE SENSES MAKES YOUR BUYERS SWOON

So, in addition to designing, staging, and creating vignettes, there is one more secret. You've got to subconsciously seduce four out of the five senses! Sight, sound, touch, and smell. The only taste you have to worry about here is your own taste in design! Remember, when they say "I just love the way this house *feels!*"—*cha-ching!* You've seduced them.

Sounds

Indoor or outdoor fountains, melodious wind chimes swinging in a light breeze, or soft music drifting throughout. Basically, any source of pleasing sound will stimulate the senses. Keep it soft, soothing, and barely audible, as it subconsciously adds a fullness and tranquillity to your home. This also helps to shut out traffic noise or sounds from the neighborhood.

Touch

A chenille throw across the back of a chair or arm of a sofa or draped on a bed feels wonderful to the touch, is very inexpensive, and says "cuddle up."

Life Is a Breeze

I love the feeling of a warm breezy day. But indoors? Why not? Ceiling fans are a fantastic addition to bedrooms and dens. They make you feel as though you are being gently caressed. And who doesn't like that? But ceiling fans are meant to be *felt*, not seen or heard, so give them a test run to make sure they are not clanging like a railroad train.

Scents

Smell is perhaps the most powerful of the senses. It can conjure grand memories of childhood or a past event, and it can remind us of bad experiences or terrible times, too. The scent that permeates every room of your house can make the difference in what price you can fetch for it.

Studies have shown that citrus scents in the home can be the most appealing when they are from natural sources—that is, real citrus! So don't go spraying an aerosol or use those overpowering plug-in things or stacked-up scented soaps. Simply squeeze a fresh lemon carefully in the sink, and wipe it out with a paper towel. Perfect. Be careful about scented soaps. They are often overused. I'm allergic to perfumes and colognes, and your buyers might be, too.

And then there's that old standby of baked bread (use Pillsbury Crescent rolls—bake just one or two before a showing) or cinnamon sticks simmering on the stove. But try these "cooking" scents only when the weather is cold. A hot oven in the middle of the summer is *not* appealing.

Cooking

Before you open your home to Realtors and potential buyers, make sure you haven't been cooking something whose aroma lingers long after dinner is done. Avoid fish, garlic, heavy curry dishes, or anything too pungent.

Smoke

When was the last time someone smoked in your home, yourself included? One Realtor told me that he immediately knocks 5 percent off the potential sale price of a house before he lists it if the owner smokes. It's *that* significant. The smell of cigarette smoke will completely and immediately turn off at least 50 percent of potential buyers. They may not say anything about it, but subconsciously they will have a negative and unpleasant experience of the house. It will *not* feel like home to them, not a place they will want to come back to and hang around.

If you are a smoker, this could be a fantastic reason to quit. And make sure you quit at least two months before you put your house on the market. Yes, it will take that long for the smell to air out. Think of this as an opportunity to be paid to quit smoking!

Sight

If you have followed the RSS techniques, you are pretty well covered with designing and staging for visual stimulation. However, during the day, make sure all the window coverings are pulled back to show as much natural light as possible. At night, put lights on dimmers to create a warm and inviting mood.

PREPARING FOR SHOWTIME—THE FINAL PREP TO SELL

Squeaky Clean

Of course your house not only has to look good, but it also needs to be *spotless*. Kiss cobwebs, dust, grime, rust, mildew, and stains good-bye! I know, no one likes to get on their hands and knees and scrub. You'll say, "I have never cleaned the house so thoroughly before!" Well, if you can make $5,000 to $10,000 more at sale time, I'd say it's worth it! You should be able to eat off the floors. The windows, glass, and mirrors must sparkle. The sinks and toilets should look five-star hotel perfect.

You Don't Have to Go It Alone

If you love to clean and are particularly good at it, you're in luck. Slap on those cleaning gloves and get cracking. But I know a lot of people who cringe at the thought of getting down and dirty with their own grime. It's okay to hire help in this department, as it's usually very cost-effective. A good cleaning team (we're talking two to three people tops, depending on the size of your home) can have your home spotless from start to finish in a day for less than it might cost you in time to go room to room, corner to corner. And it's likely that these people can do a better job than you can. They know from experience where dirt and grime hide, and they can be extremely efficient as well.

RSS Cleaning Tip: Making the Most of Your Save-It/Chuck-It Pile!

Still not sure about that box of old T-shirts that you have in your save-it pile? Instead of buying rolls of paper towels or spending wads of cash on cloth towels, just use your old T-shirts as your cleaning towels and you'll kill two birds with one stone.

YOUR PETS—HOW YOUR DOG COULD LOSE
YOU A BUYER

I love animals—dogs, especially. I have a wonderful Welsh terrier that I rescued five years ago. So, as I discuss this next section, keep in mind that this is all about you making more money and not about mistreating or neglecting your little furry family members. That said, get them out of the house!

Selling Gone Wrong: My Sweet Little Dog

Let's talk about pets and house selling. If a burglar were to climb in through a window, my dog would come over and sit by his feet and lick him. Yet my sweet mild-mannered dog goes into a frenzy whenever someone comes to the front door and rings the bell. So, whenever I put my house up for sale, I prearrange with a friend to keep my dog when there are showings.

On one occasion my Realtor arrived unannounced with two very interested buyers. This was the couple's second time back. They really liked the house and were in my *strong buyers* category. When the Realtor rang the bell, my dog went berserk—barking, howling, yelping. Needless to say, the buyers were so taken aback, they wouldn't even enter the house despite my Realtor's pleas. They never returned.

Pets Distract Your Buyers

Remember when I discussed staging your home to feel like a hotel? Well, how many hotels have you been to that leave other people's pets in the room when you arrive? It's the same principle when selling your house. Pets are a very personal part of your home, and our goal is to depersonalize your home prior to sale. You wouldn't leave your Uncle Frank sitting in a rocker in the living room while buyers wander through the house, so why would you leave your pets running rampant? After all, they are family members, too! Just as we also remove all personal photos, you need to remove all pets, be they dogs, cats, lizards, birds, or hamsters. Send them all on holiday.

Come opening day when your home hits the market, plan on board-

It's amazing that this sweet little dog could ruin a sale. Learn from my mistakes, and get your pets out of the house before any showings!

ing your pets elsewhere. You'll *at least* want your pets absent during any individual showings and certainly during any open house. Also, they can be nuisances when strangers arrive. The last thing you need is to attract a perfect buyer who happens to be highly allergic to cats or doesn't like dogs and doesn't get much farther than the front porch. Thus, be mindful of clearing out all traces of your pet throughout the house, including dog hair and cat dander, when you super-clean your house from top to bottom.

PREP TO SELL ON THE BIG SALE DAY

When shooting a movie, right before the camera rolls to film the big scene, someone out of the darkness shouts, "Last looks!" The chaos that ensues is something out of a vaudeville slapstick act. A dozen minions, makeup artists, costumers, lighting directors, and stagehands will run onto the set frantically tweaking every last wrinkle, strand of hair, and piece of set dressing into perfection. Well, welcome to your *last looks!*

Is Your Home "Camera-Ready"?

When you have finished staging, give your house a little movie screen test. Give it the "last looks." After all, if it's going to be a star, it's got to look perfect. And the camera doesn't lie. Start outside from the street where your potential buyers will park. Go ahead, be corny. Hold up your hands like you are a director checking the composition of a camera shot, or take a picture with a digital camera. How does the "shot" of your house look? Is everything perfect? This is the first impression your buyer will have of your house. Do you need more flowers? Are the new street numbers perfectly straight? Open the front door and take photos of every room. Look at them. And then make the necessary changes.

Show Prep Setup

I want to prepare you mentally for the work that sale day brings. Whether you are living in the house or not, be mentally and physically prepared to "show prep" your house for each showing. Even though my Realtors are fantastic, they are busy and they often arrive at the same time as the buyers. They may not have the opportunity or time to show prep. I do, and so should you.

When those buyers arrive, you must have this house *on!* Every light set perfectly, the music softly playing, the fireplace going if it's cold, the doors and windows open if weather permits, and the temperature exactly right. Remember, you are selling a lifestyle where everything about this house and the life a buyer would experience in it is perfect!

A Family Affair

If you have children, you have a lot of stuff. And of course your kids need to be able to play and carry on with their everyday lives. So how do you get the house looking perfect for every showing? Involve your kids. Make the process a game and get them to participate.

Children love to feel like they are part of the setup. Let them understand that it's time to put the house on display and you all need to set the stage together. Have them pick their favorite toy and stuffed animal to showcase in a perfect spot each time for the show, and put the other toys away. You will be surprised how cooperative the kids are and how much fun they have when you yell "showtime!"

The Show Prep Hit List

My busy schedule sometimes forces me to rely on Realtors or friends to do the show prep. Therefore, I take extra care to keep it in dressed-for-sale mode every day. When I leave the house in the morning, the beds are always made and the bathrooms are totally pulled together, which saves time before those last-minute showings.

In advance of every showing, just accept that you'll be nuts for about a half hour, running through the house like a white tornado! I use my show prep hit list, and so should you. Make copies, mark off items as you complete them, and you'll always be ready to show!

SHOW PREP HIT LIST

Item	Completed
Air out the house for a half hour	☐
Open doors and windows, weather permitting	☐
Vacuum and dust	☐
Kitchen	
Make sure stove, oven, and sinks are spotless	☐
All surfaces are freshly wiped down	☐
Clear all countertops	☐
Grind a fresh lemon in the garbage disposal	☐
All cabinet contents arranged face-out	☐
Floors mopped	☐
Bathrooms	
Put out fresh hand towels	☐
All cabinets' contents arranged face-out	☐
Bedrooms	
Beds made perfectly	☐
Nothing lying around	☐
Kids' toys are staged, not flung about	☐
Powder Room	
Hand towels	☐
Toilet paper	☐
Sensory Preps	
Turn on all lights, even the one above the stove	☐
Turn on all fountains	☐
Adjust the temperature	☐
Turn on or light fireplace	☐
Check on your orchids or other flowers	☐
Set the music	☐
Front Yard	
No leaves	☐
Hoses put away	☐
No cars in the driveway	☐
Backyard	
No leaves	☐
Trash cans away	☐
All toys cleared	☐
Garage	
Neat and tidy	☐

Share Your Show Prep Hit List

Review the hit list and make sure your Realtor has a copy. If there is a showing that you cannot prep yourself, then he or she will know the drill.

Get It Ready and Get Out

Once you have gone through the hit list and the house is ready for its closeup, get out! You want the potential buyers to feel that this is *their* beautiful house. After you have worked so hard to control every aspect of their experience, don't muck it up by lurking around. You'll spoil the fantasy—and the sale.

Maintain Your Privacy and Safety

Believe it or not, people will look through your drawers, closets, and medicine cabinets at open houses or showings. I guess it's just human nature. Make sure they are accompanied by a Realtor. And don't keep anything in the house that you don't want anyone else to see. That includes personal documents and valuables.

RSS Prep Tip: Stay Perfect

Keep the house looking perfect all through your buyer's inspection and contingency period. Until your buyer is *locked* in the deal, every time he or she comes to the house you want it looking exactly as it did when he or she fell in love with it.

Final Panic: "I Can't Live Like This!"—Yes, You Can!

Once you have set, dressed, staged, and prepped your home, actually continuing to live in it will feel different. You'll wonder, "How can I keep the house this perfect or this clean forever . . . and where are my things?" Well, don't worry. If you truly dress your house for sale, it's going to sell right away and you'll be moving soon. Since your things are already packed, well-organized, and edited down to what is essential, because you purged your closets and cleaned out the garage, moving will be a snap. You'll be shocked at how little you actually need for the three months you are in the sale process. And I guarantee it will change forever your relationship to your stuff, and how you live in your home. Not only have you just increased the value of your home, but you have also simplified your life.

Pali Moana Estate
SeaCliff Plantation

Your Own Private Resort

On a bluff...
Over looking Kahlll Bay...
Panoramic Pacific Ocean &
North Shore Mountain Views...

Kim D. Sain-Brady, RB
William L. Stevenson, RA
(partial owner)

Century 21
All Islands

$8,700,000

RSS Sale Success: Prep to Perfection—*This beautiful Hawaiian estate incorporated all the RSS prep-to-sell techniques. As the buyers walked into the home, they were emotionally transported. Every sense was seduced. Tropical breezes blew via the open doors and ceiling fans in every room, waterfalls and fountains gurgled, tropical music played softly, and the sweet smell of gardenia flowers wafted throughout. I was lucky enough to preview this home with Realtor Kim Brady—I didn't want to leave! And neither did the offer-writing buyers!*

Part Three

SOLD!

Thirteen

LISTING YOUR HOUSE AND SETTING THE PRICE

Ah, the all-important, make-or-break price tag. Your house is now ready and set for that final pricing. And now you have some clue as to what homes like yours are selling for in your area. If you've completed all my set-to-sell techniques, you've certainly amped up the perceived value of your home so you've got more room to price it higher. Now it's time to bring back your real estate agent, show him or her your beautifully set house, settle on your final sale price, and make sure your listing agreement is signed.

THE LISTING AGREEMENT

The first in a long list of paperwork and contracts you will be signing before the completion of the sale of your house is the *listing agreement*.

This is your contract with the Realtor, which spells out the terms of the listing and the commission rate. Before you actually put your house on the market, you need to have your contract, or listing agreement, with your Realtor completed and signed.

There is no such thing as one standard, universally accepted listing agreement. Your agent can offer you a variety of choices:

- **Exclusive Right to Sell**. This type of listing guarantees the agent a commission if the house sells. Even if *you* find the buyer, show your house to him or her while the listing is in effect, and sell the house after the listing has expired, your Realtor still gets the commission. While this may seem unfair, a Realtor with this type of listing is likely to invest 110 percent effort into the sale of your house. In exchange for giving up your right to sell the house yourself, you get the best possible service and effort from your Realtor.

- **Exclusive Agency**. This type of listing states that if your real estate agent sells the house, he or she gets the commission; if you sell the house (that is, you find a buyer and show the house), you don't have to pay a commission. Due to the risk of sticky situations emerging with this type of listing, many agents refuse to work with this type of agreement.

- **Open Listing**. This type of listing is the least desirable for Realtors, so you're not likely to sell your house efficiently through a professional agent this way. With an open listing, you agree to pay a commission to any broker who finds a buyer for you, but you pay no commission if you sell the house yourself.

Commissions—Love Them or Leave Them

I know we all hate commissions. And I agree that a 6 percent commission, which is the current standard for the industry, does seem high. It certainly seems higher than it used to. That's because ten years ago, buying a house for $100,000 was commonplace. And $6,000 to be split between the

Realtors and their respective real estate companies didn't sound like a lot. After all the splits, your Realtor may have gone home with $2,000 to $2,500, which seemed more than fair. But with homes routinely selling for $500,000 to $1.5 million, 6 percent commission translates to $30,000 to $90,000 per transaction, which means a Realtor gets $12,000 to $45,000 for doing the same work!

Why We Have to Bite the Bullet and Pay Commissions

Here's the reality: Until there is a national overhaul of real estate commissions, whether the market is hot or cold, we all need to bite the bullet and pay them. Why? Well, if you tell your Realtor you will pay only 4 percent commission for the sale, and *if* he or she accepts the listing with the reduced commission, you have now handicapped your house. Here's why.

Your house is selling for $600,000. With a 4 percent commission, that's $24,000 to the Realtors. However, there is a house down the street for sale for the same price. It may not be as nice as yours, but with a full commission of 6 percent, the Realtors are going to split $36,000 at the time of sale. Do you think a buyer's real estate agent is going to encourage his client to buy yours? He'll push for the other one, because he gets more commission for the same amount of work.

To help make your sale at that point, you'd have to drop your price. So by trying to save $12,000 you may have just lost $25,000 or more. And I promise you, a house selling with a reduced commission does not get as much Realtor and buyer traffic, which means it will sit on the market longer. Your attempt to save that 2 percent defeats everything you have done to make the house more valuable.

Understand Who Gets All That Commission

One of the ways to make those higher commissions more bearable is to understand how much your Realtor *really* gets once the sale is completed. It's not as much as you may think. By the time you sell your house, several agents and salespeople may be involved and part of the commission may be split. In most cases, at least two people are involved, but as many as four agents can take part in the split in the end. While 50/50 splits are common, sometimes a 60/40 can happen—60 percent goes to the selling agency and 40 percent goes to the listing agency. Exceptional agents can often get 80 or 90 percent of the commission, with 20 or 10 percent going to their office.

Let me give you an example of how a typical commission could be split. Let's say you sell your house for $450,000, and pay a 6 percent commission—or $27,000. Here's how that money could potentially be shared among four different people involved in this transaction:

REALTOR COMMISSION BREAKDOWN

6% commission on $450,000 house:	**$27,000**
1.5 percent (or $6,750) to the buyer's Realtor –	$6,750
1.5 percent (or $6,750) to the buyer's Realtor's company –	$6,750
1.5 percent (or $6,750) to your Realtor's company –	$6,750
Total remaining is 1.5 percent to your Realtor =	**$6,750**

In actuality, your agent isn't really walking away with a boatload of money. By the time it's all divided, the person with whom you spend the most time is taking home only a fraction of the entire commission. Which in a weird way takes some of the resentment out of paying all that commission!

Saving Money on Commission?

Despite what you might think, commissions are sometimes negotiable; there are no "minimum commission rates" by law or other sets of rules. But there are industry standards that are typically followed, and in today's terms commissions for single-family residential homes are between 3 and 7 percent. However, 6 percent is the norm in virtually all traditionally sold homes through full-service Realtors and brokers.

The key is to find out what the general commissions are for agents working in your area, and for similarly priced homes. Sliding scales, for instance, can help balance out the difference between a $1 million house, which might command a 6 percent commission in your area, and a $2+ million house, which may call for only a 5 percent commission.

There are only two situations in which I recommend negotiating on the commission:

1. **When your Realtor brings in the buyer himself or herself and no other agent is involved.** In this case include a clause in the listing agreement that if your Realtor "double ends" the deal, the commission is reduced to between 4 and 4.5 percent. This is a significant savings to you.

2. **When the buyer comes from a Realtor in your Realtor's home office.** Since the home office will receive a split on both commissions, they can offer you a break without taking any money from the Realtor's split. In this case I ask for a 0.5 to 1 percent reduction—as part of the listing agreement.

Other commission reductions you can ask for include:

Cancellation Fee. Make sure there is no cancellation fee in the contract. If there is, have it crossed out. Should you decide not to extend the agreement beyond the usual ninety days because the house hasn't sold, then you shouldn't have to pay a fee.

No Realty Agency Fee. Some realty offices include an extra $250 agency fee in the listing agreement. Look for it in the listing contract and have it crossed out.

Limit the Term of the Listing

You should ask to limit the term of the listing agreement to a maximum of ninety days. In slow markets, a good way to calculate exactly how long you should list your home, based on the temperature of your market, is to take the average days-on-market of similar homes in your area and add two to four weeks.

Stipulate That Your Realtor Be Present
for All Showings

Specify in the listing agreement that the Realtor will meet all prospective buyers and their agent and show the house himself or herself. Having your Realtor present for all showings is the optimum arrangement. The alternative is that he or she leaves a computerized lockbox with a key to the house so that prospective buyers and *their* Realtors can see it on their own. By doing this, however, you lose on several fronts. You want your Realtor present for these reasons:

- Your Realtor knows the house and will steer the buyer to its strong points.

- He or she can answer any questions or address any concerns on the spot.

- He or she can show-prep the house if you can't.

- He or she provides the extra security you need as potential buyers and their agents roam the house.

Spell Out the Realtor's Payday

Make payment due and payable when you successfully close, and have this point stipulated in the listing agreement (typically under the "remarks" section of the contract). Be specific about when the commission is earned. This protects you from having to pay a commission if the deal dies. While some agreements state that the commission is due when a buyer is "ready, willing, and able" to buy, some agreements can contain a clause that says the commission is paid only after the sale is concluded and escrow closes.

LISTING AGREEMENT DEAL POINT CHECKLIST

You should confirm that the following items are clearly stated in your listing agreement.

☐ The listing price of your home.

☐ How long you will list your home. The beginning and ending expiration dates should be clearly spelled out, with day, month, and year stated for both.

☐ The brokerage fee or percentage commission. Watch out for a *liquidated damages* clause. This states that if you take your home off the market for any reason, you owe the agent a specified fee. This clause commits you to paying a fee, sometimes a hefty one, to the agent if you decide not to sell.

☐ How long the agent is protected if he or she sells after the listing expires. Don't allow the agent-protection period to last longer than one month.

☐ Cancellation agreement. Ask the agent to include a paragraph that allows you to unconditionally cancel your agreement at any time if you're not happy.

☐ Agent disclosures. Who represents whom when an offer is received.

☐ What you authorize the agent to do, such as have keys, install lockboxes, put up signs, etc. Don't authorize the agent to do anything that can potentially cost big bucks, such as order title work or a home warranty. If a deal doesn't happen, you're out of money.

☐ Arbitration and attorneys' fees. Ask your attorney to check this clause. Most agreements stipulate the use of arbitration instead of legal action when a dispute emerges. And if a lawsuit follows, the losing party pays for all the court-related fees and attorneys' bills.

(continued)

☐ Transaction fee. Don't accept paying for this. Ask that it be removed.

☐ Signatures. All parties with an interest in the house—i.e., all named individuals on the title—should sign the agreement with the Realtor.

SETTING YOUR RSS SALE PRICE

Your Realtor is your team leader in the pricing game. I encourage you to follow along with him or her in the steps he or she takes to determine your RSS sale price. Now that you have completed all the *Ready, Set, Sold!* set-to-sell techniques, your Realtor needs to compare your ready-to-sell house to the rest of the market. Let me explain how he or she will do this.

YOUR REALTOR'S THREE SIMPLE STEPS TO SETTING YOUR RSS SALE PRICE

1. Evaluate comps—that is, evaluate your house as compared to the other houses on the market.

2. Check list versus sale prices.

3. Gauge the temperature of your market—is it moving up or down, or is it flat?

Evaluating the Comps

In part one of this book, I advised you to hunt around your neighborhood for comparable houses that have just sold or are up for sale. That got you thinking about two things: what price you could possibly attach to your house; and how much work you should put into fixing up and upgrading your house to get a top-dollar price.

Well, now your Realtor is going to re-examine those comps to determine a final valuation—your RSS sale price. When your Realtor puts your set-to-sell house through the comp test, he'll ask himself:

- What do the comps have that your house doesn't?

- What does your house have that the comps don't?

With any luck, given the work you've done, your Realtor can name a few items that put your home at the top of the comp list. It means you can command top dollar. It means you can potentially break the comps!

When analyzing the comps, your Realtor will compare the following features:

- **Square footage.** This is significant for most buyers. Some buyers will hunt for homes based on square footage alone. And when it comes to pricing, bigger house means bigger price.

- **Age and condition of the home.** Do you live in a Victorian built in 1910? Or is your house relatively new, say, circa 1997? Of course, older homes don't necessarily command cheaper prices or vice versa. But *condition* relative to *age* does factor into price. When you compare your home to others, stay within a five-year range.

- **Number of bedrooms and baths.** The number of bedrooms and baths—as well as where they are placed—can radically change the price of a home. Like square footage, families often shop for homes based on these numbers.

- **Amenities.** Obviously, the more amenities you have—such as a pool, spa, walk-in closets, gourmet kitchen, and so on—the higher the price.

- **Lot size.** Is there room for the buyer to add on to the house? Or plant a sprawling rose garden in the backyard? The exact acreage of your land correlates to price. When you compare your home to others, stay within .05 acres.

- **Condition.** Whether it's a fixer-upper, a tear-down, completely updated, or pristine, the condition of your house can be a deal maker or deal breaker. That is why applying the RSS techniques is essential.

- **Location.** This factor is multifaceted. It relates not only to your state, city, and neighborhood, but also to where your house sits on the street. Does it face a freeway or busy intersection? Have a view? Does it abut an airport, or does the noise from a nearby manufacturing plant tunnel right into your bedroom? Or does it sit on the bank of a tranquil lake?

Checking List vs. Sale Prices

Knowing the percentage difference between the actual list and sale prices for the houses in your neighborhood speaks volumes about the current market's activity. This is a strong indicator of which direction the market is moving, and will indicate how much less—or maybe even more—than your ideal asking price you can expect to get for your home.

LIST VS. SALE PRICE COMPARISON

List Price	Sale Price	Difference (%)
$180,000	$159,000	−13
$420,000	$405,000	−4
$1,200,000	$1,350,000	11
$799,000	$650,000	−23
$385,000	$400,000	4

Generally speaking, if the percentage differences for homes that sold are between −5 and −10 percent, you're in a soft market. Sellers aren't getting what they think their homes are worth. And they probably aren't selling their homes as quickly as they'd like. If the percentage differences are between −10 and −20 percent or more, the market is extremely weak. Of course, if those percentages are positive, then you're in a warm, potentially hot market.

Gauging the Temperature of Your Market

To price for a moving market, you and your Realtor will need to catch the wave whether it's going up or down. If the market is heating up, you'll raise your price a bit from recent sales figures and comps. Don't get greedy and try chasing the market—you'll never catch up! Likewise, if it's cooling down, you'll lower your price a tad so you don't overprice your home out of the market.

If all the indicators tell you that the market in your area is going up, say, roughly 10 percent a year, and you know that the last home sold four months ago in your neighborhood, don't price your home for selling four months ago. Bump up your ideal asking price for one-third of 10 percent, or 3.3 percent. Conversely, if the indicators are showing 10 percent a year devaluation, then stay ahead of the downward drop and price slightly less than what the last comp sold for.

RSS Pricing Tip: Know What's *Not* Selling

You can learn a lot when determining your price by observing not only what *is* selling, but also by observing what is *not* selling. Are these houses' true qualities hidden? Are they overpriced for what they offer? How do they compare with your house? What do they lack that yours has? Take note and take action.

Taking Inventory and Figuring Time Lag

You're probably wondering *how long* it will take to sell *your* house. That's the million-dollar question. The average amount of time it takes to sell a house differs with each market, but generally speaking is between one and four months. Your Realtor will be able to give you a realistic time frame given his or her recent experience and access to current market information:

- **How long inventory lasts.** In a hot market, an inventory of homes will last only two to three months; in a cold market an inventory can stay the same for up to eighteen months because it takes longer to sell those homes.

- **What the average list price is.** Ask how the prices compare between this year and last.

- **How long it takes to close a sale.** Obviously, the shorter the better. Long closing times, when potential deals "fall out of escrow," indicate a weak market.

PRICING CONDOS AND CO-OPS

Sales of condos and co-ops hit an all-time high in the early 2000s. But selling a condo or co-op isn't the same as selling a traditional house. Condos are part of a larger building with similar units. Thus it can be tough to price it very differently from other units up for sale. If one unit is selling for a low price, you'll have a harder time pricing yours much higher. How does your unit compare to others in the building? Is it in prime condition and dressed to sell? Where is your unit located in relation to other units? How else can it stand out as better than the rest? Getting the competitive edge over other units in the building is all about applying the same set-to-sell techniques and highlighting the best aspects of your unit as compared to the others. When pricing, you need to consider your unit's:

- general location in the building

- noise levels

- views

- natural light

- convenience for getting in and out of the building

- easy access to amenities in the building

- floor plan

- neighbors—good and bad

- number of parking spots

Understand that having the most amazing unit in the complex won't guarantee you a quick sale for top dollar. Be realistic. Find out how fast other units in the building have sold, and then decide how long you want to have your condo up for sale. If you price it too high, it may take longer.

Condos also have specific challenges that you need to consider:

- You may face limitations in advertising the sale of your home as dictated by the homeowners' association, making it more difficult to expose your condo to a wide buying audience.

- Is your building largely rented out? Lenders are more wary about financing sales in such buildings, making it more difficult for your buyer to get a mortgage.

- What's the reputation of your homeowners' association?

- Do people living in your building have good or bad things to say about living there? Your buyer will find out.

- Do buyers need to be approved by a board or association? This can make it more difficult to find a qualified buyer. Financing is also an issue with such restrictions.

PRICING THE SALE OF NEW CONSTRUCTION— YOU VERSUS THE DEVELOPER

Do you live in a planned community, an existing subdivision, or tract home community where building is still taking place? Do you own in "Phase I" and the developer is already working on "Phase II"? If so, you and your Realtor must wander over to Phase II and check out the competition. You'll find one of two scenarios:

1. **Market is soft**. You might be at a disadvantage if the market has softened and Phase II is selling for less than what you would like to get for your unit.

2. **Market is hot.** The market is hot enough that Phase II prices have increased dramatically from what you paid. For your Phase I house, you may be able to price just under the new homes' price. Keep in mind the pros and cons:

   →*Selling Plus*: Your Phase I neighborhood is already established, with grown-in landscaping and lovely, completed homes.

Some buyers will prefer that over a new phase surrounded by bulldozers, infant trees, and blowing dust.

→*Selling Minus*: You've got buyers coming in and being seduced to claim spanking new homes in Phase II.

SELLING GONE WRONG: *LET'S JUST SEE!*

"I'm putting my house on the market at a high price *just to see what I can get*. What's wrong with that? Who knows, maybe I'll get lucky!"

Well, have you ever heard the expression, "Let's throw it all against the wall and see what sticks"? This is the same principle and a very misguided approach to pricing your home. Sure, a few people do get lucky, but pricing according to realistic market prices is your best tool to make a fast and profitable sale. The former approach will cause you to miss any opportunity of attracting multiple offers. It will also prolong the time it takes to sell your home, eating up valuable time on the real estate market. You run the risk of your house sitting on the market too long. At that point it can become a dead listing and a target for vultures and bargain hunters. You could end up selling your house for less than you would have had you priced it correctly from the start.

Ocean City Dreamer - 3459 Asbury Ave.
$999,900

MLS #..274608	
Class...............................CONDOMINIUM	
Status.....................old CO OP by Member	
Asking Price.............................$999,900	
Address.........................3549 Asbury Ave	
City..Ocean City	
County.......................Cape May County	
# of Levels in Unit.............................Two	
Block #..3502	
Days On Market................................110	
Lot #...5- C2	
Original Price $1,149,000	
Rooms..9	
Bedrooms...5	
Full Baths..3	
Half Baths..1	

TheOlivaTeam

CHRIS M OLIVA
RE/MAX OF OCEAN CITY

Beautifully furnished custom built townhouse with incredible rental history. Nine weeks already rented for summer 2006! Garage plus two off street parking spaces. Two outside showers.

RSS Sale Success: The Price Was Right—*Realtor Chris Oliva of Ocean City, New Jersey, knows that the key to a profitable and fast sale is proper pricing. Especially in a vacation area with second homes, expertise in evaluating the market is critical when pricing this house. According to Chris, "If a house is priced correctly, there are no problems or challenges when it comes to selling." The proper price sold this home quickly and for top dollar.*

Fourteen

MARKETING YOUR HOME

Now let's get this baby sold. You may say, "Oh, the Realtor is a professional and it's his job to have everything ready. I'm sure he's got it all under control. I'll just sit back and wait for the offers to roll in." Listen closely now, do you hear something? That's the sound of thousands of your dollars being washed down the drain!

You've done all the work to get your house set to sell, and now you'd better take the time to be *hands-on* as you make the marketing decisions that will get your house sold! I've heard horror stories from sellers whose Realtors let some of the final details slip through the cracks. Make sure all your marketing elements and strategies are in place so that when you're prepared to put your house on the market, your Realtor has the full arsenal of selling tools at the ready.

THE THREE STAGES OF MARKETING YOUR HOUSE FOR SALE

Before you can sell your house, you need to understand the sequence of events that the Realtor will follow to get your house sold. It's all about the *marketing*—the *selling*. There are actually three stages of marketing. And you need to review each of these stages with your Realtor so that you can jointly make the decisions that will best support your fast and profitable sale. Again, don't just *assume* your Realtor will handle everything. Make it a team effort!

- Stage One: Preparing the Selling Tools and the Sale Materials
- Stage Two: Presenting Your Home to the Market
- Stage Three: Winning the Ongoing Sale Process

WHERE YOUR BUYER COMES FROM—TARGET YOUR MARKETING

Understanding where your buyer will come from is like having the answers to the test. Knowing statistically how a buyer first becomes introduced to your fabulous home for sale allows you to get the upper hand in two ways: You can put your attention, time, and effort into the productive areas, and you won't waste precious resources on avenues that yield little hope of snagging a great buyer.

Statistically, as you can see from the chart on the following page, at least 40 percent of all home sales are a direct result of a real estate agent's involvement and your property being listed in the Multiple Listing Service. That is, most homes gets sold when a buyer is introduced to a house by an agent. Thus, setting and dressing your house with Realtors in mind is just as important as preparing your house for buyers. Why? Because *Realtors* who love the house will bring you *buyers* who'll love it, too.

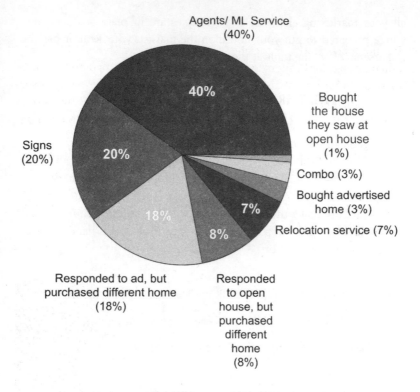

Where Do Buyers Come From?
(Source: National Association of Realtors)

STAGE ONE: PREPARING THE SELLING TOOLS AND THE SALE MATERIALS

The tools of the trade include: photos of your house, a listing on the MLS, a *brochure* or *one-sheet*, and a presence on the Internet. These are what truly showcase and represent your house to your potential buyers. Each must be in place before your house can go on the market, and must be dynamic and have all the appropriate information to snag that dream buyer.

Photos

It's not uncommon, especially with higher-priced and multimillion-dollar homes, for Realtors to invest in professional photographers to take these all-important photos. Yes, buyers do judge a "book" by its cover! The photograph of your home is the first opportunity you have to attract a buyer. If the photos are not good, this can spell disaster for a high-priced and quick sale of your home.

When I'm producing *Extra's Mansions & Millionaires*, I know how important it is to get that perfect shot of the house—the one that will represent and showcase the house in just one picture. Called the *money shot*, it's that one angle or snapshot that says "Now *this* is the house I want to see more of!"

Great photographs of your house are critical tools for snagging buyers. This terrific photo pulled in dozens of eager buyers to this condo, designed by Laguna Staging & Design.

You don't need a professional camera crew to find your money shot. Just use your eyes and a digital camera to try all the different angles of your house. Typically, your money shot is the one from the curb—but not dead-straight on. Try positioning yourself with the camera just slightly to the left or right so you get an angled shot that still shows the entire front of the house. Your Realtor should have developed a pretty good eye for this and will be able to direct the shooting. We all have "good sides," and we stand angled either to the right or left of a camera when someone takes our photograph. Well, so do houses. And if you are selling a condo, usually the living room shot will be the money shot.

Normally, the Realtor is responsible for providing all the photographs of your house. He or she will either take the photos, hire a photographer who specializes in architectural photography, or use someone who works specifically for the realty company.

RSS Marketing Tip: Go Wide

Professional photographers always shoot house photos with a special wide-angle lens. Ask to have your house photos shot with one, or at least with the widest lens setting on your camera. It gives the house and all the rooms a bigger feeling in the photograph.

The Multiple Listing Service—MLS

Think of "MLS" as standing for "Must List to Sell." The MLS is made up of hundreds of database computer systems located throughout the country for real estate agents to showcase their available listings. MLS listings in most cities are now available for viewing by the public on www.MLS.com, but to access the complete source you typically have to be a Realtor, or member of the National Association of Realtors. But thanks to the Internet we've got access to millions of free listings so buyers can easily see what they look like by going online to any real estate site and searching for homes. If you go to Realtor.com, which is run by the NAR, you can check out a typical listing.

Similar to a listing for a television program in *TV Guide*—which describes and tries to sell a show to potential viewers in two short sentences—the MLS entry cuts right to the chase and describes your house so it jumps out from all the other houses listed. Even though listings follow similar formats and detail similar facts and features of homes, your listing must somehow get buyers and Realtors to consider your house by highlighting any information that makes it truly stand out. Beyond the bullet points of your house's main aspects, it must include information that shouts "Look at me! I'm special!" It uses the same language as what's on the one-sheets/brochures (see below).

Keep in mind, however, that real estate practices vary region by region—including state by state and even county by county. In New York City, for example, three of the five boroughs (the Bronx, Staten Island, and Queens) use an MLS system, whereas Manhattan and most of Brooklyn don't pay much attention to the MLS. Buyers go from broker to broker in search of a property.

The Brochure

Often referred to as the *one-sheet*, the brochure is a critical marketing tool. It's the "take away" that prospective buyers will carry with them after they have seen your property, and it must contain a compelling profile of your home on a normal 8 1/2" × 11" piece of paper. Aim to have a few wonderful photos, preferably in glorious color, added to the brochure. The sheet lists all the essential features and highlights of your home. In large metropolitan areas, or where homes fetch high prices, brochures with color photos have become standard. In other words, they are a must! And if you don't live in a city or have an expensive house, think how much your home can stand out among the competition by adding color photos. These days, color photocopying is cheap and widely available at nearly every copy store or, better yet, at your Realtor's office.

Emotionally, brochures with color are a grabber! They allow the buyer to show off and talk about your house with friends and colleagues. "Hey, check out this house I'm thinking of buying!" It offers a visual connection to your house so that buyers continue to build an emotional attachment to your house even days after they did their first tour.

Your agent should be responsible for creating and printing the brochure. Most realty companies now have their own in-house system for creating these one-page sheets or brochures. The team of Realtors that I always work with has a wonderful three-photo template that they use for every house they sell. It looks great and includes all the pertinent information.

Here is an example of two very-well-done, eye-catching brochures. They showcase the homes, giving a brief and compelling description of the houses' best features.

Creating the Perfect Brochure or One-Sheet

The science behind these marketing sheets is pretty simple. Make sure to include:

- **Price.** Including the price weeds out buyers who are out of your range.

- **Square footage.** Exclude unfinished rooms, such as a large basement ready to be converted into a game room, and detail that feature separately.

- **Year.** When the home was built and/or remodeled.

- **Style of home.** Such as English Tudor, Contemporary, Colonial, etc.

- **Number of bedrooms.** Detail size of closets, such as "double" or "walk-in."

- **Number of baths.** Detail special features, such as spa tubs, walk-in closets, his-and-her sinks, etc. Note: A full bath has both a tub and a shower; a three-quarters bath has a shower only; and a half-bath contains a toilet and sink only.

- **Kitchen features.** Such as new appliances, granite/marble countertops, built-in wine storage, walk-in pantry, etc. List appliances and give brand names for fancy items like a Viking range or Sub-Zero refrigerator.

- **Roof.** If new, type of roof.

- **Best feature.** Create a headline that highlights the best feature of your home, such as its square footage, view, lot size, proximity to trendy areas or stores. Examples: 101 OCEAN VIEW DRIVE— BREATHTAKING 360° VIEW!; 3.4-ACRE LOT WITH FRUIT GROVES!; ROOSE- VELT SCHOOL DISTRICT; 2 BLOCKS FROM THE BOARDWALK AND PIER!

- **Additional highlights.** Any other features that should be mentioned, such as ocean or city views, river-rock/wood-burning fireplace in great room, hardwood floors, crown molding, recessed lighting, and so on.

RSS REALITY CHECK: STAY TRUE TO FORM

In order to be legally considered a bedroom, there must be a closet in the room. So don't describe your house as a four-bedroom when you simply converted an enclosed porch into another bed-room that doesn't have its own closet.

The Marketing Words That Attract the Buyers

Be very specific in describing your home. Don't be vague and use words like "fantastic," "spacious," or "charming." Boring! Avoid sweeping adjectives. Give specifics, using descriptive, straightforward terms that indicate the physical attributes of your home, such as "marble," "spiral staircase," "gourmet kitchen with new Viking appliances," and "solid bamboo flooring."

According to Levitt and Dubner in their bestselling *Freakonomics*, "An analysis of the language used in real estate ads shows that certain words are powerfully correlated with the final sale price of a house. . . . A 'fantastic' house is surely fantastic enough to warrant a high price, isn't it? What about a 'charming' and 'spacious' house in a 'great neighborhood!'? No, no, no and no."

They go on to say, "If you study the words in an ad for a real estate agent's own home . . . you see that he or she indeed emphasizes descriptive terms (especially, 'new,' 'granite,' 'maple,' and 'move-in condition') and avoids empty adjectives (including 'wonderful,' 'immaculate,' and the telltale '!')." Take their advice, and don't make it appear that you're desperate to sell by using a phrase like "must move quickly." You're going after the buyers looking for their dream home—and willing to pay for it—not the bargain hunters!

Here's the hot-button word breakdown, as described in their book:

Five Terms Correlated to a Higher Sale Price

- Granite

- State-of-the-art

- Corian

- Maple

- Gourmet

Five Terms Correlated to a Lower Sale Price

- Fantastic

- Spacious

- !
- Charming
- Lovely

RSS Marketing Tip: Keep It in the Box

Ask your Realtor to provide a Lucite or weatherproof box that holds brochures, to be placed next to the For Sale sign or attached to it. This is where curious drive-by buyers and passersby can pick up a one-sheet or a brochure. As the price is listed on the brochure, it will eliminate a lot of unnecessary and unqualified buyers. It weeds them out and saves your Realtor from fielding a ton of annoying calls that lead nowhere.

The Internet Presence

The Internet is critical. According to Nelson Gonzales of Esslinger-Wooten-Maxwell Realtors in Miami, "At least 70 percent of all buyers will look for a house at *some* point in their house search on the Internet." In 2005, 77 percent of all home buyers used the Internet to look for a home. They may not have access to the online MLS, but they will have access to Realtor.com and any other local real estate listing site.

Many home sellers are now having their Realtors create mini–Web sites or full Web pages for their homes. Sometimes they are on your Realtor's own site and sometimes your Realtor can create one just for you. This allows you to have as many shots of your house as you like, with descriptions of all the important selling information. Think of it as an online brochure. You can even include a virtual tour of your home.

It takes several days for these Internet submissions to be processed and go live. Make sure your listing is submitted a few days before sale day. The goal is to create a Web presence that gets buyers to show off their potential house to family and friends.

The Sign

Your Realtor will have this one covered. And you don't want it to contain too much information. Leave the details to your brochure or flier. Your For Sale sign simply needs to convey the fact that your home is up for sale and how to contact your real estate agent. If you belong to a home-owners' association, be sure to ask about any restrictions on putting up signs. There might be restrictions on the type and size of a sign you can put up, and where it can be placed.

RSS Marketing Tip: Move It to Lose It

If for some odd reason your house has been on the market for more than four weeks, move the location of the For Sale sign. It sounds almost unbelievable, but with the sign in a new location people who drive by your house will notice it again, as if for the first time. I've witnessed people remark, "Hey, did you just put your house on the market?" *after* the sign has been moved!

RSS SELLING SECRET: PUT THE SIGN UP BUT KEEP THE DOOR SHUT

Curt Truman of Coldwell Banker, Beverly Hills, says, "Put the For Sale sign up a week or two before the big sale day. But *never* let anyone in until the house is completely ready and set to sell. Buyers will call your Realtor for information. Your Realtor will take their name and number and tell them that as soon as the house is officially on the market, he will call them for a first look. Hopefully, you'll have built up a long list of targeted potential buyers in the weeks prior to the big sale day."

STAGE TWO: PRESENTING YOUR HOME
TO THE MARKET

Presenting your home to the market for the first time takes some planning. It's a crucial step in selling your home. This is where a Realtor's expertise and experience kicks in—and can pay you big dividends. This initial exposure to the marketplace is so important because once your house is set to sell and priced properly, you have a very good chance of selling it in this first round of buyers.

Your Realtor can employ numerous marketing and sales strategies when presenting your house on the market for the first time. Being a "new" listing actually has value. And as the newness lasts only so long, you and your Realtor need to make the most of these first few weeks.

The Caravan

The caravan is exactly what it sounds like: All the Realtors in your town are notified of your house's sale. In most cities, Realtors run from one new listing to the next in a *caravan* to preview all the houses that have just come on the market. In Los Angeles, for instance, it's not uncommon to have more than sixty Realtors come through the house in a two-hour period. Many realty companies throughout the country, especially those in densely populated areas where a large number of Realtors work, hold agent caravans to introduce newly listed homes to agents from other companies.

Caravans do work better in some regions of the country than others, so don't worry if your Realtor advises against it. If he or she doesn't even mention it, ask about it! You may live in a region where caravans aren't the norm because they aren't that successful or they don't result in gaining the seller any competitive edge. Go with your Realtor's advice on this.

For those who live in areas where caravans *are* part of the game plan, it's a crucial day for you and the sale of your house. Think of it as opening night of a Broadway show, with the Realtors as the reviewers—the critics. If they like the show they will recommend it to the public, their buying clients. If they don't like the show, you may never see an audience member come walking through that front door. Yeah, this day is *that* big. That's why I keep reinforcing to you the importance of setting your house for sale. It's not *just* for the buyers, but for the Realtors, too!

> **Think of the Realtors as the reviewers—the critics. If they like the show they will recommend it to the public, their buying clients.**

Hold Back

Different Realtors in different regions will employ different tactics when marketing your house. Be open to listening to your Realtor's ideas and recommendations when you strategize together and confirm a plan of action. When I'm selling a house in Los Angeles, for example, my Realtors like to build excitement by refusing to show it before the first caravan. This is called *holding back*. And because no one gets a sneak preview, all the interested Realtors and their buyers will rush over during the first few days and, one hopes, submit offers all at once. It works. I've had great luck with this technique. When a house is priced properly and looks sensational, this technique helps create a "feeding frenzy" mentality.

Remember that Realtors in some regions of the country don't do caravans. They merely list new properties on the MLS and then show them to interested parties. But the same effect can be generated by not showing the property until it actually appears on the MLS.

Just Say No to "Pocket Listings"

Don't fall for this one. If your agent says, "If you really want to make a quick sale and get the most out of my real estate office—and the sale of your home—let me *pocket list* your house. I'll tell people in my office about it and have a few open houses before I open it up to the MLS."

I hate when Realtors do this to unwitting sellers. A seller trusts his Realtor and is unaware that this is a selling tactic that benefits only the Realtor. Sometimes this ploy is referred to as *vest-pocketing* a listing. What your agent is trying to do is single-handedly sell your house by bringing in the buyer himself. This allows him to keep both the selling and buying agent commission.

If your house isn't listed on the MLS for a few weeks, other agents don't know that your house is up for sale. And while your agent may be working his butt off to sell your house himself, one agent versus one thousand or more is no competition. You'll have little or no chance of getting multiple offers. And with very few people actually seeing your house, there is scant excitement or buzz generated.

The worst part of all this is that the savvy *buyer* will also know that the house is not getting a lot of attention at the moment, and thus he or she has very little competition. If I were trying to buy that house, I'd offer a lot less for it right now. Translation: You lose money!

These first few weeks are an important window of opportunity. Just say *no thanks* if your Realtor wants to pocket list your house. Remember that exposure and timing are key elements to selling a house. You want full exposure and an MLS listing right from the start.

Host No-Offer Pre-showings

This one is a teaser. The Realtor offers sneak previews of your house but accepts no offers until the caravan or first day of sale. Once again, this stockpiles offers and often creates for you the seller's dream come true: the oh-so-desirable bidding war.

The "Talk It Up in the Office" Strategy

This is the strategy used when Realtors have a very good house that they know will sell quickly and for top dollar. They will announce to their office that they've got a great listing that their fellow Realtors need to see and review with their buyers. This is similar to hosting no-offer pre-showings, except that *if* the offer is really a good one, your Realtor just might go ahead and present it to you—the home seller—out of loyalty to the fellow Realtors in his or her office. This is not a bad thing for you and it generates some excitement in his or her office about your home—a good thing to have happen.

RSS SELLING SUCCESS STORY: HE TALKED AND I BENEFITED

In 2005 I wanted to sell one of my properties in Palm Springs, California. It was a 2,000-square-foot midcentury-style gem with three bedrooms, two baths, and a sunken living room with terrazzo floors. I called my Realtor, Brian Hatch of Sotheby's, who is very experienced. He came to my home armed with a list of comps from the neighborhood. He had done his homework, and had a good idea of what I should ask for the house: $769,000. I had already set the house to sell, so it was ready to go.

I had met with Brian at noon. Soon afterward, I hit the road to get back to L.A. Not long into my drive, my cell phone rang. It was Brian. "It was so nice seeing you today," he said. "I sold your house."

"What?!" I said. I had met with him only two hours ago. Well, it seems that Brian went back to his office and talked it up. One of the other Realtors in his office had a client looking for exactly that kind of house. He called the buyer, they met up at my house, and an offer was written on the spot!

But here is where a savvy and smart Realtor really gets to shine. Brian explained to the buyer that the house had not even hit the market yet, and that the only way the owner would even consider accepting an offer right now was if it were substantially above the asking price. The house sold for $789,000—$20,000 above my asking price! Who says talk is cheap?

THE ONGOING SALE PROCESS

Does It Pay to Advertise?

The good Realtor knows that advertising doesn't sell homes. Most home sellers get concerned if their house is not listed in great detail in the Sunday real estate section of their paper—especially if it's a big metro one. Well, the truth is that your home will not sell because of advertising. A

This is my Palm Springs home that sold for $20,000 over asking thanks to my Realtor "talking it up" in his office even before it went on the market!

common misconception among both buyers and sellers is that advertising sells real estate. No, uh-uh. Studies done by the National Association of Realtors consistently show that up to 72 percent of real estate sales are the result of agent contacts through previous clients, referrals, friends and family, and personal contacts.

So, what really sells a home? Utilizing the set-to-sell techniques and pricing a house properly. All the advertising in the world won't take an overpriced home off your hands. All the color photos in the Sunday real estate section won't sell a home filled with clutter and disrepair. This is why it's crucial to first set your house for sale, then price it properly.

The Open House

Your Realtor will want you to do an open house, as nearly 40 percent of all buyers go to open houses as part of the process. And if your agent is really good, he or she will attack the neighborhood and invite everyone and his mother to attend. You want your agent to send good-looking postcards and invitations. You want your nosy neighbors and the ones you've never seen before to show up. You'd be surprised how many homes sell to neighbors or to someone your neighbors know.

On open house day you don't need to do much other than prep the home for the event and get lost. If you're a control freak, it might be difficult to surrender the task of putting your home on display for all the world to see. But don't argue this one. Your Realtor will host the show from start to finish. Here's what he or she will do:

- Place an ad in the local paper for the day of the open house that includes the house's price and address.

- Create fliers advertising the open house, furnishing the date and time, and pass them around the neighborhood three to five days in advance.

- Make the brochure or one-sheet available so that potential buyers can take it with them.

- Put up as many directional signs in the area as needed to direct traffic.

- Make a sign-in sheet so that he or she can later follow up with any interested potential candidates.

- Be available to answer questions as people move through the house and take notes.

Security First

Now that your home is perfectly poised to sell, opening it to the public for showings poses a few risks—a bit of at-home shoplifting being one of them. While that shouldn't be your main worry come open house day, you don't want to tempt people, either. I have never found that anyone intentionally wants to walk off with your family jewels, but I certainly wouldn't want to leave them around as temptation. And you probably won't be able to blame your agent or brokerage; they are typically not liable for stolen property.

Let's just say that people are naturally curious, and I have indeed seen buyers open all closets and cabinets and sometimes drawers of furniture while they are touring a home. To reduce the chance that you'll return home to a few less possessions than you started with, think about the target spots: medicine cabinets, jewelry boxes, and rooms filled with little gadgets someone can easily pocket. Scan your house room by room and consider removing anything you don't want a stranger to see, including prescriptions, notes and paperwork, check-books, and the like.

I'm not one for obsessing about the security of each and every item in the house. That only keeps you in a state of anxiety. No one is going to walk out your front door carrying your plasma TV during an open house. However, it's important to safeguard yourself. If your home will be viewable over the Web via photographs or a virtual tour, don't display valuables that will tempt thieves to attend your open house. And with that in mind, here are a few more tips:

- Talk to your agent about how to safeguard your possessions. For multilevel homes, ask your agent to bring along an assistant so that all floors are manned at all times.

- Remove all valuables or store them in a safe and locked place.

- Remove all prescription medicines or lock those up, too.

- Don't forget about small electronics, such as laptops, iPods, PDAs, and other electronic devices that are easy to pocket.

- Make sure your computers are locked with a password.

- Don't use any heirlooms or valuable possessions when you stage your rooms.

- Make sure your agent uses a sign-in sheet for everyone who comes into the house.

- After open houses, insist that the Realtor lock all doors and windows, as you wouldn't want anyone "stopping by" later after they have already been through the house.

The Showings

Ask your agent exactly how he or she plans to facilitate showings. I request that my Realtor always be present for showings. Who better than my Realtor to guide a buyer through the house, pointing out its best features? Moreover, when you are not available to prep the house for showings, you'll want him or her to be there with your show prep hit list in hand.

Have a clear understanding of who will be handling appointments and buyers when they come looking. Ask your Realtor what the norm is for showing homes in your area. Is it customary to have your Realtor show your home by appointment? Be clear about how appointments are made, too. In some markets, your Realtor can't show up unannounced to exhibit the home with a prospective buyer—even if he or she has your approval to do so. The Realtor has to first register the appointment with the listing office. In other areas, however, it's enough to give you a heads-up only.

RSS House-Showing Tip: Advance Warning

Insist that the Realtor give you at least one hour's advance notice before a showing. You must have that lead time to run though your show prep hit list and get the house in perfect set-to-sell order! I would rather cancel or delay a showing if I know my house is not going to be prepped for sale when the prospective buyer arrives! You also need time to get out of the house and take the pets with you!

* *

I would rather cancel or delay a showing than have a prospective buyer arrive if my house is not going to be perfectly prepped for sale!

* *

Your Keys and Codes

If your Realtor is given a set of your keys and your house alarm system code, make sure you know how those keys and codes will be protected and secured. You don't want your keys left hanging on a bulletin board over a long weekend in a real estate office that doesn't have some kind of security system in place.

Lockboxes

A lockbox is like a mini-safe that's attached to your gate or placed near the front door. It contains the keys to your house, and only your Realtor knows its combination. He or she will give the combo to another Realtor if he or she is not available to do the showing. Your Realtor might either use a traditional lockbox or prefer one of the newer electronic models, secured with an access code that can even keep track of how many times the box is opened. That way, the listing office knows who accessed the home and when. I think this is a brilliant idea.

SALES SUCCESS CHECKLIST

☐ **Marketing plan.** Who is the buyer and what is the best way to reach him or her in terms of photography, language, style of materials? What will the Realtor do beyond the expected to attract buyers?

☐ **Photos.** Are they beautiful? Do they telegraph what's great about the home?

☐ **Brochures/one-sheets.** Are they attractive and well written? Is all the information correct? Got some color photos on it?

☐ **MLS listing.** Does it use the language of the ads/brochures/one-sheets?

☐ **Internet.** Is the house on the Realtor's Web site and other realty Web sites with full-color photos and glowing detail?

☐ **Presentation to the market.** Is your sale strategy in place?

☐ **Open houses.** What is your Realtor's strategy and schedule?

☐ **Showings.** Will your Realtor be present for all showings?

☐ **Advance warning.** Have enough notice to run through your show prep hit list before each showing.

Calling on St. Joseph

I'm not particularly superstitious but I do believe that anything you put your attention to you create. So here is an old house-selling custom for you to enjoy. If you bury a small statue of St. Joseph in the front yard upside down and facing your house, it will supposedly speed your sale! I never understood this one, especially the upside-down part. I would think St. Joseph would be very, very angry about being upside down. But people swear that this speeds the sale.

RSS Sale Success: Knowing What the Buyers Want—*The sellers knew that once inside this home the buyers would buy, and marketing the house properly would bring them to the door. Savvy Realtor Samantha Clark understood what the buyers in this area of Albuquerque were looking for. She smartly decided to market the home as a charming cottage, and advised the sellers to add gingerbread wood trim detailing to the front exterior to give the house the look. A little savvy marketing and a few dollars spent on woodwork snagged the sellers their asking price.*

Fifteen

DISCLOSE! DISCLOSE! DISCLOSE!

Disclosures play such an important role in protecting you and your assets—and, obviously, your profit in the sale of your house—that I'm devoting a whole chapter to the subject. So here's what I have to say about disclosures: Disclose! Disclose! Disclose!

WHAT ARE DISCLOSURES?

Simply put, disclosures are the written statements that disclose, inform, and reveal any and all problems or issues that a homeowner knows about his or her house. By law in Oklahoma, for instance, a defect that must be disclosed is defined as any "condition, malfunction, or problem that would have a materially adverse effect on the monetary value of the property, or that would impair the health or safety of future occupants of the property." Even if you're not selling a home in Oklahoma, this definition is a good one to remember.

I learned a valuable lesson many years ago from a very wise Realtor by the name of Rob Risher, of Coldwell Bankers in Beverly Hills. A lawyer before he become a real estate agent, Rob said to me, "When in doubt, disclose. It's always better and safer to *over*-disclose known facts about a house than to *under*-disclose. If there are any problems with the house, either repair them, or disclose them."

When in doubt, disclose. It's always better and safer to over-disclose known facts about a house than to under-disclose.

—Rob Risher of Coldwell Bankers

A disclosure statement can come in many forms. It can be as simple and basic as a handwritten list from the home seller, itemizing all known problems and defects; however, many states require a formal disclosure from the seller as an integral part of the sale process. It's often a preprinted form itemizing all the possible areas of the home that may be in need of repair or are defective. Disclosure statements vary state to state. Typically they are two- to five-page forms with lots of yes/no questions.

In New York, if a home seller fails to supply a written disclosure to the buyer prior to signing the contract, guess what: The seller gets penalized and the buyer gets an automatic $500 credit. Disclosures are that important. If you fail to disclose something, and your buyer discovers it after the close of the sale, you could be slapped with a lawsuit to pay for the repair. You may also face the more serious charge of fraud if the buyer can prove that you intentionally kept the problem secret.

. . . .

If you fail to disclose something, and your buyer discovers it after the close of the sale, you could be slapped with a lawsuit to pay for the repair.

. . . .

WHAT KINDS OF THINGS SHOULD YOU DISCLOSE?

I'm all for disclosing anything and everything. Honesty is the best policy. Like a good inspector, good disclosures are your friend. As the home seller, you are obligated to include all known problems, repairs that need to be made, outstanding permit issues, any problems with neighbors, or the fact that a serious crime has been committed in the home, even if it occurred before your owning the home. You must also disclose any known environmental problems, such as the presence of mold, radon gas, or lead paint.

Disclose Material Facts

At the root of disclosure forms is the revelation of all known *material facts*, which describe the condition and legal status of the house. Material facts also include the age of your house's components, any problems related to those components, structural defects, or encroachments—where someone has built on another's property line.

Specific examples of material facts include:

- Age of shingles and other roof components

- Leaks in the roof or foundation walls

- Any repairs that need to be made

- Existing mold or mildew within the home

- Damage from termites

- Problems with sewer or septic systems

- Proximity to an airport's flight path

- Information about a structure on the property that overlaps an adjacent property

- Presence of an oil or gas tank buried on the property

- A drainage problem during heavy rains

- Details about any individual who claims to have an interest in the property

Of course, there are limitations on what you must disclose. You don't have to share details about why you are selling and whether or not you personally have serious and potentially contagious health problems. Even if your Realtor is aware of some of your personal information, he or she is not allowed to disclose anything to the buyers unless it falls under the material facts category.

Disclose Everything Else

In addition to disclosing the standard items, I like to go one step further and list all the upgrade and renovation work that has been done to the property. I list anything that has been done without a permit as well as all the systems that have been replaced or upgraded. Why? Two big reasons: It's the honest thing to do, and it protects you. If a buyer discovers a problem after the purchase, even one the inspector misses, and he or she can show that you were aware of a problem and didn't disclose it, he or she can come after you.

For example, let's say I have put in all new copper plumbing with a licensed plumber and with permits for the entire house. However, I have a powder room whose plumbing was renovated a year later *without* a permit. I simply add into the disclosure statement "All new permitted copper plumbing throughout the house with the exception of powder room, which was completed without permit." Now I'm covered. If the buyers want to come back someday and sue me because the pipes installed were not to full code standards, I'm less liable. Why? Because they were informed of this issue at the time of purchase.

I will even disclose very general repairs or upgrades such as "new drywall added throughout, and outdoor decking added by homeowner." So I need to say this again: Disclose, disclose, disclose!

SAMPLE DISCLOSURE FORM

Most state real estate commissions provide blank templates for property disclosure forms on their Web sites. Try going to your state's main site—usually done by typing www.yourstate.gov—and then click your way to a link for your state's real estate Web site. You can also find out about your state's particular laws regarding disclosures.

The following is a small slice of a disclosure statement from Colorado. This will give you an idea of what one looks like.

Obviously, different regions of the country will require different focal points on disclosures. For example, you can expect to find questions about earthquake damage in California, whereas in South Carolina you can expect questions about flooding. Your Realtor can tell you what types of disclosures sellers are obliged to make in your area. Even if disclosures are not mandatory, prepare one anyway!

The printed portions of this form, except differentiated additions, have been approved by the Colorado Real Estate Commission (SPD 19-10-05) (Mandatory 1-06)

THIS FORM HAS IMPORTANT LEGAL CONSEQUENCES AND THE PARTIES SHOULD CONSULT LEGAL AND TAX OR OTHER COUNSEL BEFORE SIGNING.

SELLER'S PROPERTY DISCLOSURE
(ALL TYPES OF PROPERTIES)

THIS DISCLOSURE SHOULD BE COMPLETED BY SELLER, NOT BY BROKER.

Seller states that the information contained in this Disclosure is correct to the best of Seller's CURRENT ACTUAL KNOWLEDGE as of this Date. Broker may deliver a copy of this Disclosure to prospective buyers.

Date: _____

Property Address: _____

Seller: _____

I. IMPROVEMENTS				
☐ If this box is checked, there are no structures or improvements on the Property; do not complete Sections A-G.				

A.	STRUCTURAL CONDITIONS To Seller's current actual knowledge, do any of the following conditions **now exist or have they ever existed:**	Yes	No	Do Not Know	COMMENTS
1	Structural problems				
2	Moisture and/or water problems				
3	Damage due to termites, other insects or rodents				
4	Damage due to hail, wind, fire or flood				
5	Cracks, heaving or settling problems				
6	Exterior wall or window problems				
7	Exterior Artificial Stucco (EIFS)				
8	Any additions or alterations made without a required building permit				
9	Building code violations				

B.	ROOF	Yes	No	Do Not Know	COMMENTS
1	Roof problems				
2	Roof material _____ Age ____ Roof material _____ Age ____				
3	Roof leak: Past				
4	Roof leak: Present				
5	Damage to roof: Past				
6	Damage to roof: Present				
7	Roof under warranty until _____ Transferable				

RSS Disclosing Tip: Screwy Property Lines

What if you discover that your property line is wrong, and the fence separating you and your neighbor is eight feet into your neighbor's yard? Watch out. If you've been friendly with your neighbor for ten years and he's been cutting and maintaining your grass at his expense, he just might be able to claim that land as his property now. It's called *adverse possession*. Better disclose the potential problem.

Not Your Everyday Disclosures, but Necessary

If any of the following pertains to your house, you'd best mention it even if you don't want to or don't think it's necessary:

- noisy neighbors

- barking dogs

- previous death or murder in the house

- crime issues that have affected your home

- paranormal activity (poltergeists, hauntings, etc.—no kidding!)

Disclosures Are Like Insurance Policies for the Home Seller

Disclosure statements help protect you from legal perils later on, when your buyer tries to sue you for problems that emerged after the sale. For this reason, think of disclosures as risk diverters.

However, a disclosure is not by any means a "warranty" for home buyers. It's more like an insurance policy by which you can prove that you made the buyers aware of the problems and that that they have seen and understood the issues. The disclosure statement is only a statement of facts as known by you, the seller.

Chances are, your potential buyer is going to ask for this document upon acceptance of the offer and prior to doing his or her own inspection. Have it ready to go. The purchase agreement may also contain a clause that indicates a time limit for when the disclosure needs to be delivered to the buyers. Make sure your buyers respond with a signed acknowledgment that they've received it.

RSS Disclosure Tip: The More Inspections, the Better Disclosures

Encourage a buyer to get all the inspections he or she needs to feel comfortable: home, geological, chimney, sewer, foundation, termite, whatever. Ultimately, it benefits you, since once a problem has been identified and thus disclosed, you can never be accused of hiding problems after the sale.

Once You DO Know, Then You Know!

Once a buyer has done an inspection on your home and presented you with his or her official report, you must now disclose the findings in that report to any other buyers. That's right, even if the potential buyer who ordered that original inspection isn't your ultimate buyer. In other words, let's say Kay and Frank make an offer on your house and they do an inspection. Well, their inspector discovers that there is a big crack in the fireplace and it's separating from the wall. Wow! You had no idea, even when you cleaned out the old ashes and spruced up the mantel during your repair-to-sell process. This finding has made Frank and Kay very nervous. Kay lost her beloved pussycat in a tragic fireplace collapse when she was a child. So even though you offer to give them a credit or have the chimney repaired, they say sayonara and walk away.

Okay, back to square one with the next buyer, you think. *Nope!* You now have to disclose that you are now aware that the chimney has a severe crack and is separated from the wall. What do you do? My suggestion: Get it fixed immediately or have an estimate for the repairs handy and have your Realtor disclose the cost of the repairs to all interested buyers.

The Set-to-Sell Technique Puts You Ahead of the Disclosure Game

When you worked through the repair-to-sell list in Chapter 7, you should have identified problems or what could potentially be problems. If you chose not to repair something, now you have something to disclose. Simple as that! And when your buyer brings in his or her inspector, you shouldn't receive any serious surprises because you'll have already checked the same systems and elements when working through your repair list.

TIMING THE DISCLOSURES

Okay, let's say you do discover a few things that you don't want to fix. You have to disclose them. Do you disclose before or after you get an offer? Many deals are made contingent upon the inspection *and* the disclosure review. Like I said, if you've been following my RSS strategy, technically you will have already fixed most of your house's problems, so your disclosure list should be minimal.

Knowing all the problems and concerns about your property before the buyers enter the scene will save you the headaches of constant renegotiating later. People are always more open to dealing with problems if they know about them up front. No one wants to be handed the short list of complications once they are deeply involved in the sale process.

GETTING YOUR CONDO AND CO-OP FINANCIALS

I've seen many deals on condo and co-ops go awry because of the inability of condo and co-op sellers to get their homeowners' association's financials and information in order. Your Realtor will guide you through getting your paperwork ready ahead of time—fees, assessments, taxes, and so forth. Know what all these numbers are so your Realtor can answer questions when your buyer gets serious.

RSS Condo-Selling Tip: Get That Board in Order Now!

If you're about to put your condo on the market, get the homeowners' board members on the phone *now*. Corner them in the hallway or in the laundry room, or stake out the elevators. You're going to need all the current dues, condo bylaws, and, most important, information about any approaching assessments. If the board is discussing any new condo owners' additional assessments or contributions, you must disclose them. And don't think that the excuse "I didn't know, because I haven't been attending homeowners' meetings" is going to fly.

You have an obligation to any potential buyer to have all that information ready and available. Trust me, it's like drawing blood from a stone to get the board members to give you all the proper info. They really don't care and they are all busy. Do not, I repeat, do not wait until the last minute for this! An eleventh-hour discovery of an impending assessment is a deal killer.

HAVE IT READY FOR THE BUYERS

Let's map out everything you need to have ready before you go on the market. The following is a complete checklist:

RSS MUST-HAVE SELLER DISCLOSURE AND INFORMATION PACKAGE

☐ Disclosure statement

☐ Copies of all previous inspections

☐ Copies of all permits

☐ Copies of receipts or warranty info for any major improvements (roof, heating and air, etc.) and their major renovation

☐ Condo or co-op financials

☐ Copies of all covenants, conditions, and restrictions

☐ Copies of Historic Preservation Overlay Zone bylaws

CC&Rs and HPOZ—Lots of Initials and Restrictions

CC&R stands for covenants, conditions, and restrictions. HPOZ stands for Historic Preservation Overlay Zone. Each are sets of rules that specify what you can and can't do with your home or condo.

Developers create CC&Rs to establish rules when they create a subdivision and want to control what buyers will do with the land, such as how big they can build their homes, what materials they can use for construction, and the kind of landscaping allowed. The ultimate purpose of CC&Rs is to protect the homeowner's investment because a home's value is largely dependent on the other homes around it. Restrictions can also be placed on condos, co-ops, planned unit developments, and any subdivision that's governed by a homeowners' association.

HPOZs are actually very beneficial and a plus for your potential buyers because they guarantee that your neighbors will have to adhere to a strict code of design review standards. A homeowner will never have to worry that the house next door will be torn down and replaced by a behemoth "McMansion."

If you've got CC&Rs or HPOZs attached to your home, here's what you need to know and need to disclose before you sell:

- You may have to ask permission and go through a review process to make certain changes to your house, such as changing its color, structure, or landscaping.

- CC&Rs sometimes restrict to whom you can sell your home. Can you sell to an investor? An investor is any buyer who wants to use it as a rental property rather then a primary residence.

- Are there material requirements on garages, fences, or storage sheds?

- Any restrictions on parking for boats or RVs?

Presented By:
Lisa Almy
World Real Estate Exchange

100 S. Pointe Dr., Unit 2806
Miami Beach, FL 33139

RSS Sale Success: All Your Seagulls in a Row—*This Miami Beach condo went on the market as the Miami real estate market was experiencing substantial softening. The key to a sale in a soft market is having four key elements in place: the unit set to sell, the condo financials updated and current, all disclosures ready, and the unit priced to sell. Realtor Lisa Almy had everything ready to go but needed to explain to the seller the importance of pricing in a dropping market. "Don't be left on the sandbar when the tide is going out! Price according to today's values, not the value of your condo last season, when the market was stronger!" Her sage advice snagged this seller a fast and successful sale.*

Sixteen

THE BUYERS AND THE OFFERS

CLOSING

SET-TO-SELL
TECHNIQUES

$

PRICING

NEGOTIATING

FOR
SALE

MARKETING

You're finally ready to put your house on the market. You and your Realtor have your sales strategy in place. You've set your house for sale and implemented all the prep-to-sell techniques. Now, it's time to meet the potential buyers—and let the games begin!

MEET THE BUYERS

I hate to make generalizations, but it's important for you to understand the basic types of buyers out there in the marketplace. And most buyers do fall into one of three categories:

1. **The buyers searching for their dream home.** This is someone who is looking for his or her dream home and, once it is found, he or she typically makes an offer at or nearly at full price.

2. **The buyers looking for a great home at a fair price.** This is someone who seeks a nice home but will also look for a slightly discounted price. He or she rarely offers full price. When he or she finds a home he or she absolutely loves, he or she might really want the house but has the sense to try a few negotiating tricks to bring you down some in price. This is when smart negotiating on your part will often result in a sale. The buyer will think he got the deal he wants, and you'll get a price you're happy with.

3. **The bargain hunters.** This buyer is one who thrives on bargain hunting and fetching the deal of the century. He or she is looking for a potential investment that will need some work done before he or she can turn around and sell it. Maybe he or she is looking for a fixer-upper. This type of buyer searches for homes that have been getting stale on the market or that obviously need lots of improvements.

The good news is, you will have only the first two kinds of buyers showing up at your door. Why? Because now that you have set your house for sale and priced your home near the top of the comps, the bargain hunter will stay far from your door. It will be obvious that your house is no fixer-upper and is priced correctly for its current value—not as an undervalued relic.

BUYERS YOU DON'T WANT—THE THREE TYPES OF BUYERS TO RUN FROM

1. **The Zero-Percent-Down Buyer.** Chances are your house will be setting a selling-price high mark for comparable homes. A mortgage company might find it challenging to appraise your house for buyers with little or no money down and you'll have

to put your house back on the market again when your buyer's mortgage request falls through. I've seen it happen far too often.

2. **The Bully Buyer.** This buyer starts by listing all the things that he or she thinks are wrong with the house even as he or she presents an offer. He or she will be even more difficult to work with during an inspection process. Trust me, this bully approach is a prelude to endless negotiations, and his or her trying to obtain concessions by nitpicking on the disclosure and the inspection.

3. **The Sight-Unseen Buyer.** In a hot market, it's not unusual to have an offer from a buyer who has seen only photos of your house. This buyer is trying to tie up your house and get it off the market until he or she has a chance to make a decision. Don't deal with him or her.

THE OFFERS

Three Kinds of Offers to Expect

The offers you're going to receive will depend on your buyers and the market conditions. Hot markets don't call for low-ball offers. In softer markets, however, you can see a variety of offers, so be prepared—there aren't many people in this world today who don't at least *try* to get a bargain. We are all conditioned to avoid paying full price! No matter how much you brace yourself for the offerings, it's an emotional event. Grab your ego and hold on. Here are the three likely scenarios:

You get the dream offer—*full price*! It's exactly what you wanted and your buyers have all of their financing ready to go. You all agree on the closing date, too. It's a done deal.

You get the *so-so offer*—not quite what you wanted originally but you don't want to scare this buyer away. You counter the offer and hope to arrive at an agreement soon. You also are willing to find another buyer, though, if you can't persuade him or her to buy it at your bottom-line price.

You get the ridiculously **low-ball offer**—the one that makes your teeth clench because there is absolutely no way you can accept it. You don't even want to negotiate with these buyers; they are a waste of time . . . or *are* they? Every offer, no matter how low, can be a positive for you as the home seller. Even these low-ball offers allow your Realtor to say the magic words: *We have an offer coming in!* The section below on multiple offers explains why these are valuable.

HOW TO ANALYZE YOUR OFFERS

The Initial Offer

Most negotiations for sale take place in two stages: the initial offer, followed by the counteroffer or series of counteroffers.

So, a couple comes through and goes crazy for your house. As well they should. Your house is set to sell and looks fantastic. You have also grabbed your buyers emotionally and now they are making a strong offer on your home based on their emotions and not on their reason. Yes, it would be great to get a full-price offer, or better yet, over asking. Congratulations, you are getting your asking price or more! But wait, there are the other components of their offer to consider. You need to carefully review each one of the *seven components of the offer*, described on the following page. If you miss one or more of these crucial points, it can cost you thousands.

Here's another scenario. You receive your offer, your Realtor reviews it with you, and the price is below your expectations. Trust me, in that moment, all you can see is that *low price*. Your brain shuts down and you don't even hear that all the other components of the sale sound very good and that this is a very solid buyer.

In both of these scenarios, as in all others, now is the time to analyze the offer thoroughly. You're going to review *all* the components. Maybe the other elements to the offer are perfect and you needn't ask for anything more. Realistically, however, perfect offers are few and far between, so it's time to sit down with your Realtor and review.

The Seven Components of the Offer

The *highest* price offer may not be the *best* offer. There are seven components to an offer and you're going to have to understand them all to know their benefits and their value to your home sale. Sellers who focus too heavily on the price often win the battle but lose the war.

THE SEVEN COMPONENTS OF THE OFFER

- Price

- Deposit

- Down payment

- Length of escrow

- Contingencies

- Escrow and title company choices

- The strength of the buyer

What to Look for in the Initial Offer

Knowing what you want for each one of the components will help you to either accept an offer or decide to make a counteroffer. You'll want to know the following things right away from any initial offer:

1. **Price:** How much is the buyer offering to pay?

2. **Deposit:** How serious is this buyer? Is he or she putting down a sizable deposit?

3. **Down payment:** How much can the buyer put down? Is it 10 percent, 20 percent, or even more?

4. **Length of escrow:** What kind of timetable is this buyer on? Will you have to get out quickly or wait? Does it match your needs?

5. **Contingencies:** These include the inspection and mortgage contingencies. Are the timelines appropriate? (These are explained in depth later in the chapter.)

6. **Escrow and title company choices:** Do they match yours?

7. **The strength of the buyer:** Sometimes a buyer with a pre-approved mortgage letter, all-cash offer, and perfect credit, or a very motivated seasoned buyer is worth more than a higher price.

RSS Selling Tip: Don't Get Greedy!

If you can live with your buyer's offer, accept it. Haggling over minor odds and ends can kill your deal—and you! And get this: If your buyer offers you a deal at full asking price and all the terms you demanded in your listing, you could be on the hook for paying a commission even if the deal doesn't go through. You should be very mindful and watchful of your countering games.

RSS Selling Tip: Shoulda Asked for More

If you got your asking price first time around, don't lament "Oh, we should have asked for more." If you and your Realtor reviewed all the comps and set a price you were happy with, it's likely you've probably priced it *just right*. During a house's first two weeks on the market, buyers will often pay full price or even over-asking to make sure they don't lose it. *That* is why you got a full-price offer. Not because you priced it too low. Rather than see that glass as half empty, be thrilled that you were a savvy house-selling pricer!

THE COUNTEROFFER

The offer has been presented to your Realtor. As he or she is reviewing it with you, you're either elated or your blood is boiling! That means it's either close to your asking price or far from it . . . but don't get crazy here. Learn how to turn *any* offer into a great offer.

The trick to successful negotiating is accentuating the positive and trying to gradually improve the negative. When considering an offer, try to look at it from a wholly positive perspective—even when it's less than perfect. Remember that there are many creative ways of coming out a winner. If your buyer tugs at your price, you can tug on his timeline and get him or her to pony up more money to meet your bottom-line price. When there are compromises to be made, understand that what might initially seem to benefit the buyer can be made to work in your favor.

. . . .
The trick to successful negotiating is accentuating the positive and trying to gradually improve the negative.
. . . .

Counteroffer Success

Countering is an art. It's when you put your business hat on and drive a hard bargain. Step one in countering is evaluating exactly what it is about the buyer's initial offer that isn't good enough for you. List what's unacceptable. Then decide on what you're going to request in order to turn those *unacceptables* into *acceptables*. You put it in writing, sign the form, and it goes to your buyer for review. If he or she signs it, you're sold! If it comes back to you with a new offer, you may have to repeat the process.

The Rules to Making Successful Counteroffers

The basic rules to countering successfully are as follows:

- Always counter back. Keep the game going.

- Be willing to make some sacrifices—especially if you do find the perfect buyer and are hung up only on minor issues.

- Keep all changes, modifications, and deadline extensions in writing.

- Remember that in counteroffers time is *not* your friend—especially in cooler markets! Get it wrapped up quickly. Create as many strict deadlines as possible. Time limits for the buyers to respond show that you are serious.

The Counteroffer Review

Walking through the seven components of the offer will allow you to review all of your buyer's offer components and then structure your counteroffer without missing a single item. Let's review each one of them in detail.

The Strength of the Buyer

I want to specifically address this component because it's an important one! It's the component that you will have to take into consideration when evaluating offers. And it's the one component that you cannot counter back. You can only analyze and take the *strength of the buyer* into account.

You'll often hear a Realtor refer to a buyer as "strong." What does this mean? He can bench-press his own weight? No, it means that he is financially very strong. He has done his home buyers' homework and is financially ready to buy.

A strong buyer has:

- Prequalified for a mortgage

- A great credit score

- Ample money in the bank

- Shown motivation to move quickly

Having a strong buyer may sometimes outweigh one who is a little less financially stable yet offers a higher price. I always look for a strong buyer first when analyzing offers. Don't be seduced by a higher offer with a buyer who has no financial ability to follow through with the deal. You'll be left going back to square one, having lost valuable time when the deal falls apart.

Price

If you get an offer whose amount isn't want you wanted, figure out what your bottom-line price is and then counter just above that. Understand that some people low-ball their first offers in the hope that you'll counter with your bottom-line price. They do know that they risk losing the house if someone else doesn't play this game and offers a higher price closer to asking, but at least they can say they tried.

Keep in mind that some people will offer low numbers if they can't qualify for that higher price tag. And don't forget about people who have their eyes set on another home and just want to see whether they can get a bargain with yours. Don't try to interpret your buyers' motivation for low-balling. *Keep your emotions out of it.* And don't even think about getting into an ego battle with your low-balling buyer. The focus is on selling the house—period.

RSS Negotiating Tip: Halves Can Half Your Deal in Half

Avoid "splitting the difference" in your first counteroffer. Let's say your house is listed at $250,000 and your offer is for $220,000. You then decide to counter at $235,000, which is what you expected to get initially. But then your buyer counters again at $225,000—splitting the difference again. If you say that $235,000 is your bottom-line price, you risk losing the deal. Instead, when you make a counteroffer at the start, go higher than just the split. That way, you cushion your negotiations and tip the scale in your favor.

Deposit

Typical earnest-money—or good-faith—deposits can range from 3 to 6 percent of the purchase price, depending on what's standard in your area. It could be higher or lower but your Realtor will be able to tell you what's acceptable. While not necessarily a requirement, an earnest deposit shows that the buyer is serious. It's the "binder" money you get that confirms a pending transaction. But it's not technically your money; it should be held in trust by a neutral party and credited back to the buyer on the day of closing, when the house becomes theirs. Your buyer will probably roll the deposit over into the down payment.

RSS Damage-Control Tip: Watch the Wording

It's to your advantage to have a clause in your sales contract that says something along the lines of "if your buyer backs out, you get to keep the deposit." This is often called the *liquidated damages clause*. This clause offers some protection for buyers, too. It basically means that if they back out, you can't sue them for damages because you get to keep the deposit. Not all of these clauses are worded the same way or mean the same thing. Consult with your Realtor or attorney about the best way to handle this clause. You also need to figure out what kind of deposit you'll request, which needs to be reasonable to avoid scaring off buyers.

Down Payment

Obviously, you want to see a large down payment. Highly qualified buyers will have the standard 20 percent down payment ready to go. If they don't, hopefully they come close or have a solid financing plan. Fifteen or 10 percent down can also be very acceptable if you have a strong buyer with a prequalified mortgage letter in hand.

Length of Escrow

The length of escrow or the time under contract until closing and final sale can vary. Escrow is generally thirty, forty-five, sixty, or ninety days. If you're on the fast track to sale, and need to get your house sold immediately, the shorter the closing the better.

Countering with a shorter escrow can mean money in the bank to you. For example, if your buyers ask for a ninety-day escrow and you counter with a thirty-day escrow, you're saving yourself a great deal of money in carrying costs for those extra sixty days. In other words, an average house's carrying costs, including mortgage payment, utilities, taxes, and insurance, could be $3,000 a month. Shortening your escrow by two months saves you $6,000. That could allow you to compromise a bit on price without losing any money. A win-win way to close the deal!

Or let's take the reverse: Your buyer begs you for a short escrow but you aren't ready to move. Be prepared to be flexible to some extent—especially if everything else about the deal is perfect and you have only mismatched timelines to work out. Be willing to make some concessions, which can include any of the following:

- Changing your preferred timeline

- Offering your buyers a bonus for sticking to *your* timeline

- Closing the deal in their requested thirty days but then *renting back* from your buyers until you are ready to move out

Selling your home for top dollar is your ultimate goal. A little inconvenience is worth it in the long run. Think of the "big picture," as I do. Ten years from now, the minor inconveniences will pale in comparison to that extra money you made on the deal.

Contingencies

Your goal as a seller is to push for shorter contingency terms to lock your buyer into the deal as quickly as possible. This is the opposite strategy that I teach to home *buyers*, so let's just hope that your buyers have not taken one of my home-buying seminars! This is the opposite approach you would take when purchasing a home if you want the terms to give you the ability to walk away from the deal until the last possible moment.

Contingencies: Escape Clauses for Buyers

Contingencies can be tricky when writing a counteroffer. Any clause written into an offer that makes it subject to something happening is a buyer's way of building in "exit" clauses. They are classic "if/then" statements. Contingencies can be standard clauses in the sales contract that are activated simply by checking a box, writing on a blank line, or adding an addendum.

Contingencies written into offers have become very commonplace. Although you can't say no to all contingencies, you can at least *limit* them by being very specific about your timeline and expectations. If you're willing to take your house off the market and let a potential buyer settle his or her contingencies, then be firm about the deadlines and action taken.

Limiting timelines of contingencies is a way of working with your buyers, while still protecting your interests and making the offer more acceptable to you.

Types of Contingencies

Contingencies must be kept under control. You can choose to not accept any contingencies, but that can render you unable to sell your home quickly. Here are the most common contingencies you will have to manage:

Inspection contingency: Your buyer will hopefully insist on an inspection of your home. He will usually make the purchase of the house contingent upon the inspection and what he finds out as a result. He will at that point have the option to walk away if he chooses. You will want to tighten up this timeline. You don't want to give your potential buyer a long time to have the inspection done, only to learn later that the deal is off and you're back at square one. Seven to ten days to complete an inspection from the opening of escrow should be sufficient.

After the inspection, buyers should have only three days to respond to the *results* of their inspection. If there's no response from them within that time period, they lose their right to walk out of the deal based on the findings. That's a good thing for you, as it has just removed one more way for buyers to get out of the deal without penalty.

Contingent on the sale of the buyer's own home: If the market is hot in your area and your potential buyer doesn't want to seal the deal until his or her *current* home sells, forget it. If, on the other hand, you're in a lukewarm or cold market, be open to dealing with this type of contingency. In that case, be sure the home is on the market with a reputable agent, not for sale by owner. Also have your Realtor do a little detective work to ascertain that the buyer's house is reasonably priced.

Mortgage contingency: If your potential buyer is awaiting approval of his or her financing, be sure to remain strict with your deadline. Tighten up on the buyer's timeline if you can. Unfortunately, loan approval can take a few weeks, and a buyer's commitment letter or notification from a lender may not be immediately available. This should be your buyer's number-one priority once you have accepted an offer. If you have a thirty-day escrow, hopefully your buyer can have loan approval within twenty-one days. On a sixty-day escrow, he or she should get loan approval no later than forty-five days.

Remember, the mortgage contingency is yet another way that a buyer can walk away from the deal if he or she does not get his or her approval. Make sure the timeline for this contingency does not let him walk out at the eleventh hour.

Be sure to read the fine print of the offer. It should indicate what mortgage rate the buyer is willing to accept to get his or her mortgage. If a buyer says he or she will accept a maximum rate of 5.5 percent on a thirty-year fixed-rate mortgagee with one point, and the prevailing rate is 6.9 percent, then you had better counter back his or her rate limit.

Escrow and Title Company Choices

I'll discuss the details of escrow and title companies in the next chapter. You may not even have to deal with these entities if your state does the closing dance a little differently. But most sellers do encounter title companies to some degree—or at least their attorneys who are handling the closing do.

> ## RSS Counteroffer Tip: Keep the Pressure On
>
> Don't give the buyer more than 8 to 12 hours to accept, counter, or reject your counteroffer.

MORE ELEVENTH-HOUR DEAL SAVERS

You're countering back and forth, maybe now you're in round two of the counteroffers. You are getting so very close, but it's not a done deal. It seems like you are at a stalemate over silly things and very little money. It happens all the time.

Paying Your Buyer's Closing Costs Can Be a Deal Maker

Offer to pay for all or some of the buyer's closing costs. This may not sound terribly enticing to you at first. But there is some reasoning behind this idea. For most buyers, especially first-timers, the down payment is the biggest obstacle when buying a home. If you offer to pay for those closing costs, the perceived value of your deal is even greater in the eyes of your buyer. Your buyer's costs should be between 1.5 and 3 percent of the buyer's loan amount. If you're dealing with buyers who are financing their starter home with a very small down payment, say, less than 20 percent, closing costs could be more, so make sure you agree on a dollar amount.

Additional Creative Deal Savers

Here are some other ideas to consider if you're in the throes of negotiating and you need that extra little push to get the deal signed off.

- *Leave your appliances and make them part of your deal.* Appliances can be a pain to move and you can get new ones at your next place. Which appliances do I toss into the deal? Consider the following life spans. You make the decision:

  - Refrigerator: 8–14 years

  - Clothes dryer: 8–14 years

  - Washing machine: 7–12 years

  - Dishwasher: 7–12 years

  - Microwave: 9–11 years

- *Throw in some items you really don't care to keep.* These can include a big-screen TV, bedroom armoire, or bookcase and entertainment center in your living room. You can also consider other possessions that don't typically get left behind, such as a boat, RV, or some perk that comes easy to you at your job but hard to others. Let's say you're an agent working for the Lakers. You can throw in season tickets for a year. Or if you live in New York City and work for the Shuberts, throw in house seats for a half-dozen Broadway shows!

- *Offer to replace items that your buyer doesn't like.* Offer him or her new carpet in the living room or a paint job in the kitchen. Of course, put a dollar limit on what you're willing to spend.

- *Offer a home warranty.* You should do this anyway, but make note of it so you can impress your buyers.

- *Pick up the tab for the home inspection.* Cover the cost of the buyer's inspection, even though you let the buyer choose the inspector.

- *Ask your Realtor to kick in part of his commission for the cost of some of the above items.* Oftentimes, when the deal is close but not close enough, the selling Realtor will kick in the cost of the home warranty, or a credit from his commissions toward some of the closing costs for the buyer. Just as often, my selling Realtor will also get the buyer's Realtor to match amounts . . . to double the credit back!

RSS Negotiating Tip: Clarify Exactly What You Are Keeping

Don't assume that your buyer understands what he or she is—or is not—getting when he or she buys your house. Be very clear in your sales contract about items that you are taking with you, such as that fancy chandelier hanging in the foyer and antique light fixtures in the master bedroom. Take photographs to avoid any misunderstanding.

Give Your Buyers a Home Warranty

In many states, it's customary to provide a *homeowner's warranty* for your buyer. In a sense, it's an insurance policy against any first-year repairs. This is also a terrific hedge against liability. If your new buyers' heating or air-conditioning system goes out during their first year of ownership, they won't come running back to you. The $350–$600 expense is an incredible value. The policy basically covers electrical, heating, and plumbing systems. Also included are built-in appliances such as dishwashers, disposals, compactors, and ranges/ovens. For an additional cost, you can also include your refrigerator, air conditioner, washer, and dryer. With most policies, if there's a problem after the sale with a covered item, you simply call the warranty company, which then sends a repairperson selected from a local network of professionals for a minimal service fee, $35 to $50.

Home warranties are great at covering your butt for problems you don't realize you have—or are about to have. It's the third layer of protection you give yourself in addition to your disclosures and inspection report. Having a year of coverage for such uncertainties is an excellent way to prevent your buyer from coming back to you to complain that the heating system went bust and you should pay for it.

MULTIPLE OFFERS

Boy, you'd love to be in this position, wouldn't you? Pat yourself on the back! *Multiple offers* mean you've done your homework and gotten your home in top selling position. You can now even pocket a few backup offers just in case. If you're very lucky, the decision will boil down to who makes the bigger offer over your asking price. In really hot markets, you can get offers 10 percent or more above the listing price! It's enough to make your head spin. Every Realtor has his or her own technique for responding to multiple offers. He or she will guide you through the process—but you will still need to analyze each offer and counter back to ensure that the price and components are the best they can be for you.

BACKUP OFFERS

Having a *backup offer* is the next best thing to a seller's insurance. It means that just like in the Miss America pageant, if for any reason Miss America is unable to fulfill her duties, the first runner-up will wear the crown! The same is true for your home buyer's backup offer.

If you get two offers on your house, counter back and then pick the best one you receive in response. But have your Realtor advise the second-best offer that if he or she is willing, he or she can have a *backup position*. The backup is in no way obligated to buy the house if it becomes available, but that person does get right of first refusal. Even if you do not have multiple offers at the time of the first offer, I always expect my Realtor to let it be known that we are looking for backup offers.

Why Secure a Backup Offer?

- It puts your buyer on notice that if he or she asks for too many concessions, you can very easily walk away from the deal and go with your backup.

- It allows you to hold a bit firmer if the buyer asks for credits or repairs after an inspection.

- If the buyer fails to meet his or her obligations in a timely manner you can cancel the escrow, sometimes being able to keep the deposit, and move right away to open escrow with the backup offer.

- If the buyer decides to pull out of the deal, you have someone else in place and can avoid the time and cost of putting your house back on the market.

THE ESSENTIAL DOS AND DON'TS OF NEGOTIATING THE OFFER

- DO get offers in writing. DON'T expect verbal agreements to work in real estate.

- DO respond quickly. Time is of the essence.

- DON'T assume that when a buyer makes an offer, he or she has thrown the ball in your court and you can take your time thinking it out. This isn't like badminton in the English countryside, it's a fast game of tennis! Act swiftly or you'll lose the ball entirely and the game will be over. Be ready for all offers.

- DO know what your bottom-line price is, which should reflect how much you will walk away with in cash come closing day.

- DO keep your paperwork orderly and organized. Make sure all addenda are properly numbered and attached appropriately.

- DON'T be flexible on deadlines. Keep your buyers on a strict timeline. Have a list that outlines all the important deadlines and what the offer is subject to.

- DO take emotion out of the equation.

- DON'T counter with your bottom-line price. Give yourself some extra room in case your buyer counters again.

- DO be willing to meet your buyer's ideal timeline, by moving the closing date either up or back. If you have to rent back for a short while, be willing to do so.

- DON'T assume that your buyer knows exactly which items are going with you and which are part of the sale. Add an itemized list of items you are *including* in the sale, such as rugs, draperies, chandeliers, and appliances . . . and an itemized list of items you are *excluding* from the sale.

. . . .

Be prepared to let the buyer have the last word . . . which is what he or she wants!

. . . .

RSS Sale Success: Personally Educate Buyers—*This Manhattan penthouse was priced similarly to other apartments for sale in the area, but to get the buyers to hit the big asking price, Realtor Mark Samsky knew he had to educate them about the unit's strong points. He personally spent time with every potential buyer, pointing out the superior finishes and additional amenities yet lower monthly charges than the comparable apartments on the market. His hands-on attention to each buyer and offer encouraged the winning buyers to pay more and hit the seller's asking price!*

Seventeen

A WINNING ESCROW

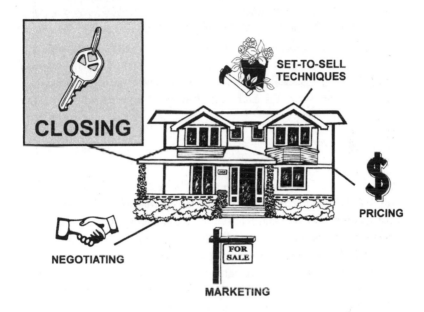

CLOSING

SET-TO-SELL
TECHNIQUES

$

PRICING

NEGOTIATING

FOR
SALE

MARKETING

After you have negotiated a price and all the other components to the deal, you're home free, right? Not by a long shot! Even before the ink is dry on the signatures, you need to be thinking about the escrow process. The *escrow* or *contract* period is everything that happens from the signing of the agreement of sale to the final closing and cash-out.

Let me warn you, a lot is about to happen. There are stacks of papers to be signed, deadlines to be met, the buyer's inspection to navigate, and one last round of possible negotiations after the inspection. For the inexperienced, this escrow process is like walking through a field of land mines. And every mine you inadvertently step on can cost you some big bucks. However, this chapter is going teach you how to avoid those mines. And you are going to learn how to squeeze thousands of extra dollars out of the process. Which all adds up and goes toward your final goal of *making more money when you sell!*

WHAT IS ESCROW?

What exactly is escrow? As defined by the Escrow Institute of California, an escrow is "a deposit of funds, a deed or other instrument by one party for the delivery to another party upon completion of a particular condition or event. It assures that no funds or property will change hands until all of the instructions in the transition have been followed." Now, *in English, please!* This means that someone is selling, someone is buying, and escrow makes sure the exchange of monies and paperwork are done properly.

Escrow vs. Under Contract

Okay, you say, I thought the lawyer and the real estate agent handle the deal? Well, if you are in Trenton, New Jersey, that's true. In New Jersey and New York, lawyers and real estate agents handle all the paperwork, as well as the exchange of the funds and title. But the type of entity that facilitates the transfer and process of exactly how it is done varies from state to state. Most West Coast states have escrow companies that handle all the paperwork transfer and distribute all the funds. Washington, D.C., and Maryland use settlement offices or settlement agents.

In these cases, once an offer has been accepted and your buyer's deposit has been handed over, the property is considered to be *under contract* rather than *in escrow*. No matter what it's called, the process to be accomplished and timeline remain the same. For simplicity, no matter where you live, I'll refer to it as the escrow process, except where noted. The chart on pages 277–278 gives a rough state-by-state guide to who's involved, but this isn't an exact science. Ask your Realtor for the details on what you can expect in your area.

WHO HANDLES CLOSINGS?

A State-by-State Look at Who's Involved

	Title Companies	Attorneys	Escrow Companies	Lenders w/ Closing Divisions	Realty Companies w/ Closing Divisions
Alabama	X	X			
Alaska	X		X	X	
Arizona	X				
Arkansas	X	X			
California	X		X	X	
Colorado	X	X			X
Connecticut		X			
Delaware		X			
District of Columbia	X	X			
Florida	X	X			
Georgia		X			
Hawaii	X	X	X		
Idaho			X		
Illinois	X	X		X	
Indiana	X	X		X	X
Iowa		X			X
Kansas	X	X	X	X	X
Kentucky		X			
Louisiana	X	X			
Maine		X			
Maryland		X			
Massachusetts		X			
Michigan	X	X		X	X
Minnesota	X	X		X	X
Mississippi		X			
Missouri	X	X	(in Kansas City area)	X	X
Montana			X		
Nebraska	X	X		X	X
Nevada			X		
New Hampshire		X			
New Jersey	X	X			
New Mexico			X		
New York		X			

(continued)

	Title Companies	Attorneys	Escrow Companies	Lenders w/ Closing Divisions	Realty Companies w/ Closing Divisions
North Carolina		X		X	
North Dakota		X		X	
Ohio	X			X	
Oklahoma	X	X		X	X
Oregon			X		
Pennsylvania	X	X			X
Rhode Island	X	X		X	
South Carolina		X			
South Dakota	X	X		X	X
Tennessee	X	X		X	
Texas	X				
Utah	X			X	
Vermont		X			
Virginia	X	X			
Washington	X	X	X	X	
West Virginia	X			X	X
Wisconsin	X	X		X	
Wyoming					X

UNDERSTANDING THE PROCESS WILL SAVE YOU THOUSANDS

I discovered some of the following money-saving tips and simple explanations of extremely complicated processes through trial and error. The rest I learned from the pros. But now *you* get them all in one place—and they will save you hours of stress and lots of money.

Escrow is full of legal language and very specific terminology. It can be daunting, to say the least. The greatest lesson I can teach you is that if you don't understand a term or a process, *just ask*. I do it all the time. Make it your business to find out why things are done in a certain manner. Approach escrow as a process you can master, not merely endure.

Two-Ring Circus

Escrow is like a circus. The circus tents get thrown together in a single day and as soon as the show begins, all kinds of things happen at once.

The Two Selling Escrow Arenas

KEEPING THE
BUYER ON TRACK

THE ESCROW PAPERWORK

There is the big finale, and then as quickly as the tents went up, they come down and move on. Well, the escrow process is just like a two-ring circus for the seller. There are two separate shows playing simultaneously, and they both relate to each other.

Think of yourself as both the ringmaster and a highly skilled juggler, jumping back and forth between the two rings. As the ringmaster, your job is to keep all the balls in the air. When it goes smoothly, everything comes together at closing for the big finale: making the sale happen!

Avoiding costly oversights, as well as finding ways to save money that most novice sellers overlook or leave unattended, is very difficult. But when you know what to look for and how to stay on top of it, it can be done.

Escrow Timeline

The key to mastering this circus is timing! With so many things happening at once and in different arenas, it's next to impossible to stay on track without a timeline of events. That's why I like to put together a calendar of target tasks and dates—to create order out of chaos. Having a big-picture timeline is very helpful when prioritizing your escrow tasks. As we review each escrow task, refer to the *escrow timeline calendar* to see exactly where on the timeline it falls.

Timelines can vary region by region. If attorneys handle the closings in your state, it could take considerably longer to close a sale—ninety days or so—especially if there are several attorneys involved. In states where title companies handle the closings, the turnaround time could be

RSS Timeline

Mon	Tues	Wed	Thurs	Fri	Sat / Sun
1 SALE AGREEMENTS SIGNED	2 ESCROW OPENS!	3 BUYER TO SCHEDULE INSPECTION AND APPRAISAL	4 SUBMIT DISCLOSURES, PLOT MAP, PERMITS	5 REQUEST ESTIMATED CLOSING COSTS	6 / 7
8 BUYER'S INSPECTION	9 BUYER'S APPRAISAL	10	11 INSPECTION CONTINGENCY EXPIRES	12	13 / 14
15	16	17	18	19	20 / 21
22 REQUEST ESTIMATED CLOSING COSTS	23 BUYER'S MORTGAGE CONTINGENCY EXPIRES	24 COMPLETE TERMITE OR OTHER BUYER-REQUESTED REPAIRS	25 CALL TO TRANSFER UTILITIES	26 REVIEW ESTIMATED CLOSING COSTS	27 / 28
29 FINAL WALK-THROUGH OF PROPERTY	30 ESCROW CLOSES!	CONGRATULATIONS			

The Escrow Timeline Calendar

shorter—fourteen to thirty days. If you're working with a good agent, it's his or her job to keep the process moving as quickly as possible.

ESCROW TIMELINE DEADLINES

- Buyer's appraisal

- The buyer's inspection contingency expiration

- Request estimated closing costs—second pass

- Loan denial deadline

- Seller to complete termite and other requested repairs

- Closing or settlement date

- Time and date you have to vacate the premises and hand over the keys

Opening Escrow

As soon as you have opened escrow, ask for the escrow company's phone number and give them a call. Ask to speak to the person who has been assigned as your escrow officer. It's important for you to establish a positive relationship with this person right away. Introduce yourself and say that you are looking forward to working together. Provide your cell phone number and say that you're available anytime you are needed. What you're really doing is forcing the officer to see you as an important person and not merely a case number.

Okay, okay . . . in other words, it's what we in the entertainment industry call schmoozing. You're going to want attention from this officer throughout the process. You're going to want him or her to stay on top of your closing paperwork and deadlines and to push your buyer to be ready with all his or her paperwork and monies. And by the time your officer issues you the second of your estimated closing statements, you're going to be hitting him or her up for some big-time fee reductions and junk fee removals. Having established a relationship ahead of time is going to save you some big bucks at closing.

RSS Tip: Don't Be Afraid of Change!

If after several days and several attempts, you're unable to get your assigned escrow officer on the phone to introduce yourself, very politely ask for the head of the escrow company. Tell him or her that it's important for you to be able to reach your escrow officer occasionally, and you would like to be transferred to one who may not currently be so overwhelmed. This will either bring you to the attention of your assigned officer, or get you one who will be more attentive. Remember, though, you are going to be asking for some money-saving favors later, so don't burn any bridges now!

KEEPING THE BUYER ON TRACK

Your Buyer's Escrow Responsibilities

- Submit the deposit

- Complete the inspection and negotiate any concessions from you

- Review and approve the title report

- Request and review estimated closing-costs statements

- Secure the mortgage

- Remove the contingencies

- Select and secure property insurance

- Prepare and transfer the funds to escrow

- Sign the final closing documents

Make Sure the Buyer Does His or Her Inspections Quickly

The buyer's inspection is something that you want done and out of the way as soon as possible. It's in your interest to get this contingency covered and signed off on immediately. Have your Realtor encourage the buyer to schedule his or her inspection as soon as escrow is opened. Also, the sooner your buyer has invested the money and effort in a purchase via appraisals and inspections, the less likely he or she is to walk away over minor differences or negotiations.

RSS Escrow Tip: Pass in Writing

If your buyer refuses to conduct his or her own inspection, get his or her refusal *in writing!* If a problem arises later, you will want to show that the buyer willingly refused an inspection.

Get Ready to Negotiate One Last Time

If you've been following my plan of attack since the beginning of this book, you should be able to breathe a sigh of relief. You'll either sail through your buyer's inspection or be ready for whatever comes up as part of it.

After the buyer has completed his inspection, he will want to negotiate *something*. He will want you to repair *something*. Be prepared and don't take it personally. Chances are that you have completely fixed, replaced, or upgraded everything in the house and it's flawless. But, personally, I am suspicious of a buyer who *doesn't* ask for something to be addressed, even if it's minor.

However, if the buyer presents a litany of expensive requests, then you need to examine your bargaining position. Is this a good buyer with a prequalified loan and a good deposit? Do you have a backup offer to turn to? I usually find that most buyers are willing to split the cost of any requests. Weigh the expense of any concessions against the carrying costs of putting the house back on the market. But whatever you decide, do it *quickly*. The clock is ticking.

KEEPING THE BUYER ON SCHEDULE

Keeping your buyer on track and on time is your real estate agent's responsibility. However, one of the best pieces of advice I can give you in the selling escrow process is: Make it your business as well to stay on top of your buyer's progress. Find out from your Realtor, your escrow officer, or your lawyer exactly what the buyer's deadlines are for submitting deposit money, signing off on inspection contingencies, and obtaining the mortgage. Mark them down in your RSS timeline calendar.

You know the old adage "If you want something done right, then do it yourself!" I'm a big believer in that. Yes, the buyer has his or her own list of responsibilities. But it's a very important money-saving approach to be well aware of his or her "to-do list" and stay informed about his or her progress. You should check in often with your Realtor and your escrow officer or lawyer to make sure your buyer is on track.

Even though the buyer and his or her loan officer are responsible for scheduling the appraisal, it will benefit you to have your Realtor help move that along. You will want to know as soon as possible if your house is appraising at your sale price. Chances are, you are selling this house at the top of the comps and it can sometimes be a push to justify the price. You will also want to make sure that your Realtor, escrow officer, or lawyer constantly checks the status of the buyer and timelines, including the title policy, termite inspection report, the buyer's mortgage commitment, and the buyer's insurance.

Who Chases Whom?

When you start making exceptions to your rules—that is, your timeline and when you expect deadlines to be met—you open yourself up to trouble. The moment something begins to go awry, if the deal has reached an impasse or has otherwise become stalled, your agent should be on the prowl and getting things moving. Bring in your attorney, too, so you're ready to apply serious pressure if your buyer has one foot out the door.

What If the Buyer Can't Get Financing Lined Up in Time?

What if your calendar ticks past an important deadline and your buyer is having a hard time securing his or her loan? The first question to ask yourself is *why*. Who tied up the process? The bank? Your buyer? Is the buyer getting cold feet? How much of an extension you choose to allow is up to you. I say, have some flexibility here if it's a matter of mere logistics, but ask your Realtor for advice on how long an extension you should give. It will depend on what the holdup is, and how long your buyer thinks it can take to settle the problem. That said, if you've got a backup offer that ain't so bad and you're nervous about this particular sale, you can always refuse to give an extension and move on to your second-best offer.

YOUR SELLER'S ESCROW PAPERWORK

Yep, now it's all about *your* paperwork. Your selling contract is the most important document in the sale of your home. Whether referred to as a

The Two Selling Escrow Arenas

KEEPING THE BUYER ON TRACK

THE ESCROW PAPERWORK

contract of sale, purchase agreement, or settlement agreement, it's all the same. Your escrow paperwork contains the entire agreement between you and your buyer. Nothing is binding for either you or your buyer if it's not explicitly spelled out in the agreement.

Review the Escrow Instruction

As when you first purchased your house, you will be asked to sign the *escrow instructions*. These should reflect all the items that you have agreed to via your buyer's offer and subsequent counteroffers. Review them with your real estate agent before you sign.

Supply Your Disclosure Statement

Make sure that within the first few days of escrow opening—at the latest— you send in your disclosure statement to both the buyer and the escrow office. It's important that escrow gets a copy to keep in your file. That way the buyer can never come back later to say he or she never received it.

Deliver All Permits

If you have not already presented them, make sure you get copies of all the signed permits from your contractor or tradesperson. Have them ready to present to your buyer.

Get the Termite Certification

You can't avoid this one. It's pretty much standard protocol to do a termite inspection. A buyer's lender will likely require it before approving the loan, and this is on your bill. If the inspection results in a problem, you'll have to do the necessary repairs. Make sure you hire a licensed termite inspector and be sure you know for how long the report is valid. You don't want the inspection to expire before you sell the house—or you'll have to pay for another one.

RSS Termite Tip: Use Your Original Company

If you have owned the house for only a few years, go back to the same termite company that did *your* inspection when you purchased. By renewing your inspection and warranty yearly, you can have the termite company pay for any damage and repairs because you'll still be under warranty. That could be a *big* money savings.

UNDERSTAND YOUR SELLING COSTS

Every transfer of funds and property entails fees, whether through an escrow, a settlement company, or a lawyer. The *estimated closing statement*, technically known as the "HUD-1 settlement statement" closing form, is the summary of the financial portion of your house sale. It lists the purchase price, loan amount, fees, charges, and expenses for both buyer and seller, and shows all pro-rations and sums to be disbursed by the title company to both you and your buyer.

Most of these fees are valid and necessary, but when you know what to look for, you unearth a plethora of what are known in the business as "junk fees" or "garbage fees." You will save yourself thousands of dollars when selling if you review and analyze each and every fee itemized on that statement. I know this sounds daunting, but it's not. Tackling them one by one is the way to do it.

Request and Review the Estimated Closing
Costs Statements

It's *imperative* that you request and carefully review your estimated closing costs statement. It's also imperative to ask for an updated copy at three different times: at the *beginning* of escrow, *during* escrow, and right *before* closing. This gives you a chance to review all the charges and credits throughout the escrow period and have opportunities to negotiate them.

If you really want to save money on all those closing costs and fees, you need to be reviewing the statement long before the closing date, and you should ask as many questions as you need to. Just to familiarize yourself, let's examine the closing costs statement on pages 289–290, taken from the U.S. Department of Housing.

The top part of page 1 contains the names and addresses of the buyers, sellers, closer, and mortgage company. The rest of the form is divided into two columns: the left column, or Section J, is called the Summary of Buyer's Transaction; the right column, or Section K, is called the Summary of Seller's Transaction.

In your column, the seller's side, you'll find lines numbered from 400 to 603.

- The lines in the 400 section all relate to money owed to you.

- The lines in the 500 section all relate to money you owe, or that comes out of the sale of your home. These can include paying off the balance of your mortgage and an equity line of credit.

- Line 507 shows any county/property tax owed by you.

- Then, the 600 section does the math for you and gives you your bottom-line number. The number on line 603 is your golden dollar sign—it's what you walk away with in cash at the close of the deal. Assuming you had some nice equity in your home, you'll get a check written out to you from the closing agent.

Page 2 of the form lists the commission and related costs in the 700 section.

- Commissions paid to a real estate company show up in lines 700 to 704. Make sure these numbers reflect what you and your agent agreed upon in advance.

- Costs that your buyer is responsible for will be in lines 800, 900, and 1000. These are payable through the buyer's loan, but may also include costs you agreed to bear during your negotiating. For example, if you agreed pay for the inspection, that fee will be listed on your side. But if you've made no concessions, there won't be any entries on your side.

- You'll find more costs listed on your side when you reach lines 1100 to 1117. These are your title and closing costs, and both you and your buyer will have responsibilities listed in these sections. The person closing the loan will review each of these charges with you. Be very careful about each and every one of them, and ask questions if you don't understand anything.

- Lines 1200 to 1206 cover the costs of recording the transfer title and any related fees. You may live in an area that requires a real estate transfer tax, which would then appear in this section.

- Look at lines 1300 to 1314 carefully. This is where any additional fees may be listed. Make sure nothing has been charged to you that should go on the buyer's side.

- Last, line 1400 tallies up the total on the page, which then gets listed on line 502 on page 1.

A. **Settlement Statement**

U.S. Department of Housing and Urban Development

OMB Approval No. 2502-0265
(expires 9/30/2006)

B. Type of Loan

| 1. ☐ FHA 2. ☐ FmHA 3. ☐ Conv. Unins. | 6. File Number: | 7. Loan Number: | 8. Mortgage Insurance Case Number: |
| 4. ☐ VA 5. ☐ Conv. Ins. | | | |

C. Note: This form is furnished to give you a statement of actual settlement costs. Amounts paid to and by the settlement agent are shown. Items marked "(p.o.c.)" were paid outside the closing; they are shown here for informational purposes and are not included in the totals.

D. Name & Address of Borrower:	E. Name & Address of Seller:	F. Name & Address of Lender:

G. Property Location:	H. Settlement Agent:	
	Place of Settlement:	I. Settlement Date:

J. Summary of Borrower's Transaction	**K. Summary of Seller's Transaction**
100. Gross Amount Due From Borrower	**400. Gross Amount Due To Seller**
101. Contract sales price	401. Contract sales price
102. Personal property	402. Personal property
103. Settlement charges to borrower (line 1400)	403.
104.	404.
105.	405.
Adjustments for items paid by seller in advance	**Adjustments for items paid by seller in advance**
106. City/town taxes to	406. City/town taxes to
107. County taxes to	407. County taxes to
108. Assessments to	408. Assessments to
109.	409.
110.	410.
111.	411.
112.	412.
120. Gross Amount Due From Borrower	**420. Gross Amount Due To Seller**
200. Amounts Paid By Or In Behalf Of Borrower	**500. Reductions In Amount Due To Seller**
201. Deposit or earnest money	501. Excess deposit (see instructions)
202. Principal amount of new loan(s)	502. Settlement charges to seller (line 1400)
203. Existing loan(s) taken subject to	503. Existing loan(s) taken subject to
204.	504. Payoff of first mortgage loan
205.	505. Payoff of second mortgage loan
206.	506.
207.	507.
208.	508.
209.	509.
Adjustments for items unpaid by seller	**Adjustments for items unpaid by seller**
210. City/town taxes to	510. City/town taxes to
211. County taxes to	511. County taxes to
212. Assessments to	512. Assessments to
213.	513.
214.	514.
215.	515.
216.	516.
217.	517.
218.	518.
219.	519.
220. Total Paid By/For Borrower	**520. Total Reduction Amount Due Seller**
300. Cash At Settlement From/To Borrower	**600. Cash At Settlement To/From Seller**
301. Gross Amount due from borrower (line 120)	601. Gross amount due to seller (line 420)
302. Less amounts paid by/for borrower (line 220) ( )	602. Less reductions in amt. due seller (line 520) ( )
303. Cash ☐ From ☐ To Borrower	**603. Cash** ☐ To ☐ From Seller

Section 5 of the Real Estate Settlement Procedures Act (RESPA) requires the following: • HUD must develop a Special Information Booklet to help persons borrowing money to finance the purchase of residential real estate to better understand the nature and costs of real estate settlement services; • Each lender must provide the booklet to all applicants from whom it receives or for whom it prepares a written application to borrow money to finance the purchase of residential real estate; • Lenders must prepare and distribute with the Booklet a Good Faith Estimate of the settlement costs that the borrower is likely to incur in connection with the settlement. These disclosures are mandatory.

Section 4(a) of RESPA mandates that HUD develop and prescribe this standard form to be used at the time of loan settlement to provide full disclosure of all charges imposed upon the borrower and seller. These are third party disclosures that are designed to provide the borrower with pertinent information during the settlement process in order to be a better shopper.

The Public Reporting Burden for this collection of information is estimated to average one hour per response, including the time for reviewing instructions, searching existing data sources, gathering and maintaining the data needed, and completing and reviewing the collection of information.

This agency may not collect this information, and you are not required to complete this form, unless it displays a currently valid OMB control number. The information requested does not lend itself to confidentiality.

L. Settlement Charges

700. Total Sales/Broker's Commission based on price $ @ % =	Paid From Borrowers Funds at Settlement	Paid From Seller's Funds at Settlement
Division of Commission (line 700) as follows:		
701. $ to		
702. $ to		
703. Commission paid at Settlement		
704.		
800. Items Payable In Connection With Loan		
801. Loan Origination Fee %		
802. Loan Discount %		
803. Appraisal Fee to		
804. Credit Report to		
805. Lender's Inspection Fee		
806. Mortgage Insurance Application Fee to		
807. Assumption Fee		
808.		
809.		
810.		
811.		
900. Items Required By Lender To Be Paid In Advance		
901. Interest from to @$ /day		
902. Mortgage Insurance Premium for months to		
903. Hazard Insurance Premium for years to		
904. years to		
905.		
1000. Reserves Deposited With Lender		
1001. Hazard insurance months@$ per month		
1002. Mortgage insurance months@$ per month		
1003. City property taxes months@$ per month		
1004. County property taxes months@$ per month		
1005. Annual assessments months@$ per month		
1006. months@$ per month		
1007. months@$ per month		
1008. months@$ per month		
1100. Title Charges		
1101. Settlement or closing fee to		
1102. Abstract or title search to		
1103. Title examination to		
1104. Title insurance binder to		
1105. Document preparation to		
1106. Notary fees to		
1107. Attorney's fees to		
(includes above items numbers:)		
1108. Title insurance to		
(includes above items numbers:)		
1109. Lender's coverage $		
1110. Owner's coverage $		
1111.		
1112.		
1113.		
1200. Government Recording and Transfer Charges		
1201. Recording fees: Deed $; Mortgage $; Releases $		
1202. City/county tax/stamps: Deed $; Mortgage $		
1203. State tax/stamps: Deed $; Mortgage $		
1204.		
1205.		
1300. Additional Settlement Charges		
1301. Survey to		
1302. Pest inspection to		
1303.		
1304.		
1305.		
1400. Total Settlement Charges (enter on lines 103, Section J and 502, Section K)		

Hidden Fees

Be vigilant! Although your eyes are glazing over as you examine all those documents, make sure the mortgage company hasn't mistakenly added buyers' fees to your side of the form. Mortgage companies and title companies often pad a sales transaction.

Be strong about questioning every listed fee. In some cases you can point your finger at your buyer. In others, you may be able to get the fee lowered or removed entirely. Start questioning those fees when you do your first review of the statement at the beginning of escrow. The *final* estimated closing costs statement should come a few days before closing. Review it immediately! Are there any junk fees remaining? Keep time on your side. Do not wait until the day before closing day to question fees. All parties involved will be scrambling to tie up loose ends and will not have the time to give you the service you need.

Fees to Review and Fees to Junk!

- **Tax service fee.** To verify that your property taxes are current (should be no more than $30 to $50).

- **Underwriter fee.** This should be on the buyer's side.

- **Administrative fee.** A junk fee; try to get rid of it.

- **Assignment fee.** This should be on the buyer's side.

- **Flood certification fee.** This should be on the buyer's side.

- **Recording fees.** Don't get bullied into paying more than what it costs to record your releases on your mortgage with the county; always ask to reduce.

- **Processing fees.** Try to avoid this one entirely.

- **Courier fee.** Was a courier ever used and is this necessary? Ask for details.

- **Document prep fee.** Scrutinize this one, as it's often way too high.

- **Download document fee.** Request this to be waived.

- **Escrow charges.** Check to make sure these aren't too high; ask that they be discounted.

- **Impound setup.** This is an extra junk fee.

- **Warehousing fee.** This is a junk fee that covers the cost of storing your documents. Ask to have it removed.

- **Writing and managing documents fee.** Request that this be removed.

- **Sub-escrow fee.** Request that this be waived.

Miscellaneous other fees to scrutinize:

- **Realtor commission.** Make sure it's accurate.

- **Closing review fee.** Ask to have this waived.

- **Document drawing/signing fee.** This is often too high.

• •

Even though you may have carefully reviewed these closing documents numerous times, don't put pen to paper until you've skimmed through them once more just to be sure!

• •

RSS Insider Tip: Don't Freak Out!

Escrow expert Rex Berkebile of Escrow Exchange West advises sellers not to "freak out" when they first review their estimated closing costs statement. Escrow companies intentionally estimate high to make sure they are in the black at closing. So review early—and save big!

Title Insurance

Title insurance is a necessary cost of selling a home. No matter who handles the closing, you must obtain *title insurance* to help cover any serious problems related to the ownership of the home once you've passed it on to your buyer. A title search has to be done to make sure the title is clear of liens, back taxes, or any other judgments against you. In other words, the title report shows who really owns the property—every square inch. It can indicate restrictions to the property regarding use or development, such as height restrictions or an easement that could keep an owner from developing certain parts of the property.

In some states, the company that provides the title insurance also handles the escrow funds and closing paperwork. But if you've got an attorney or escrow company who's closing your deal and they don't offer title insurance, you'll have to go elsewhere.

Why Is Title Insurance Necessary?

Title insurance is more important than most people think. Let say you've just sold your home but forgot to mention that the city bought an easement in the corner of your lot for purposes of reconfiguring the water lines. This easement means you lose about 200 square feet of land and your back property line gets moved up by two feet. Your buyers don't know anything about this easement until they start planning to redo the backyard and make room for a deck and hot tub in that very corner. One day, there's a confrontation with a city planner who shows up at the start of the water-line improvement project. What do the buyers do? The title company settles with the buyers and you are not liable to pay part of the claim. If there was no title insurance, you would have found yourself in court paying enormous legal fees and probably damages as well.

How Much Does It Cost?

The cost of title insurance varies state to state, and your agent should be able to advise you about the average costs in your area, as well as who normally pays for it. You do, however, want to err on the side of caution and ask for more coverage than the bare minimum. It's that old "you get what you pay for" thing. If you obtain a cheap policy, it may not be there to save you if you run into serious troubles later on. So spend wisely.

RSS TITLE INSURANCE MONEY-SAVER: ASK FOR A REDUCTION

If you have owned your home for only a year or two, you had a title search and title insurance policy issued to you relatively recently. This means less work for the title company now. Accordingly, ask for a reduction in fees!

Seven RSS Tips for a Smooth Closing

☐ Get and review your estimated closing costs three times during escrow. Don't wait until the last week.

☐ Stay on top of the escrow company to make sure the buyer is keeping to schedule.

☐ Make sure all contingencies are removed in a timely fashion.

☐ Stay in touch with your Realtor and be updated frequently on the status of the process, especially if anything is holding up the final closing.

☐ Don't miss a deadline or leave a document unsigned. It could cost you your sale.

☐ Review every document sent to you and return it immediately. Time is of the essence and you need to be ahead of schedule at all times.

☐ Don't schedule anything for at least two days after the preferred closing date. Things always go wrong, and escrows are often held up.

RSS Selling Tip: Never on Friday

Always schedule a closing on a Wednesday or Thursday. Last-minute items often get delayed. Closing on a Wednesday allows for two extra days, just in case.

RSS Selling Tip: Don't Leave Money Behind

When you sell your house, make sure you contact your home-owner's insurance company to find out if you have any prorated money due you from the insurance you have already paid in advance. This could be substantial. You may also be able to transfer your fire and homeowner's policy over to your buyer. In that case, be sure you are reimbursed for any unused portion by your buyer. This also can be part of your settlement agreement.

OPEN TUESDAY 11:00 - 2:00

Attention celebrities, developers and privacy nuts!
Double-gated, private view estate in the "A List" Bird Streets on its own private promontory.

Significant architectural contemporary with incredible city and ocean views. Gourmet kitchen, hardwood floors, two fireplaces, soaring vaulted ceilings, disappearing pocket doors with Bali influences and professionally designed interiors. All access security system.

25,000 sq. ft. lot. Multi-level viewing decks and magnificent large flat useable lot. Expand and increase the value on this property by millions - just look at Collingwood, Thrasher, Blue Jay, Oriole, Sierra Mar - this is the next big one on the Sunset Strip.

Full surround sound system, plasma TVs, outdoor living rooms. Seller has a new property survey. All offers in by June 9, 2006 5:00 PM

offered at $4,500,000

TRUMAN ESTATES
COLDWELL BANKER PREVIEWS
International

CURT TRUMAN
Estates Director

RSS Sale Success: Be One Step Ahead—*This gorgeous Hollywood Hills property had a very complex escrow and closing, which is typical of very high-priced properties. This multimillion-dollar mansion, once owned by Richard Gere, was no exception. Knowing that the way to avoid any delay is to be proactive, the seller and his Realtor made a preemptive check-in with escrow two days prior to each one of the buyer's deadlines. The house sailed to a smooth closing.*

Eighteen

CLOSING DAY, CASHING OUT, AND MOVING OUT

You're almost home! Well, actually, almost *out* of your home. Hopefully, your settlement or escrow process has gone smoothly, you've kept your buyer on track, and you have managed to stay on top of all your paperwork. By now your buyer's loan paperwork is done, you've finished all of your negotiations, and you've reviewed your estimated closing costs statement. Everything is spelled out as you've negotiated. All you have to do now is show up to sign the final paperwork and you're done. There is a light at the end of the tunnel. Closing day is fast approaching.

THE FINAL WALK-THROUGH

The final walk-through is the opportunity just before closing for the buyer, the buyer's Realtor, your Realtor, and sometimes even you, to literally *walk through* the house to make sure that everything is in order and ready to sell. The walk-through is usually scheduled at some time after the removal of all the buyer's contingencies and before the closing day.

Things the buyer will expect:

- All requested repairs were completed.

- The house has been maintained in good condition.

- The house is in the same good physical condition as it was during the negotiation.

- Any and all appliances that were contracted to be left for the buyer are still in place.

- Any and all pieces of furniture that were contracted to be left for the buyer are still in place.

- The buyer is given instructions about the use of all systems in the house, such as security alarms, timers, heating and air systems, outdoor lighting, and so on.

RSS Selling Tip: Until the Bitter End

I like to make sure the house looks as good as possible on the final walk-through. Even if I have started to move out, I want to be certain that the house is neat and clean, and looks as wonderful as possible. After all, the deal isn't completely done yet, and even though a snafu is unlikely at this point, anything could happen. Better to keep your buyer excited about his or her new home until you have the cash in your account.

WHAT TO EXPECT ON CLOSING DAY

Whether you live in an area that calls the "big" day the *closing* day or the *settlement day* makes no difference. This is the day that brings the deal to the *cash-out*. It's when you and all those involved in your transaction show up at the same place to sign the finalized documents.

The actual location of your closing will depend on where you live and how the selling process works in your area. It could be at the title or escrow company, at the realty company, at a lender's office, or at an attorney's office. Your Realtor will tell you where you need to go.

It's a very emotional day. Be prepared. You may be signing away your home with only the escrow officer present. Just you, the officer, the final papers, and a pen. It's a little weird, actually—especially if you've lived in your home for many years.

In some states you will actually be in the room with your buyers as you all sign the final documents concurrently. But no matter where this takes place, by the end of it all, your transaction will be complete and you will be presented with a check. Now all you need to do is turn over your home to the new owners, and move out. No small task!

RSS Money-Saving Tip: Saving Money Down to the Wire

Here's one final money-saving tip—even after you have completed the closing! Always have the funds from your sale *wired* into your account. You start accumulating interest faster, there's no chance of costly holds on large checks, and there's never a chance that you'll lose the check on the way to the bank—delaying your deposit and interest even further.

MOVING OUT—MOVING IN

The day the buyers take possession and the day escrow closes are two separate matters, yet both are key to the entire transaction. Standard real estate contracts generally provide separate provisions for the date of closing and the date of possession. Unless you've negotiated a special move-out date in your agreement, it's common for possessions deadlines to strike within a few days of escrow closing. Many buyers want to move in as soon as possible, as their loan payments can begin immediately.

In some cases buyers request to move in before the close of escrow. How shall I say this? *Don't agree to it!* So many things could happen at the last second to delay or to mess up the deal, and now you've got tenants mucking up a house that needs to go back on the market.

Technically, the buyers are officially the new owners by 5:00 P.M. the day of the closing and as soon as their funds have been received. The actual *possession* occurs when the keys are handed over to the new owners. Even if you're ready to hand those keys over on the day of the closing, your Realtor might wait until the deed is recorded, which makes the change of ownership official.

But if you're *not* ready to release possession and you arrive at your closing with buyers who think they get the house that night . . . oops! You'll have some fast packing, boxing, and heavy lifting ahead of you. Be prepared. As a new buyer, I've been known to run over immediately to my newly purchased home with keys in hand directly from the closing! There are some buyers who may do the same, so you had better be packed and out the door.

Here's my advice: Be very clear about when you plan to allow your buyers to take possession *before arriving for the final closing*. If your ideal move-out dates were never discussed during your negotiations, you need to come to an agreement with your buyers about when they can expect to get the keys. If you assume you automatically get a week to organize your stuff and call the moving trucks after the official closing, think again!

DELIVERING THE PROPERTY

Delivering the property is an important issue. Just because you have sold the property doesn't mean you should hand over the keys and yell "good luck" as you drive away. I'm a big believer that you need to *over-deliver* what you promise. And when creating a home and lifestyle, you want to deliver just that.

The Buyer's Welcome Package

I always like to prepare an information booklet for the buyers. You can have this prepared in advance of closing day and hand it to them at that time. Items to include are:

- The alarm codes
- The location and current schedules for any sprinklers, light timers, pool equipment, or other timed mechanisms
- The contact info for:
  - Gardener
  - Utility companies

- Cable or digital satellite provider

- Garage door company

- The day trash is picked up

- Paint color chart (This is the chart that lists room by room all the names and brands of the paints used throughout the house. Fortunately, when you follow my three-color indoor and outdoor paint technique, you won't have dozens of different paints to list.)

Also provide an envelope with:

- All the warranties and instruction booklets for all appliances, alarm system, built-ins, etc.

- The keys

- The garage door openers

The Final Touches

The very last thing you want to do before the sale day or the day before the owner takes possession is to make the house look as terrific as possible for their move-in day. Not only is this a wonderful thing to do for your buyer, it is also a very smart way to hedge against the buyers' finding last-minute things wrong after they have moved in. Leave the buyers thinking, "Oh, the seller took such care when he moved out. Let's not bother him with this or that."

- Touch up any paint scratches or scuffs.

- Make sure the front and backyards are trimmed and beautiful.

- Remove any trash or garbage from the property.

- Clean the house from top to bottom.

And for the final touch, put a lovely orchid on the kitchen counter with a note that says simply, "Enjoy!" It's a $20 investment that may be just the gesture that keeps those new buyers from tracking you down months later to complain that the garbage disposal doesn't work as well as they thought it would . . . or the hot-water pressure isn't really the cascading waterfall that they had anticipated.

MOVING OUT!

Surely you haven't just sold your house without having at least some idea where you're going. Hopefully, the timing all works itself out from the day you snag that buyer to the day you move out and into another place. If you used all of my set-to-sell techniques, then you also don't have a whole lot to pack up, because many of your belongings will already be in boxes ready for the actual moving day.

Timing and Preparing to Move

Given the timeline you created for yourself and the expectations you've agreed upon with your buyer, plan your packing and moving well in advance. Shop around for professional movers and start by asking friends and family members for referrals. The moving industry has been plagued with stories of consumers getting ripped off, or worse, getting poor service that results in damaged or lost possessions. I suggest you use a well-known moving company that plenty of people you trust can vouch for. And before letting any moving team into your home, make sure you have checked their references thoroughly. You want to make sure these are the people you can trust with your family heirlooms, entertainment centers, antiques, china collections, and grandma's rocker.

Get a Firm Estimate Up Front

Get your moving estimates in writing and request that what you agree upon is binding. Don't get sucked into paying more on moving day because the movers suddenly decide "You have more stuff than we thought" or "It took us longer to load up your stuff." Moving can be a tremendously stressful and pressure-filled experience. Some argue that it's the most stressful event to endure in selling a house—almost more than selling! You don't need the hassle of renegotiating rates and charges on the day of the move.

When your moving rep gives you an estimate, show him or her *everything* that will be moved. Don't hide the exercise equipment and boxes of heavy books in the basement closet. Let him or her determine any special handling and packaging that should be taken into account, and double-check size concerns that can make moving large items through doors problematic. If you recall having trouble getting that four-poster bed to fit through your bedroom door, even when disassembled, you're going to have the same trouble moving it out!

Also, understand exactly what's included in the estimate and what will be billed as separate charges, such as packing materials, travel time . . . including the movers' lunch break! Most movers charge by weight and distance (the weight will determine how big a truck—and how many trucks—they need to use). If your move doesn't entail a long distance or remains in-state, a mover will typically charge per man-hour. If that's the case, be sure to ask how many hours *total* they think it will take to get the job done.

Make sure you ask the question: Will this cover *everything*, no extra charges? Having a detailed and thorough estimate will be big money and stress saved on moving day!

AFTER THE BIG CASH-OUT—USE YOUR MONEY WISELY

If you've just walked away with more cash than you've ever seen in your bank account before, *congratulations!* You get an A from the school of *Ready, Set, Sold!* But here's a word of warning: Watch out. Don't go spending it all tomorrow on a fancy car or a vacation to Easter Island. Think about rolling that money over into a new investment, whether it be your next house or maybe just filling your retirement accounts. Your house was your financial security up until the day you sold it, so now this money is your financial security until you transfer it into your next home or into something else.

We all work very hard to pay the bills while striving to bring in additional money and to build financial security. Selling a house and cashing out your equity is a *huge* stepping-stone in that financial game plan. But you have to nurture the selling success that you've worked so hard to achieve. Use this money wisely.

Think of it this way: You've got your hands on the most liquid form of money—cold hard cash—so please use it wisely. I know it's tempting. Cold hard cash is powerful stuff. You start dreaming of all the things you can buy with it *right this minute*.

If you're not moving into another home and transferring the proceeds from the sale of your old house to your new home, be very careful about how you protect those funds until you purchase another piece of property in the future. If you've chosen to hang out and rent for a while, don't rent the penthouse unit! Hold that cash in reserve for the down payment on your next house. Coming up with a solid down payment of 20 percent is very difficult for many buyers—especially in expensive markets—and if you've got that amount or more already covered, you allow for significant savings when you purchase your next home.

MY PERSONAL CONGRATULATIONS

Again, congratulations! I know that reading this book has empowered you. And empowered me, too. Knowing that I've been able to share my knowledge, as well as the insider secrets that the real estate pros use every day, has made writing this book worthwhile for me.

I said in the Introduction that *Ready, Set, Sold!* is the book *every* home-owner *must* read before putting his or her house on the market. Why? Because now all homeowners can maximize the value of their house, capture money they would have otherwise have thrown away, and save thousands of dollars in unnecessary fees.

I'm confident that if you follow the steps and tips in this book when putting your house up for sale, you are able to maximize your home's value, identify a more solid buyer, and traverse the path to closing day more smoothly and economically. In other words, when you Ready, Set, Sell! . . . *you make more money when you sell your house!*

Send me your stories! I'd love to hear from you. Write to me from my Web site at www.MichaelCorbett.com and share your RSS success!

MY *READY, SET, SOLD!* EXPERTS

LISA ALMY

Lisa Almy, a Realtor since 1996 and currently with World Real Estate Exchange, specializes in South Beach, Middle Beach, and Miami Biscayne corridor properties. Most of Lisa's success has been in commercial apartment buildings in South Beach. www.worldrealty.com

ROBERT "BOBBY" CIPOLLONI AND MICHAEL EMERY, THE LA HOME BOYS

Having joined with Keller Williams Realty, the LA Home Boys is a realty group of professional agents and assistants. Cipolloni's team handles the transactions—"List & Sell"—while Emery's crew handles the "Repair & Prepare" of a property. They provide a value-added service that's unique to the industry. www.thelahomeboys.com

SAMANTHA CLARK

Samantha Clark has a background in design, freelance writing, and art. She's an associate broker at Coldwell Banker Legacy in Albuquerque, New Mexico, specializing in mature neighborhoods and historic homes. www.cblegacy.com/sclark

ROBERT W. CRAWFORD JR.

In 1979, Robert W. Crawford Jr. founded Brook Furniture Rental, Inc. He currently is the chairman and chief executive officer. By 1985, Brook had become the area's largest furniture rental provider. www.bfr.com

RICK GEHA AND COCO LEWIS

Rick Geha and Coco Lewis, in real estate for more than twenty-five years, run the successful real estate group Keller Williams Benchmark Properties in Fremont, California, which has fourteen team members, ten full-time professional Realtors, and four administrative officers. www.rickandcoco. com

JIM GILLESPIE

Jim Gillespie is the president and CEO of the Coldwell Banker Real Estate Corporation, and is responsible for the company's more than 3,500 independently owned and operated residential and commercial real estate offices and 112,000 sales associates globally.

NELSON GONZALEZ

Gonzalez is the senior vice president of Esslinger-Wooten-Maxwell Realtors, Inc. He has nineteen years of real estate experience. From 1998 to the present he has been the top producer at EWM Realtors' Miami Beach office, consistently selling more than $100 million per year.

RUSS GRIEVE

Russ Grieve has lived in Las Vegas for twelve years, specializing in residential and land real estate. Grieve had the distinction, in only his second year in real estate, of receiving the largest commission of any Coldwell Banker agent in the state of Nevada. www.cbwardley.com

KATE HART, ASP, IAHSP

Kate Hart is the president and principal real estate stager of Hart & Associates Staging and Design, helping Realtors and homeowners to prepare their homes for sale. Hart earned the ASP Designation and has trained local Realtors and stagers as a trainer for Stagedhomes.com. www.hartstaging.com

BRIAN HATCH

Brian Hatch is a successful Realtor specializing in residential real estate. He's the top-producing Realtor with Pacific Union GMAC Real Estate in Palm Springs, California. His background in design and construction makes him a triple-threat Realtor for anyone looking to invest in real estate in the Palm Springs area.

MICHAEL J. LARIO

Michael Lario has been a general practitioner attorney for the past sixteen years. He specializes in real estate law, and is one of South New Jersey's top real estate attorneys.

AARON LEIDER

Aaron Leider is the owner and broker of Keller Williams Brentwood. He's been a real estate professional for more than twenty years. His office is one the West Coast's top producers. His knowledge and expertise have been described in features in *Forbes, New York Times, Los Angeles Times,* and many other publications. www.aaronleider.com

JOHN LIVESAY

John Livesay has been the West Coast director for *W* magazine for the past nine years. He is also the author of *The 7 Most Powerful Selling Secrets,* which combines spiritual concepts with selling. He is a motivational speaker as well. www.johnlivesay.com

MICHAEL MALONEY

Maloney opened Maison Luxe in Manhattan Beach, California, with all things luxurious from France and Italy, and has now formed Castle Keepers home staging company.

CHRIS OLIVA

Specializing in customer service and vacation home sales, Oliva has been a successful Realtor for eighteen years with the the Oliva Team of RE/MAX in Ocean City, New Jersey, assisting buyers and sellers in achieving their real estate goals through his dynamic market knowledge. www.theolivateam.com

SUZE ORMAN

Suze Orman is an internationally acclaimed personal finance expert whom *USA Today* has called a "one-woman financial advice power-house" and "a force in the world of personal finance." From her earliest childhood years and the stress of her father losing his business, to her post-college job working as a waitress, to climbing the ranks in the in-vestment world, to becoming a bestselling author, Orman has lived and learned many hard financial lessons. She has translated these experi-ences into frank, savvy financial advice that has transformed the lives of millions around the world. www.suzeorman.com

DOUG RAGO

Working as a Realtor with Rodeo Realty out of Studio City and Beverly Hills, California, Rago has a commitment to excellence that continues to produce multimillion-dollar sales and an extremely satisfied clientele. www.dougrago.com.

ANTHONY ROBBINS

For more than a quarter of a century, Anthony Robbins has served as an advisor to leaders around the world. A recognized authority on the psy-chology of leadership, negotiations, organizational turnaround, and peak performance, Robbins has directly impacted the lives of nearly fifty million people from eighty countries with his bestselling books and au-diotapes, public speaking engagements, and live appearances. Since fa-thering the life coaching industry, Robbins has produced the number-one audio coaching system of all time. www.tonyrobbins.com

ALAN SKLAR

With more than fourteen years of experience, Sklar has renovated more than twenty-four properties in southern California. Sklar's firm, CA Modern Living, can be hired for interior design projects both large and small.

CURT TRUMAN

Curt Truman is a previews international estates director at Coldwell Banker Beverly Hills North and a member of the prestigious International President's Elite. He is ranked in the top 4 percent of all sales associates internationally, and was named by *Los Angeles Magazine* as one of LA's Real Estate Super Agents. He specializes in luxury home sales in Sunset Strip, Beverly Hills, and West Los Angeles.

CLARE TUDOR

Australian designer Clare Tudor came to California in 1997. She is cofounder of Laguna Staging and Design. Since that time she has worked on various projects including ground-up construction, major remodels, and interior design for homes and corporate offices, as well as staging homes for resale. www.lagunastaging.com

MARK SAMSKY

A top-producing Realtor with Corcoran Group, Samsky works closely with several world-renowned architects and interior designers. His background is interior design and construction management. www.corcoran.com

JOYCE TAPSCOTT

Joyce Tapscott is a million-dollar producer with Coldwell Banker Wallace & Wallace. She specializes in corporate relocation opportunities. www.joycetapscott.com

BARB SCHWARZ

Barb Schwarz is the CEO and founder of StagedHomes.com. She is also a professional real estate broker and the creator of the Accredited Staging Professional Course, which sets standards for the home staging industry. An award-winning professional speaker and bestselling author herself, Schwarz has personally staged and sold more than 3,000 homes in the greater Seattle area. www.stagedhomes.com

JULIE WELKER

Julie Welker, Realtor, CRS, CRB, has been president of Coldwell Banker Welker Real Estate since 1977. In 1996, Welker was honored by the State of Pennsylvania as one of Pennsylvania's top fifty businesswomen. www.welkerre.com

STEVEN WILDER

Steven Wilder is a registered building contractor and architectural interior designer. He is co-founder of Laguna Staging and Design. Australian-born and -educated designer Wilder primarily specializes in the creative remodeling of homes and has experience in remodeling bars, restaurants, and nightclubs. www.somethingwilder.com

TOBY WOLTER

One of Carson Realty Group, Inc.'s top producers, Toby Wolter has been in the real estate industry since 1987. Wolter recently affiliated with Carson Realty Group and specializes in both residential and investment properties on and off the beach. www.tobywolter.com